Ten Philosophical Essays
in the Christian Tradition

FREDERICK J. CROSSON

(1926–2009)

TEN PHILOSOPHICAL ESSAYS
in the CHRISTIAN TRADITION

Frederick J. Crosson

Edited by

MICHAEL J. CROWE

and

NICHOLAS AYO, C.S.C.

University of Notre Dame Press
Notre Dame, Indiana

Manufactured in the United States of America

The Press gratefully acknowledges the support of the Institute for Scholarship
in the Liberal Arts, University of Notre Dame, in the publication of this book.

Library of Congress Cataloging-in-Publication Data

Crosson, Frederick James, 1926–2009.
[Essays. Selections]
Ten philosophical essays in the Christian tradition / Frederick J. Crosson ;
edited by Michael J. Crowe and Nicholas Ayo, C.S.C. ;
tribute by Mary Katherine Tillman ; introduction by Mark Moes.
pages   cm
Includes bibliographical references and index.
ISBN 978-0-268-02311-9 (pbk. : alk. paper)
ISBN 0-268-02311-5 (pbk. : alk. paper)
1. Philosophy and religion.   I. Crowe, Michael J., joint editor.   II. Title.
BL51.C717   2015
210—dc23
2015005762

CONTENTS

PREFACE

Discussions in late 2007 between Frederick Crosson, a distinguished emeritus professor at the University of Notre Dame, and his friend Jude Dougherty, Dean Emeritus of the School of Philosophy at The Catholic University of America, generated the suggestion that Fred select a number of his best essays for republication as a book. Shortly before leaving for Florida in late January 2008, Fred made his selection and delivered ten essays to a Notre Dame secretarial center requesting that an electronic version of the essays be prepared. Fred had done light editing of the essays, e.g., correcting some typographical errors. His idea clearly was that an electronic copy would facilitate publication. Before leaving South Bend, he asked his long-time colleague Professor Michael Crowe (the author of these comments) to serve as an intermediary with the secretarial staff in case questions arose.

In early February 2008, shortly after arriving in Florida, Fred suffered a series of falls, seriously injuring his head. These injuries made it impossible to consult with him on this project and necessitated that he enter a facility providing full-time care. Ultimately, they led to his death on December 9, 2009.

In late March 2008, I shared information on Fred's medical condition with Jude Dougherty, who expressed hope that the project might yet succeed.

Because Fred was so widely known for the quality of his insights and the sensitivity of his writings, because he had been a friend and mentor to me for over five decades, and because he had shared his hopes for these essays with me, it seemed proper that I should do what I could to keep alive Fred's hope for their republication. Wary of taking on this important responsibility alone, I asked my colleague Fr. Nicholas Ayo, C.S.C., a wise and well-published scholar and close colleague to Fred, to work with me on this project.

After receiving in mid-July 2008 the scanned copies of the essays, we launched the project, encouraged by Fred's wife, Dr. Patricia Crosson. At that time, I had made efforts (only partially successful) to secure an up-to-date bibliography of Fred's publications. Although we had copies (typically photocopies of the published essays) and of course knew their titles and author, we had no clear idea of where they had been published. Moreover, one essay (that on Cicero) was in typescript, suggesting that Fred had not yet published it. Another reason for securing a bibliography was our belief that readers of this collection may wish to read more of the writings of this thoughtful and wise scholar. (An enhanced and verified version of Professor Crosson's bibliography appears at the end this volume.)

Nicholas and I then discussed what steps we should take next. Because our fields are respectively theology and history of science, we realized that we needed input from other scholars, both in the Program of Liberal Studies (a Great Books program in which Fred, Nicholas, and I have taught for many years) and in Philosophy. To this end, we prepared a draft edition of the volume (naming it *Ten Philosophical Essays in the Christian Tradition*), sought start-up funding from Notre Dame's Program of Liberal Studies, and circulated copies to a few scholars.

We also sought a philosopher capable of commenting on these broad-ranging essays. This need led us to contact a Program of Liberal Studies colleague, who is not only a philosopher but who also shared with Fred a long-time interest in phenomenology, philosophy of religion, and classical philosophy. Through a generosity based on their three decades of friendship and an admiration of Fred's wisdom, Professor Mary Katherine Tillman agreed. The tribute she prepared appears in this volume and sets Fred's essays into a broad context, which illuminates them in a variety of ways, especially by showing how they interrelate.

We also decided that the volume would be strengthened by the addition of an introduction written by a philosopher who has used some of the essays in his classroom at another university. This led us to contact Professor Mark Moes, who teaches in the Philosophy Department at Grand Valley State University. Mark knew Fred from Mark's studies in Notre Dame's Program of Liberal Studies and graduate program in Phi-

losophy. We were very pleased that Mark agreed to supply this introduction.

Greatly helped by Katherine, Nicholas and I checked the scanned
electronic text for typographical errors, finding and correcting hundreds.
We also submitted a funding proposal for our project to Notre Dame's
Institute for Scholarship in the Liberal Arts. The proposal was promptly
and fully funded.

In editing these essays, we have above all sought to ensure the pres-
ervation of Fred's message. We have carefully compared each of the
published essays with the electronic copies to ensure their accuracy.
When we have made alterations, they were minimal and were such that
we were convinced that Fred or a careful copyeditor would also have
made these changes. In short, we are confident that these are the ten
essays that Fred would have wanted published, and that they are in the
form he would have preferred for their publication. Moreover, in preparing these essays for publication, we have been motivated both by our
attachment to Fred Crosson as a splendid colleague and impressive
scholar, and by our conviction that these insightful essays deserve increased circulation.

In submitting these collected essays to the University of Notre
Dame Press, we were aware of the prestige it has attained as a publisher
both in philosophy and in scholarship in the Christian tradition. Moreover, we believed that securing publication from this press would also be
especially appropriate because of Fred's numerous contributions to
Notre Dame. Not only did he teach here for many years, he also served
as the first lay dean of the College of Arts and Letters (1968–75), as
editor of Notre Dame's *Review of Politics* (1976–82), as the holder of
the Cardinal O'Hara Endowed Chair for Philosophy (1976–84), and
later of the Rev. John J. Cavanaugh, C.S.C., Chair in the Humanities
(1984–98). Notre Dame recognized the excellence of his teaching by
awarding him a Sheedy Prize for outstanding teaching and also a Presi-
dential Award for his overall contributions to Notre Dame. To mention
only one of Fred's contributions beyond the university, it is noteworthy
that Fred served as the first Catholic president of the Phi Beta Kappa
National Society (1997–2000). Thus we intend this publication not only
as itself an important contribution to scholarship but also as a tribute to

this brilliant and beloved teacher, able administrator, and generous scholar.

Before closing this preface, we wish to extend special thanks to two people who contributed significantly to this project. These are Father Kevin Grove, C.S.C., who encouraged the publication of these essays, and Elizabeth Sain of the University of Notre Dame Press, who very carefully copyedited the final manuscript for this book. And finally, we thank Fred's department, Notre Dame's Program of Liberal Studies, chaired by Professor Gretchen Reydams-Schils. At numerous times during this project, they have supported this project with generosity and enthusiasm.

MICHAEL J. CROWE
Cavanaugh Professor Emeritus, Program of Liberal Studies

in collaboration with

REV. NICHOLAS AYO, C.S.C.
Professor Emeritus, Program of Liberal Studies

TRIBUTE

Entering the cool building on a sunny afternoon, one is perhaps first struck by the multicolored patches of light that cast their stretched transparencies across the long wooden table and benches. Two students study there munching on their sandwiches. The diffuse light splashes along a bit of floor, then travels partway up the high walls opposite. Here are the modern stained glass windows of the vast portal called the Great Hall, the main entryway to Notre Dame's College of Arts and Letters. The Tudor-Gothic edifice was dedicated in 1953 as the O'Shaughnessy Hall of Liberal and Fine Arts.

In the same year that the century-old college moved into its new home, there settled into this place a young instructor, a faculty member whose entire professional life, over half a century, would be situated and thrive in the halls of this building—in its classrooms and at its seminar tables, in its dean's office, its Philosophy Department, and its Program of Liberal Studies. Teacher par excellence and dean of the college from 1968 to 1975, scholar, author, and dedicated contributor to American higher education, Professor Frederick J. Crosson was partial to and decidedly trained in the liberal arts, necessary as they are to every academic pursuit, especially to philosophy, his field, as well as to the practical endeavors and objectives of human life in general.

Set high up in the Great Hall's north and west walls, and thus often barely noticed, the seven stained-glass panels represent symbolically the seven liberal arts: grammar, logic, and rhetoric; arithmetic, geometry, music, and astronomy. The figures colorfully portrayed on the Great Hall's glass represent the tools and appliances involved in the practice of the arts, and each long panel is topped by the names of celebrated liberal artists of the early Western tradition, such as Euclid and Atlas, Aristotle and Cicero. Frederick Crosson loved this Great Hall of O'Shaughnessy, through which he as dean often walked on his way to and from his office down the hall.

The liberal artistry of Professor Frederick Crosson is brilliantly confirmed in the essays of this book. Although his expertise in the arts of grammar and logic is obvious here, it is the art of rhetoric that he exercises with the skill of a master. Rhetoric is his own highly-honed instrument and it is also the pervasive method he discerns, often concealed, yet silently effectual, in the writings of his selected authors. Here rhetoric is no longer simply the pedagogical art of expression through writing and public speaking, but it has returned to its original, broad significance as the art of persuasion embedded in lived experience, in the political and cultural lives of ordinary people. The "sense of things" required by good rhetoric enhances reason, for through attentive listening, understanding, and interpretation, its power expands and enriches the everyday human being in the world—"like the turning-on of a new light, extending the range of what is to be taken into account" (Hans-Georg Gadamer, *Truth and Method* [New York: Seabury, 1975], 442).

The practitioner of rhetoric (the art of persuasion) must be able to read and interpret the nonconceptual senses of lived experience and put forth not arguments so much as verisimilitudes—that is, likenesses, what resembles or approximates truth (for instance, metaphors, stories, analogies, aphorisms, and so forth)—in order to sway ordinary people to what could never be demonstrated by reason alone or empirically tested. In chapter 2 Crosson cites Augustine's *City of God*, "no one doubts that things are perceived more readily through similitudes," and in chapter 1 he quotes St. Thomas Aquinas, "Under similitudes and figures [of speech], there lies latent (*latet*) the truth that is thus figured." This manner of persuasion, states Crosson, provides "a picture which is not intended to be deceptive, which gives some sense of what it's like" (chapter 1).

From approximations then, from multiple and layered senses, from obvious and concealed meanings, and from an abundance of viewpoints, one interprets, discerns, and attempts to disclose truth, which, in its fullness, cannot be determined by exact concepts and formulations alone.

These are some of the reasons, it seems to Crosson, why for Cicero there is no philosophical *knowledge*, for "philosophy lives in the disputed questions of the schools and the best it can hope for is to eliminate some positions as untenable and reach those more probable" (chapter 5). Even from something that seems as limited and skeptical as Cicero's position, there is still much that can be learned.

Perhaps one may conclude that the dialogue and its two sequels offer us insights into the roots of the natural inclination to believe in gods, into the weakness of the philosophers' explanations of divine existence, and into the human and political role of such beliefs, as well as into how *religio* tends to well over into a superstition that needs to be criticized and pruned.

Empirical study, scientific explanation, and objectivity are not viewed negatively by Crosson, but they are considered to be fundamentally incomplete. What is personal is not always subjective; it is often possessed of a universality that speaks to human beings precisely as human. In his essay on "Proof and Presence," Crosson writes: "Joy is the awareness of the presence of the beloved [God]. While that awareness is personal, it is not merely subjective in a psychological sense. For it derives not from private intimations but from a public source: the propositions which are handed on to us by a historical tradition."

Crosson's conclusions on the existence of God, the sense of God's presence or absence, and God's mysterious providence are the implicit grounds upon which Crosson stands firm, as throughout these ten essays he focuses upon disclosing various kinds of "hiddenness," above all in great texts such as those by Cicero, Augustine, Aquinas, Hume, and Newman. "Great works of literature commonly have a dimension of meaning that appears clearly only when one reflects on the text, connects up different loci, and 'puts two and two together'" (chapter 1).

Crosson is interested throughout the essays in what Giambattista Vico called the "*sensus communis*," that is, in the practical wisdom of the public forum—political and cultural—that people take for granted, what might be called "the view of the man on the street." There is a stock of ideas and a repertory of convictions that constitute an individual's living context and shared inheritance. What Plato understood as the world of mere opinion and belief (*doxa*) is thus shown to have a legitimacy and rationality of its own. Rhetoric defends the everyday, the probable, and the commonplace, what is convincing to ordinary reason by whatever means available, against the claim of science to accept as true only what can be conceptualized, proved, and tested. Rhetoric recognizes the commonly held beliefs of the city and the culture as expressed in tradition and custom by the elders and by the public in general.

Besides the hiddenness of "common sense," still other types of concealment are dwelt upon by Crosson, such as the actual absence, yet potential presence, involved in teaching as reminding, and the hiddenness of nature in its gradual self-revelation to the scientist and to the poet.

In chapters 9 and 10, Crosson reflects upon concealment in the moral domain, what Pope John Paul II refers to in his encyclical *Evangelium Vitae* as the "tragic obscuring of the collective conscience" in liberal democracies today. Crosson says that "we no longer form one political community, sharing a sense of one human good which we seek together and which we argue about within a common set of moral principles" (chapter 10).

But that which is concealed within the written text is Crosson's main, pervasive concern. For one thing, the dialogue form, be it Cicero's, Augustine's, or Hume's, "allows the author to recede from view or to hide" (chapter 8). Crosson details how the presence of a hidden meaning in a text can be indicated by an author in many ways: by the structure of the text, by qualifications, by irony and double meaning, by the genre chosen, by hints and allusions, by the implications of assertions, by allegory, by the connections of its parts, by its relation to other writings of the same author, and by modifying subsequently what had been stated earlier.

Importantly for Crosson, the audience of a work is a major factor in attempting any interpretation of a text, but this is especially true for dialogue. "If we take into account the form of a work—for example, the dramatic structure of a dialogue—then different meanings of what is said may derive not only from what is said but to whom and when and in what circumstances it is said." In Hume's *Dialogues Concerning Natural Religion*, for example, "What Philo says to Demea and what he says to Cleanthes and what he says to Pamphilus may have to be evaluated differently.... Philo makes an explicit point several times of allying himself with Demea" (chapter 8). When Demea leaves the conversation, however, Philo switches his allegiance to Cleanthes. Does Philo change his argument? Though it may seem to be a reversal, Crosson argues convincingly that its appearance of change is only because Hume has recast the argument rhetorically.

Attentive listening to an entire situation, "keeping an ear to the ground," as it were, is required for adequate interpretation. Significantly in a dialogue, "what leads to the difference between the two antagonists is not the empirical evidence or the logic of the argument but the inclinations that carry each one beyond the evidence" (chapter 8). In addition to the minute elements of the text, there is the *Gestaltung*, the sense of the whole, "and only as these come together do we approach *scientiam*, the fullness of knowledge" (chapter 4). What is being said in an undertone, so to speak, what is set apart in parentheses or as presuppositions, may slowly become evident, and perhaps even central, as one makes connections and gradually realizes a whole within which the seeming minutiae make sense.

Professor Crosson's ten philosophical essays taken altogether are his reflections upon some of the many kinds of textual shaping that are concealed in discourse and that require interpretation. The common theme in the essays about the disclosure of hiddenness has been perennially understood as a central task of philosophy: *aletheia*, an unveiling of what is concealed, a showing. "Classical love of wisdom," Crosson writes, "sought understanding through what showed itself to be true or false, what was evident, or was evidently implied by what is known" (chapter 4). In our time, Martin Heidegger "has retrieved this Platonic teaching and characterized truth (*aletheia*) as disclosure, as opening up beings to our comprehension" (chapter 3).

One of the most common themes of Crosson's essays is the prominent fact of Cicero's influence on Augustine, on Hume, on Newman, and as the primary pre-Christian source of natural law teaching. Another theme is the view of an author's work from the vantage point of philosophy of religion through considerations of the nature of religion, its history and its forms, and its distinction from belief and religious faith. In a word, however, all of the essays are about the discovery and showing of what is concealed within a great text. These themes, made explicit and manifest, become interpretive lenses through which the thoughtful reader may learn and develop a viewpoint. Crosson understands that "some readers will ponder and assemble into an interpretation, a perspective from which to read and understand the text" (chapter 1). After all, that is what he has done here so remarkably well.

MARY KATHERINE TILLMAN
Professor Emerita, Program of Liberal Studies

Introduction

Even if my first encounter with Frederick Crosson in early September 1969 did not have the same degree of significance to my life as hearing Saint Ambrose had for Saint Augustine, or as the uproar over *Tract 90* had for Newman, it nevertheless was an important turning point in my life. Sitting in Notre Dame's library auditorium at the outset of freshman orientation, embarking on my undergraduate career, I heard Crosson talk about the history of religion and about the history of the term "religion." More than forty years later, I still remember fragments of what he said about the ways in which Catholic Christianity took up the pre-Christian agricultural calendar and absorbed it into its liturgical year by correlating its key moments with key moments in the life of Christ and the life of the Church. I was at the time not yet able to understand him in the light of Augustine's reflections on history, time, eternity, memory, and narrative in the later books of the *Confessions* or in the light of Christopher Dawson's story of the history of religion in *Progress and Religion*. The deeper meanings of Crosson's talk were hidden from me. Hidden too was the role his talk, and others of his I would hear later, would play in my life, spurring me to read many of his favorite authors, including Plato, Aristotle, Augustine, Aquinas, Hume, and Newman.

Latent teaching and hidden providence were among Crosson's primary preoccupations, acquired from reading Saint Augustine, who

1

taught us to learn from the Johannine Prologue that all reality is spoken by a Master Teacher and Master Craftsman in whose creative action thinking and making and teaching are all identical. "I wonder what sort of tale we've fallen into," said Sam to Frodo on the stairs of Cirith Ungol, in that story by another master teacher who was devoted to John the Evangelist, J. R. R. Tolkien. Another name for latent teaching is artful rhetoric, and Katherine Tillman wisely draws attention to how Crosson not only exercised rhetoric with the skill of a master but also discerned with the skill of a master reader the rhetoric of the writings of his favorite authors. Like Gadamer, Crosson learned—from Plato's dialogues, from Aristotle and Cicero and Vico—the importance to all human crafts, not least the crafts of rhetoric and interpretation, of a tacit and not-merely-theoretical understanding that unites theory and practice in *phronesis* or wise judgment. In the ten essays in this volume, Crosson shows us that understanding the works of master writers requires us to recognize the rhetorical craftsmanship in their works in the form of textual genres and structures, hints and allusions, unstated implications, organic unity of design, figures and allegories, ironies, multiple meanings, and the like. Taking for granted the Johannine analogy between text and world, Crosson shows how something like Newman's *illative sense* is needed as much to recognize the cumulative significance of the details of a rhetorically well-constructed human text as to recognize the workings of providence in the created world.

Crosson's approach to the interpretation of philosophical texts differs in important ways from Leo Strauss's. Crosson found that Strauss's distinction between the esoteric and the exoteric meanings of philosophical texts was a different kind of distinction from that between the latent and the manifest meanings of rhetorically well-constructed texts in general. Strauss maintained that certain philosophers intended the esoteric meanings of their texts to remain inaccessible and hidden to all but a relatively small number of their readers, behind a cloak of politically and religiously less disturbing and conventionally more acceptable meanings. Crosson tries to make clear in the first essay that many of the best philosophers and persons of letters in human history expressed hidden meanings in their oral or written teachings for *pedagogical* rather than for politically self-protective purposes. Crosson emphasizes what

Socrates taught in the *Phaedrus*, that the effective philosophical rhetorician takes into account the different moral and intellectual capacities of his or her readers and attends to their different degrees of readiness to grasp or to accept certain truths. The rhetorician aims to express both latent and manifest meanings in order that auditors and readers at all levels of understanding and moral development—both the captains and the troops, so to speak—receive something edifying. He will sometimes even construct discourses in ways designed to elicit from readers and hearers the active exercise of their intellectual interpretive capacities—sometimes providing clues but leaving them to do the integrating and the "gestalting," sometimes presenting fallacious arguments and leaving them to discern the fallacies, and so on. *Ars est celare artem* ("it is artful to conceal art") or *Ars latet sua arte* ("art hides its artfulness"). The rhetorician's task is to communicate insight, and insight is a personal achievement by the learner and cannot be "poured," as Socrates remarks to Agathon in the *Symposium*, from one head into another. Without the insight that goes with them, the words of a teacher become dogmatic in a negative sense of the word and can at worst even provide obstacles to learning.

Crosson's groundbreaking essay on Augustine's *Confessions* brings to light subtleties of composition in the book that attest to Augustine's rhetorical skill for *showing* the workings of an initially hidden divine providence in his own life story, while at the same time *training* readers to develop, in the very act of reading the book carefully, their own capacities to recognize the workings of hidden providence in history and in their own lives and not only in literature. Augustine does this by first building hidden chiastic thematic structures into the narrative of Books 1–9 and then in Books 10–13 providing profound reflections upon the narrative significance of those books in light of the natures of memory and language and time and eternity. These reflections are designed to cast light on the ways in which the scriptural narrative, both as a whole and in the opening chapters of Genesis, provides the key to understanding every narrative. Augustine shows that revelation can provide a light in which the believer can hear God speaking to him directly *in the events of his life*, enabling him to understand for himself the meaning of the narrative that his own life enacts, to understand his own life as one of the subplots taking its place in the larger narrative provided by the Scriptures (as Sam and Frodo came to understand on the stairs of Cirith Ungol the place of their own journey within the larger metanarrative of Middle Earth). Crosson's Augustine, through persistent reflection upon Scripture, comes to look beyond reason's capacity to recognize timeless patterns or *universalia ante res*, and instead to focus on and to develop reason's capacity to recognize narrative patterns in time.

Augustine's reason for focusing upon narrative temporal patterns, according to Crosson, is that he is trying to solve the (Ciceronian) puzzle of how Plotinus' "One" (or even Aristotle's *noesis noeseos* or "thought thinking itself") might be conceived of as going out to rescue mankind by speaking a divine "Word" within the world, the puzzle of how it might be possible for a transcendent, immaterial, bodiless God to nevertheless speak in the world and to offer aid to mankind. For unlike Neo-Platonism, Hinduism, and Buddhism, Scripture depicts the ascent to God not only as an ascetic individual effort but also as assisted by divine grace. Augustine attends to the fact that any utterance is a structured whole that unfolds in time a non-temporal meaning that cannot be fully grasped until the utterance has been concluded. To hear and to recognize the Logos of God cannot therefore consist merely in hearing or seeing some isolated paranormal event but must involve coming to see the entire temporal Creation, including crucial event sequences within it and the (revealed) Last Things, in the light of its meaning as a whole (with the aid of Scripture and of the life and teaching of Christ). Coming from outside of time and preserving all things in existence (including fallen superhuman intelligences), God's utterance is an expression of the creative *phronesis* or wise judgment at work in history as a whole as well as in the life of an individual human being. The *Confessions* (aptly formed as an act of prayer and worship) narrates the growth of Augustine's own consciousness of self and world as deriving from God.

The only earlier writing of his own that Augustine mentions in the *Confessions* is the *De Magistro*. In his third essay, Crosson gives a careful reading of the latter book in order to bring to light its latent "germinating conception." Crosson tries to show us how for Augustine teaching is a way of using discourse in order to quicken and guide the student's own capacity for recognizing real aspects of extramental reality *and their interrelationships.* (Crosson writes: "*Intelligere* is not so much *intus legere*, to read within, as *inter legere*, to bring together.") Teaching for Augustine goes beyond the mere exploration of the network of inferential role relations among man-made concepts, and so escapes the "self-referential network of signifiers" which provides the sole horizon for idealists such as Derrida, Brandom, and all the proponents of "inferential role semantics." Crosson's Augustine takes his place in the tradition of Socrates, who, after articulating the Parable of the Cave, insisted that teaching is not putting or "pouring" something into the mind of the learner but rather a process of turning around his "inner eye" in such a way that the learner can achieve insight for himself.

Crosson's fourth essay, a careful reading of Augustine's *De Utilitate Credendi*, explores all that is involved in the human act of believing revealed truths inaccessible to unaided human reason. In contemporary analytic philosophy, belief is usually analyzed as a two-place relation between a person's mental act or disposition, on the one hand, and a proposition, on the other. But, like Josef Pieper in his *Belief and Faith*, Crosson analyzes belief as a *three-place relation* involving (1) a person's mental act or disposition, (2) a proposition, and (3) another person on whose authority the proposition is believed. This analysis cuts right through the individualism built into modern epistemology and philosophy of mind by showing that belief essentially involves the believer in interpersonal relationships. In human craft communities, apprentices believe their teachers until they can come to grasp for themselves the reasons for belief. But in the Church the objects of belief are truths that are in principle beyond any human capacity to prove.

Yet an inability to prove, Crosson reminds us, is not the same thing as the inability to offer good reasons for belief. The believer in religious revelation can have good reasons to believe the truths of faith, just as the apprentice can have good reasons for trusting his master and can eventually come to have his own insights into the subject matter of his craft. The deposit of faith is credible not only on the authority of a teacher whose life is a good life but also to the extent that it is consistent, highly illuminating, and provides guidelines to a way of life that bears good fruits. Crosson insists that what makes a religious belief illuminating is its power to catalyze intelligent understanding of the world in all its many and complex aspects. What Augustine means by the maxim "unless you believe you will not understand" is that accepting and reflecting upon the truths of the Catholic faith will enable the believer to "gestalt" into a beautiful whole the contents of the faith together with what he already knows without the aid of faith-belief and to elucidate the meaning of particular propositions, sayings, and narratives by the mutual light they can cast on each other. Reflection on the faith not only makes use of philosophy—by justifying inferences, making arguments, and interpreting texts—but also serves philosophy by casting light on the problems of philosophy that can point philosophers toward insights that might otherwise have been overlooked.

The relationship between philosophy and theology receives further treatment in Crosson's fifth essay, "Cicero and the Philosophy of Religion," which reads the *De Natura Deorum* as a compendium of puzzles in philosophical theology. Crosson maintains that the statement made by the Cicero-persona in the last line of the dialogue—that the Stoic arguments in the dialogue appear closer to the truth than the Epicurean and Skeptical ones—does not express Cicero's own opinion as author but rather is meant to protect Cicero against censure for dogmatic atheism. In Crosson's reading, Cicero is skeptical about the truth of all philosophical theologies known to him, Platonic or Aristotelian or Epicurean or Stoic, but nevertheless is open to the possibility of the emergence of some better and truer one in the future. Crosson's Cicero remains a religious man and a holder of a religious office in Roman society despite his theoretical skepticism because he is convinced that the practical benefit of religious rites and ceremonies counts as much toward rational justification as does adequate theory.

The sixth essay in the collection examines in tandem two classics of Western literature—Augustine's *Confessions* and Newman's *Apologia Pro Vita Sua*. Crosson discovers four important structural similarities between the two books that derive from the kind of story each author is trying to tell: (1) neither book is an autobiography; (2) each book divides into a narrative section describing the past and a non-narrative section which deals with the author's thoughts at a later time reflecting back on the narrative; (3) in each book the narrative section is organized around an axial event or *peripeteia*, for Augustine the encounter with Faustus and for Newman the negative reception of *Tract 90*; and (4) in each book the original and final religious positions are separated by a period of uncertainty and drift, and the final religious position coalesces around a dawning realization that God's action was involved in the axial moment, and that God's intention was different from the author's intention at the axial moment.

Returning to questions already discussed in the fourth essay, Crosson's seventh essay, "Proof and Presence," turns to Aquinas's teachings on faith. For Aquinas the merit of faith is diminished if a person believes only when human reasons are provided, because faith is belief in truths as revealed by a God whom one has encountered, whom one loves and trusts, and on whose authority one relies in believing. In Crosson's reading, Aquinas holds that people can reasonably judge the propositions of faith to be true even without a prior demonstration of the "preambles"—those truths about God knowable in principle without being revealed (God's existence, oneness, truthfulness, etc.). Readers of Aquinas have thought that Aquinas took knowledge of the preambles to be a necessary condition for the *act* of believing, when in fact he held only that knowledge of the preambles was a necessary condition for the fullest understanding of all the necessary conditions for the truth of the articles of faith.

Crosson defends his reading of Aquinas by emphasizing that Aquinas divides the act of faith into (1) a belief that God exists, (2) a belief that the propositional content of what God has revealed is true, and (3) a trusting and loving stance toward the God who reveals Himself. For Aquinas a demonstration of the divine existence is neither necessary for faith (though he believed such a demonstration was possible for some people capable of achieving it) nor sufficient for it, since faith involves an intuitive awareness of the presence of God that is a special kind of cognition, outside the realm of proof (it needn't be a direct mystical perception of God, but might be mediated by the Church). The content of faith is a self-revelation of God to man, rather like the self-revelation to a person by another person who says "I love you." Believing *that* cannot consist merely in accepting a coercive knock-down drag-out demonstrative argument. God's self-revelation speaks to the heart as well as the intellect (as is implied in Aquinas's third component of faith), and there are many ways of shutting the doors of mind and heart. (For a masterful discussion of this affective dimension of faith, see Dietrich von Hildebrand's *The Nature of Love*.)

Setting aside the affective and personal aspects of the act of faith, Crosson returns at the end of the essay to the topic of proofs for God's existence. Aquinas believed that the discovery of an adequate demonstration of God's existence becomes more likely in the light of a pre-existing faith-apprehension of God. For only by knowing what it is we want to prove, on other grounds than demonstration, do we stand a chance of finding a proper demonstration. Crosson discusses two episodes from the history of science—the acceptance of Copernicus' heliocentric astronomy and the acceptance of Cantor's transfinite mathematics—that illustrate this Thomistic teaching on the "retrospective character of the search for truth," episodes in which demonstrations were presented and rejected because of disbelief in the conclusion, but later came to be accepted as demonstrations after the conclusions had become acceptable. (For an interesting complement to Crosson's discussion here, see M. W. Sinnett, "Another Mathematician's Apology: Theological Reflections Upon the Role of Proof in Mathematics," *Scottish Journal of Theology* 46, no. 3 [1993].)

David Hume's philosophy of religion is an example of how little force a proof for the existence of God can have for a person without faith. Crosson's eighth essay, returning to the issue of latent versus manifest meaning in literature, offers an insightful analysis of the rhetorical strategies used by David Hume in his major writings about religion—the *Essays Concerning Human Understanding* (Chapters 10 and 11), the *Natural History of Religion*, and the *Dialogues Concerning Natural Religion* (the latter modeled in important ways on Cicero's *De Natura Deorum*). One of Hume's aims, realized in the *Dialogues*, is to attempt to discredit positive religion and especially Christianity by claiming that flaws in the design argument, the reality and amount of evil in the world, and the morally bad behavior on the part of theists show that theism is irrational, indemonstrable, and unable to provide a compass for human life. Another of his aims, realized in the *Natural History*, is to attempt to show that the real explanation of why theistic belief is so wide-spread is that it arises from irrational human propensities toward fear, flattery, and anthropomorphic projection in response to the vicissitudes of life (presaging the works of Feuerbach, Marx, Nietzsche, and Freud). A third aim is to found a non-ritualistic, non-theistic, man-centered "philosophical religion" as the basis for a secular liberal worldview and politics. Crosson shows that Hume's intentions are latently and not manifestly expressed in his works. (For a treatment providing an ex-cellent complement to Crosson's view of the latent implications of the *Dialogues*, see Anders Jeffner, *Butler and Hume on Religion*.)

Crosson's ninth and tenth essays offer two short histories. The first traces conceptions of the "natural law" from Philo's theologically based conception to Locke's conception, with its agnosticism about the human good, to Mill's liberal conception. The other traces the history of Ameri-can Catholic social teaching from a time when it holds to a conception of the state as a moral agent responsible for seeking the common good to a time when it holds that the state's only roles are to protect the im-munity rights of its citizens (rights conceived as providing immunity against the violation of preferences, as opposed to rights conceived as enabling one to participate in a substantive common good), to secure public order (e.g., by protecting religious liberty), and to ignore distribu-tive justice as a constitutive component of the common good by taking a laissez-faire attitude towards the market. Crosson ends with a sympa-thetic discussion of Alasdair MacIntyre's critique of the liberal state.

I am delighted to introduce this volume of essays by Frederick Crosson, who was an important influence on my generation of Phi-losophy and Liberal Studies students at Notre Dame; we revered him as an approachable teacher and a person of *gravitas* and great intelligence. The volume will be especially useful for courses in the history of phi-losophy and in the philosophy of religion. The essays on the *Confessions*, on the *De Magistro*, and on *De Utilitate Credendi* are minor classics in the secondary literature; they taught many of us how to read Augustine. All the essays together express a distinctive historical approach to the philosophy of religion. It is an approach that attends to the historical changes in the meaning of "religion," to Hume's important role in that history, to the importance of the philosophy of mind to the philosophy of religion, and to a variety of important interrelations between metaphysical arguments, proofs, Newman-style cumulative-case arguments, and "inferences to the best explanation," on the one hand, and historical/biographical narratives and personal life experiences, on the other. Those of us who knew him and his work continue to be grateful to him.

MARK MOES

CHAPTER ONE

Esoteric versus Latent Teaching

One of the ideas to which Leo Strauss drew the attention of many readers in the last century is that of a difference between exoteric and esoteric philosophical writing. These terms can refer to different kinds of philosophical teaching, one kind intended for a general and the other kind for a more restricted audience. Indeed, it seems to be the case historically that it was Aristotle who first used (perhaps coined) one of the terms in such a sense, as will be discussed below.

Alternatively, the terms can also be used to describe a single text that incorporates both levels of communication—such a text would have the capacity to address simultaneously two different kinds of readers. In this alternative case, the presence of an esoteric aspect of the text, one intended for a more restricted readership, can be indicated by hints, the structure of the text, allusions, and so forth, that most readers will not pay attention to but which some readers will ponder and assemble into an interpretation, a perspective from which to read and understand the text.

Of course any kind of text that is written with dimensions of meaning that are not immediately evident might be called "esoteric" in a broader sense, the term here suggesting that the reader does not readily see the connections, the implications of its assertions, even though the author did not intend to hide anything from most readers. I have this experience when I read some literary works: as I reread and ponder them, I come to see new implications in what the author has written. Think of reading Sophocles or *Moby Dick*. Some of what is being said in an undertone, so to speak, slowly becomes evident, as one makes connections.

Of course a less apparent or "esoteric" meaning may also be intended by the writer or speaker to be discovered by as many readers as possible, so that its covert character is a kind of challenge to the reader. In a work attributed to the fourth-century Athenian orator Demetrius, we read,

> not all possible points should be punctiliously and tediously elaborated, but some should be left to the comprehension and inference of the hearer, who when he perceives what you have left unsaid becomes not only your hearer but your witness. . . . For he thinks himself intelligent because you have afforded him the means of showing his intelligence. It seems like a slur on your hearer to tell him everything as though he were a simpleton.[1]

Great works of literature commonly have a dimension of meaning that appears clearly only when one reflects on the text, connects up different loci, and "puts two and two together."

But to call these last examples "esoteric" in the present context would be to muddle the sense of the term that we are trying to articulate. Strauss uses the term "esoteric" to refer primarily to a level of meaning that is intended by the philosophical author to remain inaccessible to all but a relatively small number of readers.[2] In this case of a text with these two levels of meaning intended for different audiences, we can say that for most readers the esoteric meaning is and remains unnoticed.

Why would an author want to speak to two disparate audiences in this way? Well, that difference may depend (as Strauss believed) on two senses of the phrase "political philosophy." One is its common meaning, philosophizing about the political community, about its *telos* and its matter and form. The other sense of "political philosophy" refers to the "politic" self-presentation of philosophy and philosophers to the political community in which they live. Why do philosophers have to think about that, to be concerned with that?

Because philosophy is the project, the undertaking, to replace opinions about all things and the whole with knowledge of all things and of the whole. As Socrates says in the *Phaedrus* when he is asked a question about what actions are pleasing to the gods,

> I can tell you what I've heard from our ancestors. Whether it's true or not, I don't know. But if we could find out the truth for ourselves, should we still bother about human opinions?[3]

"A ridiculous question!" Phaedrus responds.

But opinion is the foundation-element of our common life, of the political community. As Tocqueville wrote in *Democracy in America*, "[U]nder no circumstances will dogmatical belief cease to exist. . . . [M]en will never cease to entertain some opinions on trust and without discussion. . . . [W]ithout ideas [about what is right and wrong, good and bad] held in common there is no common action, and without common action there may still be men, but there is no social body."[4] So the endeavor to call into question those foundational beliefs can be perceived as a threat to the existence of a society, as Socrates learned. Philosophers in the classical world learned from his fate to respect those fundamental ideas to which a political community is dedicated,[5] not just from fear of Socrates' fate but from the recognition that the common life of the community, the good of the community, presupposed those dogmatical beliefs. Paramount among those beliefs are religious doctrines about the divine and what actions are pleasing to God or the gods.

In Strauss's view, the creation of esoteric writing, of esoteric communication, was the philosopher's response to that situation. If such esoteric communication hidden within the published writings is possible, then philosophers can awaken their progeny, the young potential philosophers, to the love of wisdom and to the task of trying to replace common opinion about what is so and what is good with the quest for knowledge of these things. Meanwhile the exoteric dimension of their writings would leave undisturbed the dogmatical (that is, unquestioned) beliefs that the community needed. Indeed, the exoteric dimension could be read as helping to support those beliefs. And, in Strauss's view, prominent among the esoteric teachings of many philosophers was the true nature of religion and the divine (for example, Cicero's *De Natura Deorum* and Spinoza's *Tractatus Theologico-Politicus*).[6]

In order to get a clearer picture of the historical origin of this terminology, we need to go back to the classical Greek and Roman philosophers.

I

The term *exoterikoi logoi* occurs at least eight times in Aristotle's writings.[7] It is commonly translated as "extraneous discourses" or "popular arguments" because *exoterikos* refers generally to something external, or outside.[8] It is not clear what the discourses referred to are external to, but the general assumption is that the reference is to discussions or writings external to the Lyceum (where Aristotle's students were taught), or perhaps to writings by Aristotle but for an audience outside the Lyceum. In the latter case, one could distinguish between Aristotle's writings for an external audience—and so *exoterikoi logoi*—and his lectures and writings within the Lyceum, intended for his students.

So, for example, one scholar (Bernays) argued that the term referred to Aristotle's dialogues, praised by Cicero, but of which we possess only fragments. They were written apparently while he was still at the Academy of Plato and, like Plato's dialogues, written with the awareness that they would be available to a wide audience. Others believe that the term refers to some of our extant treatises of Aristotle (such as the *Ethics* and *Politics*) that were written to be accessible to readers who were not students of the Lyceum. Still other scholars (for example, Rackham) think the term refers to arguments or doctrine that were not peculiar to the Peripatetic school but would be known to the generally informed reader.

Unfortunately, in only one of the eight uses which Aristotle makes of the term does he contrast it with any other kind of discourse. This is in the *Eudemian Ethics*:

> to assert the existence of a Form not only of the good but of anything else is a mere idle abstraction (but this has been considered in various ways both in extraneous discourses and in those along philosophical lines [*kata philosophian*]).[9]

Although this does not cast much light on the source of the extraneous discourses, it implies that they are less rigorously philosophical than discourses in the Lyceum.

Cicero supplies a similar term of contrast in Latin (though he quotes the term for extraneous works in Greek), three centuries later. In his dialogue *De Finibus*, one of his characters (Marcus Piso), speaking of the Peripatetics, says

> Their books on the subject of the highest good fall into two classes, one popular in style, and this class they used to call *exoterikon*, the other *limatius* [a Latin word meaning more carefully worked].[10]

But this Latin term seems not to have been used by others to designate the class opposed to the Greek *exoterikon*. About a century and a half later, Plutarch takes the extraneous writings to include the ethical and political treatises of Aristotle, but he contrasts that category with the *aporreton* (that is, secret, not to be spoken about) teachings which he says philosophers designate by the name *akroamatikas* (meaning for hearers, not readers).[11]

Toward the end of the second century A.D., in one of his satiric dialogues, the Greek writer Lucian uses the term that has become common to contrast with exoteric. Speaking of the Peripatetic philosopher, one of Lucian's characters says,

> Viewed from the outside, he seems to be one man, and from the inside, another; so if you buy him, be sure to call the one exoteric [*exoterikon*] and the other esoteric [*esoterikon*].[12]

So there we have the now familiar term of esoteric and its contrast with exoteric. That terminology passes on into the Eastern Greek tradition and is used by Clement of Alexandria, Simplicius, Origen, Iamblichus, and others.

It is a curious fact that those terms do not seem to be have been appropriated by the Latin tradition, classical or medieval. As noted above, Cicero cites the term *exoterikon* but does not transliterate it into Latin. Two centuries later, the Latin writer Aulus Gellius mentions (using the Greek words) the tradition that Aristotle had two forms of teachings, *exoterika* and *akroatika*, and he transliterates these into Latin:

> He also divided his books on all these subjects into two divisions, calling one set exoteric (*exoterici*), the other acroatic (*acroatici*).[13]

There is also a letter written to St. Augustine which seems to use, in Latin, the word *esotericam*, but there is no responding letter of Augustine.[14]

According to the *Thesaurus Linguae Latinae*, these are the only three instances of Roman writers who use forms of the Greek terms. A last instance occurs in the twelfth-century writings of John of Salisbury (d. 1180) who, speaking of Aristotle in his *Polycraticus*, says:

> He is said to have been the first to have divided the kinds of studies into acroatic (*acroaticum*) and exoteric (*exotericum*).[15]

So it seems that for over a thousand years, the Greek terms (and their Latin transliterations) never took root in the Latin of the Western world. (According to the *Oxford English Dictionary*, esoteric and its variants first appear in English only once in the seventeenth century, and more general use in the eighteenth.) As a result, the medieval recovery of the writings of some of the classical Greek philosophers presented translation problems, as we shall see.

In the Eastern and then Byzantine Empire and Church, where Greek remained for some time the language of philosophy and theology and, for another thousand years, the official language of Church and Empire, the distinction of doctrines that are termed *exoterikoi* or *esoterikoi* continued. Clement of Alexandria, Origen, and their successors apply the distinction to their discussions of both philosophers and Christian doctrine. However, it is interesting and relevant to note that, for example, Origen vigorously denies that there is any secret (*kruphion*) Christian teaching, that is, teaching passed down orally from the time of the Apostles to some inner circle of followers, as was traditionally asserted of Pythagoras and his students.[16] At the same time, he asserts the presence of an exoteric and esoteric dimension to the Scriptures and the teaching of Jesus.

II

Saint Augustine knows of this distinction, of a philosopher's work being different on the surface from what the author himself thought (though he never uses the terminology of exoteric and esoteric). In the *City of God*, for example, he discusses the writings of Plato, Cicero, Varro, and others as sometimes concealing what they really thought.

> Plato makes a point of preserving the manner of his master Socrates. . . . It is well known that Socrates was in the habit of concealing his knowledge or his beliefs: and Plato approved of that habit. The result is that it is not easy to discover his own opinion, even on important matters.[17]

Cicero believed that it would not be reasonable for a religion to pray or sacrifice to a God who had no foreknowledge of the future or power over it. Such a being could not respond effectively no matter what our entreaty or offering—indeed in such a case one might deny that there is a god (in the sense of a superior being who had such knowledge and power).

> Cicero himself realized this, and almost ventured on the denial. . . . But he did not say it in his own person; he knew that such an assertion would disturb people, and incur odium. And so he represents Cotta as arguing this point against the Stoics, in the book *On the Nature of the Gods*.

Cicero himself is a character in (and narrator of) the dialogue of that book, and at the end of it Cicero the character votes against Cotta's atheistic position, but, Augustine continues, that was not the thought of Cicero the author. Indeed, in his book *On Divination*, Cicero comes out openly in his own name in an attack on the notion of foreknowledge.[18]

Augustine says that Varro, a prolific writer on Roman culture and practices, admits to feeling bound to write conventionally about the traditional deities, although if he were founding a city, he would have named deities according to the rule of nature. But in "speaking like this he hints ... that he is not revealing all that he knows." Augustine adds,

> I should rightly be suspected of indulging in conjecture here, if Varro had not openly declared in another place, on the subject of religious rites, that there are many truths which it is not expedient for the general public to know, and further, many falsehoods which it is good for the people to believe true.[19]

Similar comments are made about Apuleius and others, but mention will be made here only of Augustine's persistent view about the "Platonists." These "Academics" (as they were called during the late Academy) held the view that the truth about virtue and knowledge and divinity could not be effectively presented to skeptics and men addicted to pleasures, so their energy was spent instead criticizing the Epicureans and Stoics. They acted rightly, in Augustine's view, "in concealing completely the doctrine of the Academy and burying it as gold to be found at some later time."[20]

But Augustine does not unfold, by commenting on it, the text of any of these writers as possessing both an esoteric and an exoteric teaching. Rather, he treats them as exoteric discourses whose teaching is not what the author himself truly thought, as the author indicates by what he hints and by what he says elsewhere. But there is sufficient indication for the thoughtful reader that this is not the truth, the whole truth, and nothing but the truth.

However, Augustine has learned and knows of a text and a tradition of its interpretation that does rest on a distinction between a manifest and a latent level of meaning. He learned of this the hard way, by first reading the manifest meaning and finding it inferior to Cicero's writing, and turning away from the text. What he turned away from was, of course, the Scriptures, to which he had turned after being inspired by Cicero's exhortation to the pursuit of wisdom in his *Hortensius*. He writes in the *Confessions*:

> I [now] see something within them [the Scriptures] that was neither revealed to the proud nor made plain to children, that was

lowly on one's entrance but lofty on further advance, and that was veiled over in mysteries. . . . I did not feel towards it then as I am speaking now, but it seemed to me unworthy of comparison with the nobility of Cicero's writings. My swelling pride turned away from its humble style and my sharp gaze did not penetrate into its inner meaning.[21]

But after learning to read the latent meaning of the Scriptures from listening to the sermons of St. Ambrose, his ability to read and to understand is metamorphosed:

[The Scriptures] were easy for everyone to read and yet safeguarded the dignity of their hidden truth within a deeper meaning, by words completely clear and by a lowly style of speech making itself accessible to all men, and drawing the attention of those who are not light of heart. Thus it can receive all men into its generous bosom and by narrow passages lead on to you [God] a small number of them.[22]

So for Augustine, the paradigm or prime analogate of this combining of a latent and a manifest meaning in a single text was the way in which the Old Testament discloses a new significance when read from the perspective of the New Testament.

This is the sacrament, the hidden meaning, of the Old Testament, where the New Testament lay concealed. In the Old Testament the promises and gifts are of earthly things; but even then men of spiritual perception realized, although they did not yet proclaim the fact for all to hear, that by these temporal goods eternity was signified; they understood also what were the gifts of God which constituted true felicity.[23]

One could say that for this tradition of reading and interpretation, the paradigm of the opening up of the latent meaning is the recounting in Luke's Gospel of Jesus revealing the latent meaning of the Hebrew Scriptures for the disciples on the road to Emmaus.[24]

Of course that distinction regarding Scripture (both Old and New Testaments) of manifest and latent, of overt and hidden, if it is for the good of the different kinds of hearers and readers, will also have to apply to preaching and writing about those things. So in his work *On Christian Doctrine*, Augustine remarks that in the case of speaking to a public audience,

> There are some things which with their full implications are not understood or are hardly understood, no matter how eloquently they are spoken. . . . [T]hese things should never, or only rarely on account of some necessity, be set before a public audience.[25]

In such public speaking where one knows something about the character of the audience, it is easy to pass over or touch lightly on issues which may be misunderstood or disturbing to some.

But as Plato had noted, the situation is different in the case of writing, because one cannot know in advance the character of the (unknown) reading audience. Still, it is possible to write in such a way that those who understand are held by that which they read, while those who do not understand are disinclined to read further. However, Augustine adds, there is a duty, not to be neglected, to bring one's understanding to the knowledge of others, provided they have a desire to learn and the capacity to learn.[26]

Perhaps an example of such writing would be Boethius' treatise *On the Trinity*. In the proemium to that work, Boethius addresses his father-in-law, a distinguished Roman consul and senator, and says he is not writing for everyone. The topic is difficult; the philosophical vocabulary required is technical and unknown to most. So, he writes,

> I purposely use brevity and wrap up the issues that I draw from the deep questionings of philosophy in new and unfamiliar words such as speak only to you and to myself. . . . The rest of the world I simply disregard since those who cannot understand them seem unworthy even to read them.[27]

To judge from the text of the treatise, Boethius (probably rightly) believed that the technical terminology and concepts regarding substance and property, identity and difference, relations, and similar terms would be off-putting to anyone not trained in philosophical sources. But in terms of the language of the categories we have been adumbrating, it would perhaps be more appropriate to designate such a work as simply esoteric—that is, not intended for a broad readership but for only a small one. We could then contrast such a work with, say, the *Confessions* of St. Augustine, which not only has but was intended to have both manifest and latent levels of understanding.[28]

I mention Boethius' work also because it provided the occasion for one of Thomas Aquinas's few discussions of latent teaching. In his commentary on Boethius' treatise, Thomas has an article on the topic, "Whether Divine Things Ought to Be Concealed by New and Obscure Words."

After advancing some opinions pro and con, Aquinas begins his own response:

> A teacher should so moderate his words that they tend to the benefit and not the detriment of his hearers. Now there are some things that can harm no one when heard, for example the truths that everyone is responsible to know, and these should not be concealed (*occultanda*) but openly (*manifeste*) proposed to all. There are others which if presented openly would be harmful to those hearing them. . . . These matters should be concealed from those to whom they might do harm.

Thomas remarks that in oral face-to-face communication, one can decide how to speak because one can discern the nature of the hearer or hearers, and one can moderate one's words accordingly. But, he continues,

> In writing, this distinction does not apply, because a book once written down can come into the hands of anyone; and therefore such matters should be concealed by obscure words so that they may benefit the wise who will understand them and be hidden (*occultentur*) from the uneducated (*simplicibus*) who will not be able to grasp them.[29]

So, he comments that teachers of Sacred Scripture are not obliged to propose the same things to both the wise and the unwise, but to tell to each what is accessible to them. His model for this is the way that Scripture and Christ communicated sacred doctrine.

In the very first question of the *Summa Theologiae*, Aquinas inquires whether sacred doctrine should employ metaphorical language, and his response is yes, it is appropriate because we human beings learn of spiritual things through material images and metaphors. It is also appropriate to Sacred Scripture,

> which is proposed to all of us without distinction of persons . . . that spiritual things be taught by means of similitudes taken from corporeal things, so that thereby even the simple (*rudes*) who are unable to grasp intellectual truths by themselves may be able to understand them.[30]

It is natural for human beings, although they are intellectual creatures, to understand what is hidden within (latent) the sensible appearance of things—for example, the substantial nature of the thing—in terms of metaphors taken from the perceptual world: "under similitudes and figures [of speech], there lies latent (*latet*) the truth that is thus figured."[31] What is latent is hidden, but in the sense of potentially present, potentially manifest; it can become actually known, manifestly present, if it can be regarded from the right perspective. In contrast to Boethius, who offers his readers not metaphors but rigorous logical and metaphysical analyses, Sacred Scripture latently offers, as Aquinas says in the very next article, figurative as well as literal senses of its words.

In the third part of the *Summa Theologiae*, Aquinas inquires whether Christ should have taught (*docere*) all things publicly, as he did. Well, Thomas says, there are three ways in which someone's doctrine might be hidden. One way is by deliberately, intentionally not communicating it to anyone, but this was not the way of Christ. A second way to hide a doctrine is by telling it only to a few, but Christ discoursed to many. In a third way, he says,

> doctrine is concealed by the way in which it is taught (*modum docendi*), and thus Christ spoke of certain things in hidden ways to the

crowds, by using parables in announcing spiritual mysteries to them which they were either not capable of or not worthy to grasp. Yet it was better for them to hear the expounding of spiritual things in the form of parables than to be deprived of it completely. However, the Lord opened up the parables and explained the unveiled truth of them to the disciples, so that they might present it to others who were ready for it.[32]

Note that Aquinas says that Christ taught certain things in hidden ways—because of course he declared many things without parables or metaphors, presented them openly to all. And, Aquinas adds, "whatever things out of his wisdom he judged it right to make known to others, he proclaimed not in secret but openly, although he was not understood by all."

This manner of teaching something that is beyond the capacity of some persons to understand is similar to, for example, the way in which a scientist might try to explain quantum theory to a readership mathematically and scientifically unprepared to understand it directly. So the scientific writer would imagine various commonsense similitudes to illustrate the uncertainty principle or the particle-like properties of light waves, and so forth. "Is it really like that?" one might ask, and be answered, "Well, no, but it's sort of analogous to that." It does provide a picture which is not intended to be deceptive, which gives some sense of what it's like. One might add that even if the writer could provide a mathematical physics account of these quantum phenomena for an audience prepared to understand it, still that account would convey neither all there was to be understood about quantum phenomena nor what lay in the future understanding of them. Just so, the explanations that a teacher like Jesus gave to his disciples were not the end of understanding what was being said.[33]

III

So Aquinas and Augustine are quite aware of latent teaching, of a discourse having both a hidden dimension and a manifest dimension.

They both think that it is sometimes appropriate to write and speak in that way for the good of those receiving the words. Augustine, at least, sometimes writes in that two-level way himself. But their position on latent teaching in the Christian tradition is, in my judgment, quite different from that of Leo Strauss on esoteric writing and the philosophical tradition he tries to trace.

A central difference is that in the Christian tradition the manifest teaching expressed in similitudes and metaphors and parables aims at communicating the truth, at bearing witness to the truth, in a form in which it is able to be understood (at least partially) by all. There is only one doctrine, presented in different depths of meaning to the two audiences. In contrast, the esoteric philosophical tradition that Strauss discusses typically allots to its exoteric dimension the favorable presentation of the socially orthodox views (the dogmatical beliefs) while the esoteric dimension may present a quite different position.[34]

A second difference is linked with this: in such a context, it would be morally wrong to deceive those who understand only the manifest level because they need to know what is being made known. Aquinas follows Augustine in maintaining that although it is never permissible to conceal the truth by lying, it may be licit to hide the truth prudently, by keeping it back, by keeping silent. But he also follows (and quotes) Augustine that it is not a lie to do or say a thing figuratively "because . . . when a thing is said or done figuratively, it means what those who apprehend it understand it to signify."[35] No deliberate misrepresentation of what is so, or misrepresentation of the convictions of the speaker or author, is compatible with the responsibility to bear truthful witness. If they were so compatible, then Dostoievski's Grand Inquisitor would be an appropriate model for the Christian teacher—deceiving the many for what the teacher deems to be their good.

That is why, as noted previously, Augustine speaks of the moral responsibility of one who expounds sacred doctrine to go as far as possible in seeking the understanding of those addressed:

> [I]n conversations, the duty should not be neglected of bringing the truth which we have perceived, no matter how difficult it may be to comprehend or how much labor may be involved, to the under-

standing of others, provided that the listener or interlocutor wishes to learn and has the capacity to do so.[36]

It is not inconsistent with this position to indicate to the audience of the manifest level that there's "more here than meets the eye." So, St. Paul writes back to the new Christians of Corinth about his first proclaiming of the "good news":

> I myself was unable to speak to you as people of the spirit, but treated you as carnal-minded, still infants in Christ. What I fed you with was milk, not solid food, for you were not ready for that.[37]

For Augustine and Aquinas, *some* hearers of the word must learn how the similitudes and parables and metaphors are to be understood (and how not to be understood) and know when and how to go beyond the literal to what is figured by it. Their responsibility would be to preserve and extend a tradition of interpretation and reflective understanding that originates with the apostles and guides the presentation of the scriptural doctrine. Theology and the development of doctrine play an essential role in this process.

The classical conception of esoteric writing is inflected by some later philosophers who, convinced of the possible benefits of enlightenment and consequently of a wider capacity for understanding the truth, desired a gradual replacement of the accepted opinion by the truth or an approximation to the truth.[38] Strauss believed that not a few European philosophers in the modern period adopted this standpoint, and while they retained the difference between exoteric and esoteric communication, they desired to reach as many readers as possible who could be made aware of the esoteric teaching.

A third difference between the philosophical tradition of esotericism and the religious tradition of latent teaching is their distinct origins, reflected in the absence of and ignorance of esoteric/exoteric terminology in the Latin tradition. As I shall try to show, a thinker like Thomas Aquinas, for example, can know and teach the distinction between overt or manifest communication and hidden or latent communication and not know of the philosophical tradition.[39] These are, historically, in origin and practice, distinct traditions.

IV

Although Augustine and Aquinas share common views about manifest and latent teaching and the usefulness of both under certain conditions when communicating Christian doctrine, they seem to differ in regard to the teaching of philosophers. Augustine, as has been noted, thought it was not uncommon for philosophers to conceal what they truly thought about certain things for the sake of not disturbing some of their readers. At the same time they might provide hints, to those able to discern them, that there was a different way of regarding the issues. Augustine himself certainly writes on two levels and does not simply hint that there is another (latent) level in some of his own works,[40] but he articulates that latent level at some length. But then all of his works that we have were written after he had turned to Christianity, so one might expect that he would feel free to follow the counsel he offers in his work *On Christian Doctrine* about latent and manifest doctrine. Indeed, in the *Confessions* he uses the same language to describe both the text of the Scriptures and of his own writing:

> Provided, therefore, that each person tries to ascertain in the holy scriptures the meaning the author intended, what harm is there if a reader holds an opinion which you, the light of all truthful minds, show to be true, even though it is not intended by the [human] author, who himself meant something true, but not exactly that?

A few pages later he adds,

> Of this I am certain, and I am not afraid to declare it from my heart, that if I had to write something to which the highest authority would be attributed, I would rather write it in such a way that my words would reinforce for each reader whatever truth he was able to grasp about these matters, provided there was no falsity to offend me.[41]

It is not clear to what extent he read philosophers as articulating and unfolding a hidden teaching in addition to their hinting or saying elsewhere that there was another perspective on the issues being discussed. The philosopher he was most likely to have been able to learn that from was Plato in his dialogues, but Augustine knew little Greek and it seems clear that, apart from Cicero's translation of the *Timaeus*, his knowledge of the dialogues is mostly secondhand, through secondary sources. To judge from his own early dialogues, he certainly could and did develop a latent teaching in the dialogue form.

While he shared with Augustine the acknowledgement of latent and manifest teaching in the same discourse (exemplified in the parables of the Gospels), Thomas Aquinas does not seem to have written in a latent/manifest way. If that is so, the reason may be simply that virtually all that he wrote was (1) intended for theologians and students of theology who would need to know what the simple and uneducated might not need to know; and (2) unlike Augustine and Boethius, for example, he wrote in a language (Latin) restricted, in practice, to those prepared by their studies to learn from it. He wrote, in short, for persons well aware of the niceties of technical and subtle language in discussing such mysteries as the Trinity and the Incarnation, and familiar with apt philosophical distinctions (as did Boethius in his *De Trinitate*).

But there is another aspect to the problem presently being discussed, and that is the status of philosophy in relation to the religious tradition in which it is carried on. Leo Strauss maintained that there was a significant difference in this respect between Judaism and Islam, on one hand, and Christianity on the other. For Judaism and Islam, he said, revelation has primarily the character of *nomos*, of law, and so of the constituting of an earthly community governed by that law, while for Christianity, revelation has primarily the character of *logos*, of truth. No political community is established by that *logos*, but at most an *ecclesia*, distinct from the realm governed by Caesar's laws.

Clearly philosophy, as the quest to understand the nature of the whole and its parts, has more in common with revelation as *logos* than with revelation as law. First, with respect to the hearing of what is proposed to faith, philosophy's treasure-trove of reflections on language and meaning and logic and on what there is, is indispensable in unfolding the proper meaning of the words of revelation. Second, with respect to the elaboration of those proper meanings into a coherent and systematic doctrine of theology, philosophy is indispensable. It is no accident that from the early centuries, philosophy in the Christian world came into an ever closer dialogue with revelation.

For Judaism and Islam, in contrast, it is as commentary on divine law, as Talmud and Fiqh (jurisprudence or commentary on the law) that reflection on revelation takes its primary form. Greek philosophy as it became known to the expanding Islamic society was a more precarious, or less necessary, study than jurisprudence. In contrast, as a Christian society and culture developed, the study of philosophy became an essential and required part of the education of theologians. Strauss comments:

> This difference explains partly the eventual collapse of philosophical inquiry in the Islamic and in the Jewish world, a collapse which has no parallel in the Western Christian world.[42]

It is against this background that Ernest Fortin, a careful student of Strauss and of the Christian tradition, wrote that

> [t]he canonical status which philosophy enjoyed in the Christian world helps to explain . . . why Aquinas was able to discard as unnecessary or irrelevant the esotericism common to much of the ancient philosophical tradition and purposely affected by many of the Church Fathers with whose works he was acquainted.[43]

My hesitation about this statement is with the word discard, because I do not think that Aquinas was aware of a practice of esotericism in the ancient philosophical tradition (nor of the role of persecution or the danger of persecution in its development). I do not think that he ever discusses the esoteric writing of philosophers or reads the texts of those ancient philosophers (whose texts he knows) as having a hidden dimension of meaning.

He certainly acknowledged the cryptic character of Boethius' treatise on the Trinity, but then he never called any Christian thinker a "philosopher."[44] It is generally accepted that he did not know any of the dialogues of Plato at first hand. Robert Henle concluded after a long study that "[i]t is certain that Saint Thomas did not use [of the three works of Plato in Latin translation] either the *Meno* or the *Phaedo* and there is no convincing evidence that he was directly acquainted with either Cicero's or Chalcidius' translations of the *Timaeus*."[45] Aquinas has only two indirect references (from Augustine and Isidore) to any of the three dialogues of Cicero on the gods and religious practice (*De Natura Deorum, De Fato, De Divinatione*), and no references to the *De Rerum Natura* of Lucretius. These are mentioned simply to indicate that Aquinas seems to have had little direct encounter with the texts of classical philosophers who are taken by Strauss and others to exemplify esoteric writing.

One might have thought that Aquinas's close study of and commentaries on Aristotle's works could have provided an encounter with the idea, especially since Aristotle refers eight times to exoteric discourses.[46] Unfortunately, no translation of the *Eudemian Ethics*, the only work in which Aristotle provides a contrasting term for exoteric discourses (namely, more philosophical) was available to Aquinas, and of the other seven occurrences of the term *exoterikoi logoi*, Aquinas has commentaries on only four of them. The translations he worked from are not much help: they translate the Greek by exterior discourses, extraneous arguments, external conversations. Aquinas sometimes takes them to mean other discussions of the same subject but in other works of Aristotle, or sometimes arguments given by others, or sophistical arguments, or even texts written for someone living far away.

A striking instance that seems to reinforce the view that Aquinas was unaware of a tradition of philosophical esoteric writing is encountered in some of his comments on Plato's manner of writing. It has been remarked above that in the first question of the *Summa Theologiae* Aquinas commends the use of metaphorical language and similitudes in theological teaching to convey the truth about intellectual things, because under similitudes and figures, there lies latent (*latet*) the truth that is thus figured.[47] But while commenting on Aristotle's *De Anima*, in a section where Aristotle is criticizing Plato's *Timaeus* for describing the world-soul as a circle divided into parts, Aquinas describes Aristotle as criticizing the literal sense of Plato's language rather than its intention. The problem is not with Aristotle, he says, it is with Plato's use of language:

Plato had a bad way of teaching (*habuit malum modum docendi*) for he says everything by figures of speech (*figurate*) and teaches through symbols, intending something other by his words than their literal sense.[48]

This would seem to imply that philosophers ought to write straightforwardly, avoiding figures and metaphors that could mislead. Any idea of philosophy's being written in such a way in order not to disturb the dogmatical opinions of possible readers seems absent.

Fortin, in a work written a decade after the words quoted from him above, seems to have had some second thoughts. He still believed that Aquinas had a bookish knowledge of secret writing

through certain ancient authors such as Cicero, Boethius and Pseudo-Dionysius, [but he himself] did not deal with it and merely stated that it was no longer in use among his contemporaries: *apud modernos est inconsuetus* [in our time it is not customary]. One can even ask whether he understood it aright. Although he speaks of it a number of times, he seems to have seen in it no more than a pedagogical device used to make the truth more appreciated by making it more difficult to attain and keeping it at a distance from those who would be unworthy of it.[49]

But Boethius and Pseudo-Dionysius belong to the theological tradition in which, as we have seen, Aquinas justifies latent teaching by reference to the model of the Scriptures and to the way of teaching (*modum docendi*) of Christ who concealed (*in occulto*) some of his teaching in parables. This is not the same as the intention to make the truth more appreciated because one has to work at discerning it—the position that Demetrius was quoted earlier as approving—although that motivation can play a role in some teaching.

There do not appear to be grounds for identifying Aquinas's conception of how and why Christ and the Scriptures concealed a deeper meaning with the conception of a philosophical tradition of esoteric meaning. There do not appear to be grounds for asserting that Aquinas knew of such a tradition.

So our conclusion is that the theological tradition which Aquinas knows, of concealing a latent dimension of meaning, is, in the West at least, historically independent of a tradition of philosophical writing that incorporates both esoteric and exoteric meanings in a single text. It is different in origin since its roots lie in the disclosure by Christ of a latent meaning in the Old Testament and in his own teaching by parables and similitudes. It is different in structure since the same truth is taught in both latent and manifest dimensions—there is only one doctrine, taught in two different modes. It is different in its moral dimension because the philosophical tradition of esotericism not only allows but requires that the socially useful dogmatical opinions of the many be left undisturbed, for their good as well as that of the community, while the theological tradition, since it deals with revealed truths concerning the salvation of each and all, must hand on (*tradere*) what all must know.

CHAPTER TWO

The Disclosure of Hidden Providence

Introduction: Composition and Hermeneutics

It has been a commonplace for some scholars to say that the *Confessions* is not carefully composed. It is "a badly composed book," Augustine "was not able to plan a book," he "composes badly. . . . the ancients generally did not give to composition the attention that we do."[1] If one has such views, it is unlikely that subtler indications of meaningful structure in the text being read will be noted. And if those structures are not attended to, it is likely that the text may seem to lack design, to lack unity. But as Ovid said, "It is art to conceal art," and some of Augustine's art is easy to overlook.

Perhaps part of the reason for some modern inattention to such factors is the decline of a tradition that considers the possible intention of an author to speak differently to different kinds of readers using the same words. Augustine was familiar with such a tradition from his long and careful study of the classical rhetorical and philosophical authors, even before he first came to learn how to read the Scriptures from Ambrose. So, for example, he comments in the *City of God* on the practice of philosophers of communicating on two levels: Socrates and Plato, Cicero, Varro, and Apuleius.[2] But already much earlier he speaks of the Scriptures and of the practice of Jesus as exemplifying the method of "all rational disciplines"; such a practice, he says, "teaches partly quite openly and partly by similitudes," and he adds, "If there was nothing that could not be understood with perfect ease, there would be no studious search for truth and no pleasure in finding it."[3]

It is the understanding of Scripture that is paradigmatic for Augustine in the *Confessions*. Thus, he speaks of how he came to think of the authority of the Scriptures:

> scripture was easily accessible to every reader, while yet guarding a mysterious dignity in its deeper sense. In plain words and very humble modes of speech it offered itself to everyone, yet stretched the understanding of those who were not shallow-minded. It welcomed all comers to its hospitable embrace, yet through narrow openings attracted a few to you.[4]

Indeed he speaks of his own desire to be so read:

> Of this I am certain . . . that if I had to write something to which the highest authority would be attributed, I would rather write it in such a way that my words would reinforce for each reader whatever truth he was able to grasp about these matters, than express a single idea so unambiguously as to exclude others, provided these did not offend me by their falsehood.[5]

This hermeneutical attitude stands in a mean between the position that thinks the words of a teacher need not be moderated in this way—and so everything is on the same depth level, so to speak—and the position of someone who believes that what is to be taught is not determined by what is so, but by what the student/reader should hear.

Augustine's view that these two attitudes may sometimes need to be blended is explicitly stated in a slightly different context in *Christian Instruction*.

> Where certain truths are, by reason of their own character, not comprehensible, or scarcely so, even when explained with every effort on the part of the speaker to make them clear, these one rarely dwells on with a general audience, or never mentions at all: but in writing,

the same distinction cannot be adhered to, because a book, once published, can fall into the hands of any one at all, and therefore some truths should be shielded by obscuring words, so that they may profit those who will understand them and be hidden from the simple who will not comprehend them. (4.9.23)

This view is reaffirmed by Thomas Aquinas in his commentary on Boethius' *On the Trinity*. There he maintains that

the words of a teacher ought to be so moderated that they result to the profit and not to the detriment of the one hearing him. Now there are certain things which on being heard harm no one, as are the truths which all are responsible to know; and such ought not to be hidden but openly proposed to all. But there are others which, if openly presented, cause harm in those hearing them.

Citing the text from *Christian Instruction* just quoted, he adds, "by this procedure no harm is done to anyone, because those who understand are held by that which they read, but those who do not understand are not compelled to continue reading."[6] Clearly this is a different basis for writing with two levels of address than the one suggested above for Augustine writing the *Confessions*. But it makes clear Augustine's understanding of such writing, and Aquinas's confirmation of it.

Granting for the moment that Augustine was aware of a way of writing (and reading) that permits a structure, a dimension of meaning in a text to remain latent, why would he want to do that in a work intended "to give you glory that [my soul] may love you the more, and let it confess to you your own merciful dealings" (5.1.1)? Why would he do that in a work addressed to "the ears of believing men and women . . . my fellow citizens still on pilgrimage with me" (10.4.6)? Because Augustine wants to show the hidden character of that providence: "I must not omit to confess to you the reasons why I was so persuaded [to move to Rome], because in them your deep, secret providence was at work, and your ever-present mercy, and these are to be pondered and proclaimed" (5.8.14). Augustine wants to present that hidden providence for the reader not only by asserting it but by leaving partially hidden what he has discovered about God's providence in the events of his life through the process of thinking back on that life and writing the story of his confessions, by indicating to the alert reader the latent dimensions of his story. In such a case, part of the confession of God's secret providence will be explicit, but part will remain implicit.

The Center as Structuring Principle

So what would be an example of structure that might help to guide the reading of a work? Well, a simple one might be the center of the text, in either (or both) the sense of halfway through, or the sense of where the argument turns, where the course of the first part gives way to a different course for the second part. For instance, Augustine's work *The Usefulness of Believing* (*De utilitate credendi*) is divided into two parts exactly in the middle of the text. That locus marks the place where the issue of the first half is dropped (the need to find teachers from whom to learn how to read texts appropriately, and to be taught wisdom) and the issue of the second half is introduced (how to seek and find a preceptor, a preacher of true religiousness in whom to believe). Between these two topics (one about seeing, the other about believing), Augustine inserts an autobiographical section, recounting in brief compass the intellectual and spiritual journey of what is related (ten years later) in the first five books of the *Confessions*, just the point in the latter work where he begins to reflect about the indispensability of believing some things, as opposed to the Manichean ridicule of the Christian requirement to believe.

Of course, the axial or transition point of a text need not lie at its physical center. It might lie at the climax, for example, at the moment of recognition and reversal in a Greek tragedy like *Oedipus Rex*, where the climax comes three-quarters of the way through the play. If we were to follow that analogy, the central point or event of the *Confessions* could seem to lie in Book Eight, the scene in the garden where Augustine recognizes God speaking to him and turns his life around.[7] That scene may well be the dramatic center of the story Augustine is telling, the moment when his long quest for wisdom and for true religiousness are at once fulfilled and metamorphosed by a fervent and moving experience of faith.

But is it that dramatic narrative that is the object of Augustine's writing? Is it to tell the story of his life, of his childhood, education, teaching, affiliation with Manicheism, the quest for wisdom, of its *peripeteia* in the garden, of the new life that began to open to him? What is the purpose of his confession? At the beginning of Book Five he writes, "Accept the sacrifice of my confessions . . . to confess to you your own merciful dealings, that it may give you glory."[8] The perspective that has been disclosed to Augustine as he meditated on the course of his life up to his conversion is a dimension that he had not been aware of during those years. One *could* describe those years by saying that the desire and quest for wisdom, aroused in him by reading Cicero, led to the Manichees, then to the Platonists, then to the Scriptures he had learned to read from Ambrose, and finally to the fulfillment of his quest in the encounter with God, the hearing of God's word, in the garden.

But that description would put the initiative for the searching on Augustine, whereas what he came to see, reflecting on those years with the eyes of faith, was that it was God who had brought it all about. "You acted on me that I might be persuaded to go to Rome,"[9] he writes in the middle of Book Five, but the motive that moved *him* at the time was what he heard about students in Rome, and *his* motive for leaving Rome to become master of rhetoric in Milan, in turn, was to advance his career. Looking back, he discerns the providential hand of God as the reason for the journey to Milan, but he little knew it at the time: "Unknowingly I was led by you to [Ambrose], so that through him I might be led, knowingly, to you."[10]

Indeed, when one thinks about it, the conception of a providential, loving God, who created us to come to him, who made us so that our hearts would be restless until they rest in him, who—unlike the One of Plotinus and the Platonists—comes seeking us, calling us,[11] such a conception entails that God will have been working to bring us to him long before we become aware of it.[12] Such are the "merciful dealings" referred to above, which Augustine wants to confess in order to give glory to God's love and providential care.

If we think of the *Confessions* from this perspective, it becomes apparent why it is not an autobiography, why the scene in the garden is not the center of the narrative, and why the axis of the narrative is in Book

Five, when God brings it about that Augustine is turned away from the Manichees and (although he does not know it yet) toward Ambrose. Book Five is in fact also the middle book of the historical narrative, Books One through Nine. Book Ten is not part of the historical narrative, but deals with the philosophical questions about memory, and with Augustine's spiritual situation at the time of writing. It mentions nothing of the years that have intervened between that time and the end of Book Nine, the waiting in Ostia for a ship to Africa, or the death of Monica.

We have been using spatial metaphors, of turning, of going toward, and so forth. In doing so, we are, of course, only following the lead of the author himself, who regularly introduces the basic image of journeying away from and toward God: "Small wonder, then, that I was swept off helplessly . . . and borne away from you, my God" (1.18.28); "I was wandering away from you, yet you let me go my way. . . . I continued to wander far from you" (2.2.2). After reading Cicero, "I began to rise up, in order to return to you" (3.4.7). But he encounters the Manichees and, becoming a hearer in their sect, he "supposed that I was approaching the truth when I was in fact moving away from it" (3.7.12). These few examples are among many uses of this fundamental spatial metaphor, which is complemented by matching it with a literal spatial journey to Italy.

So let us think about Book Five, about the center.

The Center of Book Five

First of all, Book Five itself has a center, a midpoint. And it happens that that middle of the book is the point where the narrator, looking back, first attributes to God's acting on him, to God's guiding him, something he had decided to do for what seemed at the time purely his own reasons—to go to Rome.[13] God uses the motives of Augustine's moving (primarily, to find better behaved students), for his own ends, namely the good of his prodigal son, the return of his son. The passage from Carthage to Rome not only divides Book Five in the middle, it divides the narrative Books One to Nine in the middle of the middle book, so that the narrative is neatly divided between Africa and Italy. Although the

Confessions is written a decade later in Africa, we are not told anything of his return there or of the events of the intervening years.

Second, immediately preceding his decision to go to Rome (in "God's secret providence," 5.8.14), he tells us that because of his encounters with Faustus, he had become disillusioned with the teachings of Mani,[14] so that Faustus unintentionally began his emancipation from the Manichees—"thanks to your hidden providence, O my God" (5.7.13). It is interesting and worth noting that the encounters with the two bishops, Faustus and Ambrose, are placed symmetrically around the center of Book Five. Three paragraphs from the beginning of this book we meet Faustus, three paragraphs from the end of the book we meet Ambrose, the two critical figures in the reorientation of Augustine's journey, a journey before Book Five away from God, and now turning toward him.[15] Without committing himself to either Manicheism or Catholic Christianity, he at first decides to remain loosely attached to the Manichean teaching: "since I had found nothing better than this sect [Manichees] into which I had more or less blundered, I resolved to be content with it for the time being, unless some preferable option presented itself" (5.7.13). Then at the end of the book, he decides to return to the status of a catechumen in the Catholic Church: "I resolved therefore to live as a catechumen in the Catholic Church, which was what my parents had wished for me, until some kind of certainty dawned by which I might direct my steps aright" (5.12.25).[16]

Third, this indecision is reflected in another facet that also marks Five as the center book, as a point of equilibrium between two balanced alternatives, two directions of motion, namely his opting in the final chapter for the Academic philosophy. "Accordingly I adopted what is popularly thought[17] to be the Academic position, doubting everything and wavering" (5.12.25). The inability to be sure, to know, was a consequence of his discussions with Faustus. He had had many problems about the teachings of Mani and had been told to wait until Faustus came, who would answer his questions. The Manichees he had spoken with over the years had ridiculed the Christian requirement for belief and promised to provide reasons for the teachings of Mani. But after Faustus, he gave up hope of *knowing*, being shown, why those teachings were true. He began to think that the skeptical philosophers (i.e., the

Academics) were wiser than the self-styled teachers of wisdom (5.10.19). So Book Five ends with Augustine's deciding that it was best to remain uncommitted until something certain enlightened him.

Book Five and Books Three through Seven

This third aspect of Book Five as a midpoint can lead us out to a different and broader way in which it functions as an axial book. The last chapter of the book, as noted, deals with Augustine's being drawn to the teachings of the Academic philosophers. But if we look at the endings of the surrounding books, we discover that all of the books from Three to Eight conclude with the reading or discussion of different philosophers or teachers of wisdom. Not only is it remarkable that these books all close on this note, but the teachings discussed mark off stages in Augustine's journey away from and toward truth. The import of the end of Book Five has already been indicated: the Academic counsel to remain uncommitted, since the truth cannot be known, aptly fitted Augustine's mind at that time.

Book Three deals with his being inspired by Cicero with the love of wisdom (the literal meaning of "philosophy," as Augustine notes), and to search for wisdom as a guide to life, and how this in turn led him to the Manichean sect, in which he became a hearer. In addition to listening to their teaching he read their "huge copious tomes" (3.6.10).[18] In the last chapter of Book Three his mother, concerned at his increasing affiliation with the sect, goes to visit a bishop who had formerly been a Manichee and had "read nearly all their books" (3.12.21), to ask him to speak with her son and show him the error of his ways. But Augustine was not yet ready to listen, as the bishop rightly judged, and he replied that her son would discover, through further reading, how wrong his present ideas were.

In Book Four, he reflects on the beginning of his (nine) Manichean years, on (as he now sees it) the false conception of God and the world that Mani taught. At the base of the Manichean teaching was a story of God as light, a kingdom of light, having been long ago attacked and scattered by the forces of darkness, so that the scattered divine particles of light constituted (and were dispersed through) the universe, mixed and jumbled with the particles of darkness. This mixture explained, among other things, why creatures (who were mixtures of such particles), and especially human beings, had impulses toward evil as well as toward good. Apparently this doctrine appealed to Augustine's own experience of not only doing wrong but doing gratuitous wrong (the pear tree of 2.6.12).

After some reflections on these ideas, he tells us the story of a boyhood friend (of the same age as Augustine) who died during an illness. Deeply moved by the death, Augustine meditates on the transience not only of life, but of all creaturely existence. All creatures "belong to a society of things that do not exist all at once, but in their passing away and succession together form a whole" (4.10.15), just as our speaking requires that one word die away to be replaced by another, in order that a whole sentence (the unity of a thought) can be. Just so, what we were in the past must die away in order that what we are now can come into being.

In the last chapter of Book Four, he says that when he was about twenty, a copy of Aristotle's book on the *Categories* had been handed to him. It is striking that he relates this now, since he has been telling about his departure from Thagaste (where his friend dies) to go to Carthage in order to resume his teaching career, and—just at the end of the next-to-last chapter—how he wrote his first book during his years there, at the age of "twenty-six or twenty-seven." Why, having narrated the story of his life up to that age, would he go back six or seven years to tell of reading Aristotle?

Perhaps because that book—highly praised as it was by his teachers and rightly understood by Augustine—was of no more help in freeing him from the erroneous conception of God he had acquired from reading Mani than the bishop of Book Three had been. For the *Categories* is an exposition of the ten ways in which things can be said to exist—either as substance or as one of the nine kinds of accidental attributes or qualities of a substance. In logical terms, in the most fundamental sense the substance is indicated by the subject of a sentence and the attributes or accidents by the respective predicates asserted of or ascribed to the subject.

As has been noted just above, the accidental qualities of a creature, of a substance, naturally change over time, so that, for example, what I once weighed (say 6 pounds at birth or 170 pounds some years ago) I no longer do. Now I weigh 150 pounds. Indeed, Aristotle says in chapter five of the work, "The most distinctive mark of substance appears to be that, while remaining numerically one and the same, it is capable of having contrary qualities," i.e., at different times.[19]

If we try to understand God in terms of such categories, misconceptions of the divine nature follow. One is that we can tell a narrative about what status or qualities the divine substance once had and what it subsequently became and what it is now, just as we can about my life. And of course that is just what Mani did, tell the story of how the divine light was attacked and dispersed and is being re-collected, stage by stage. Aristotle's metaphysical analysis of subjects and predicates supported such a telling of a story. But God is simple. There is in him no distinction of substance and accidental qualities: "I mistakenly attempted to understand even you, my God, in terms of [these ten categories], you who are wonderfully simple and changeless, imagining that you were the subject of your greatness and beauty, and that these attributes inhered in you as their subject."[20] So while reading Aristotle's work and understanding it without any help was a tribute to Augustine's intelligence, it not only left him with the Manichean misunderstandings of God but actually provided support for them.

Book Five, as we have noted, ends appropriately with him being drawn toward the Academic skeptics (as they were popularly understood), who recommended suspending judgment as long as there was no certainty to be found.[21]

Book Six deals with Augustine's increasing dissatisfaction with the busyness that his post as master of rhetoric in Milan required—not only teaching, but cultivating contacts with officeholders and influential persons in government. Thirsting for wisdom and the time to think about its pursuit as he was, his time was taken up not with study but with making a successful career. Coming across a drunken beggar in the streets, he comments to his companions on the contrast between the beggar's temporary happiness and his unhappiness. For the moment at least, the beggar is carefree and tranquil, and his pleasure seems preferable to the stress and strain associated with Augustine's pursuit of worldly success (6.9.10).

In a vivid dialogue with himself, Augustine presents the stressful demands that keep him from his real desire (6.6.9–10). He was living with his closest friends at the time, Alypius and Nebridius, all of them seeking some free hours for the same pursuit of wisdom and truth, and they talked about a life in community where responsibilities would be shared in turn, allowing some leisure to the others. But marriage plans and liaisons kept getting in the way, and nothing came of it.

So it is no surprise that, in the last chapter of Book Six where Augustine relates discussing these philosophical questions with his friends, he decides that Epicurus would win the debate among the philosophers about the way of life one should seek, if it were not for the soul and what would happen to it after death: "If we were immortal, and lived in a state of perpetual bodily pleasure without any fear of losing it, why should we not be happy?" (6.16.26). For Epicurus had taught the need for withdrawal from the worldly competitive and acquisitive life, and the pursuit of a state of undisturbed tranquillity, or pleasure (the absence of discomfort or dissatisfaction, which absence Epicurus identified with pleasure). He also insisted that friendship was basic to such pleasure or happiness, so that friends should share a common life.[22] One can see why, at this point in his life, Augustine could have found that position persuasive.

Book Seven is the culmination of this journey through the tutors of wisdom. Like the first of the series, Book Three, it goes from a philosophical wisdom that turns Augustine toward God to a disclosure of a religious path, a Tao. In Book Three the philosopher is Cicero (3.4.7), who first inspires the love of wisdom in Augustine, and the religious path he comes across is the teachings of Mani. In Book Seven, it is the "books of the Platonists" that set him on the final ascent toward the conception of God's nature that overthrows the Manichean doctrine of God's spatiality and mutability, and the religious path is laid out by reading the letters of St. Paul.

Perhaps the most crucial insight he derives from the books of the Platonists is the conception of God as spirit, as immaterial, and so not present everywhere by occupying space, but rather by not being in any place at all. Before he reads those books, he could not imagine a non-material thing: "anything to which I must deny these spatial dimensions seemed to me to be nothing at all, absolutely nothing, not even a void [empty place in space]" (7.1.1).[23] Now he comes to see that God is immaterial and immutable, a transcendent, unchangeable, and timeless Truth, and so eternal, an infinite Being who is the source of all finite beings. The question of the Manichees to Christianity, "Where did evil come from if it were not eternal?" which had plagued him earlier (3.7.12), he now resolves. Moreover, he feels confident in borrowing the language of the Scriptures to describe what the Platonists taught. Seizing the writings of St. Paul, "I began to read and discovered that every truth I had read in those other books was taught here also" (7.21.27).

But there were problems in the other direction: there were things in St. Paul's writings that were not in those of the Platonists. Two were crucial, and related. One was the incarnation of the Logos. Augustine (and Alypius) had difficulty in conceiving how the transcendent, immaterial, immutable divinity of the Platonists and Christians could be this human being who lived in space and time and like other humans ate and drank and slept. So he thought of Christ as a human person, excellent and wise, but human (7.18.24–19.25).

The second problem is not unrelated to the first. It is that in the Platonist teaching, as Augustine says, "no one there hears a voice calling 'Come to me'" (7.21.27). It is, as Plotinus taught, the task of the individual soul to make its way of ascent toward a return to the One, the ultimate eternal principle of all things. But Christianity taught that God came seeking us, came to call us to turn and come together to share God's life. How could a timeless, immutable, transcendent Being act in the world of space and time?

It is, of course, that question that is responded to not by philosophy, but by a personal experience in Book Eight, in the garden where Augustine hears a voice uttering what he takes to be a divine command, a call to open the book of Paul's writings and read. But here at the end of Book Eight it is not the reading of a book of wisdom that moves him, it is the experience of being called, spoken to by the words of the Eternal Word.

Book Five and Books Two through Eight

What has been primarily intended here is not the exposition of the stages of the philosophical encounters that close each of the books from three to seven, but rather the symmetrical structuring of those around a center, Book Five. This is exemplified by this symmetry and by the centricity of Book Five for the whole division of the journey into African and Italian phases, but also by the philosophy (skepticism) that marks his in-between state.

There is another structuring around this center book that reinforces the analysis thus far, and indeed advances it. There is a symmetrical gathering of the themes of his progressive alienation from God around that center. The stages of this alienation and return are those of the triad that runs through the text, as well as in other books of Augustine from the early *True Religion* to the late *Enchiridion*. This triad is the one discussed at length in the second half of Book Ten: concupiscence of the flesh, of the eyes, and of the pride of life (as St. John calls it).[24] It derives from Scripture, but it correlates with the three parts of the human soul that Plato had delineated in the *Republic*,[25] where the three sources of human action, the three principles for explaining why people do things, are identified as desire, reason, and aspiration. Desire is the appetite for what will please or satisfy us physically, whether it be food or sex or sleep; reason is thinking about what we ought to seek and why, and what we should do to achieve that end (whether it be contrary to our desires or not); aspiration is what moves us when we seek to rise above others, above a lower status, whether that be economic or political or educational or moral (e.g., doing something because it would be dishonorable or demeaning not to do it). In the view that Socrates puts forth in the *Republic*, disorder in one's behavior or conduct is the result of conflict in us between these three sources of action. So, for example, the sexual appetite can overpower reason's judgment that this behavior is morally wrong, or is shameful.

Augustine does not deny that wrongful behavior results from such disorder and conflict among these parts of the soul, but following St. John and the teaching of Catholic Christianity he also thinks that those three sources of action can be—and are, as a result of original sin—

individually disordered or corrupted, so that they acquire an unnatural power in our behavior. Even reason has weaknesses that can lead us astray, for example, an inordinate curiosity about things not deserving our attention and study.

The three books before Book Five each record Augustine's succumbing to one of these three types of concupiscence, so that his increasing distance from God is traced by his alienation through sin in three stages: in Book Two, concupiscence of the flesh; in Book Three, concupiscence of the eyes or mind; and in Book Four, concupiscence of worldly ambition. He regains his freedom from these states of alienation in the three books following Five: ambition in Book Six, the mind in Book Seven, and his bondage to the flesh in Book Eight. Thus the symmetry around Five in this case is chiasmic, i.e., the liberation occurs step-by-step but in reverse order, and the stages mark his ascent toward God, culminating in the scene in the garden at the end of Book Eight.

Book Two opens, in fact, with the explicit statement of its theme: "Now I want to call to mind the foul deeds I committed, those sins of the flesh that corrupted my soul" (2.1.1), and how in this sixteenth year of his age "the frenzy of lust imposed its rule on me" (2.2.4). And for sixteen years he remained under the scepter of this concupiscence.

The second concupiscence (of "the eyes") is the compelling desire to see and to know. The desire to see, in the literal sense, produced Augustine's passion for theatrical shows in Carthage, where he went to continue his studies (3.2.2). But Augustine found the metaphorical sense of "to see," i.e., to know or understand, an even more consuming passion:

> There is still another temptation, one more fraught with danger. In addition to all the concupiscence of the flesh, which lures us to indulge in all the pleasures of the senses, and brings disaster on its slaves who flee far from you, there is also concupiscence of the mind, a frivolous, avid curiosity. . . . it masquerades as a zeal for knowledge and learning. Since it is rooted in a thirst for firsthand information about everything, and since the eyes are paramount among the senses in acquiring information, this inquisitive tendency is called in holy scripture concupiscence of the eyes. (10.35.54)

Book Three, as has already been noted, tells of his reading of Cicero's *Hortensius* in the course of his studies in rhetoric, and tells how it inspired in him the desire for wisdom, for knowledge of how one should live to be happy. He turned at first to the Scriptures, but was put off by their lowly and unpretentious prose style and so did not perceive their "inner meaning": "I disdained to be a little child and in my high and mighty arrogance regarded myself as grown up" (3.5.9). He was an apt candidate for the "proud madmen" who proclaimed the wisdom of Mani, with their pretentious trappings of pseudoscientific astronomy and biology. Looking back, he now calls the Manichean teachings "chimera," "figments of my imagination," "inanities" (3.6.10). But they posed questions about Christian doctrine that were problems for him, for example, whether humanity's being made in the image of God meant that God had a body like a human, or (as mentioned earlier) how evil could emerge in a world made by a perfect creator, if it were not as eternal as God.

Book Four opens with relating how through his nine years with the Manichees, while teaching the liberal arts, he pursued empty popular acclaim and "the contest for ephemeral wreaths" (4.1.1), entering dramatic poetry contests and similar attempts to win renown (4.1.3). He "admired people simply because they were judged praiseworthy by others." He wrote a book on the nature of beauty, dedicating it to a man of "splendid reputation" who found favor with others, an eminent orator in Rome:

> This orator, however, was the sort of man I loved in the sense of wanting to be like him. I was driven off course by my pride and tossed about by every wind. . . . I had come to love him more for the love he aroused in those who sang his praises than for the achievements by which he won them. . . . Accordingly I set great store by bringing my oratory and my research to this man's notice. (4.14.21–23)

But by Book Six, although still "hankering after honors," the race is beginning to pale. Augustine describes himself as "preparing to deliver a eulogy upon the emperor in which I would tell plenty of lies with the object of winning favor with the well-informed by my lying. . . . my heart was panting with anxiety and seething with feverish, corruptive thoughts" (6.6.9). It is at this point that he encounters the drunken beggar, mentioned above, and wonders which of them is the happier. He re-creates the dialogue with himself that these thoughts engender:

> [W]hen are we to pay court to our important friends, whose patronage we need? When prepare the lessons we sell to our students? When refresh ourselves and relax our minds from concentrating on these problems? . . . Why are we so slow to abandon worldly ambition and apply ourselves singlemindedly to the search for God and a life of happiness? Wait a little, for those things are very pleasant, too; they hold no slight sweetness. . . . Consider what a fine thing it is for a person to win a reputation. What prize could be more desirable? We have plenty of influential friends: without setting our sights unduly high, one may expect at least a governorship to come one's way. (6.11.18–19)

Alypius plays a role in this debate in Book Six about worldly ambition. He has become Assessor to the Chancellor of the Italian Treasury and refuses a bribe from a very powerful senator. He thus exemplifies the choice of doing the right thing at the cost of gaining help from influential figures in advancing his career (6.10.16). By the end of the book, as we have seen, Augustine is ready to side with the Epicureans in their counsel of withdrawal from public life in the pursuit of happiness. Although he continues his career, it no longer has attraction for him: "I was irked by the secular business I was conducting, for no longer was I fired by ambition, and prepared on that account to endure such heavy servitude in the hope of reputation and wealth, as had formerly been the case" (8.1.2). So the events and reflections of Book Six undermine the desires described in Book Four for praise and reputation, and lead to the abandonment of those aspirations. The busyness involved in advancing his success has become a burden and the goal itself ephemeral.[26]

Book Seven is striking in that in it there is not a word about his sexual concupiscence (which is the theme of Books Three [Two] and Eight) or about the concupiscence of worldly fame that is now fading away (the theme of Books Four and Six). Every other book between Three and Eight touches on or deals with more than one of the three concupiscences.[27] Book Seven is wholly focused on the philosophical inquiry that guides Augustine toward God, that frees him from astrology and the Manichean "figments of imagination." Book Seven explicitly takes up the Manichean questions that had motivated his joining the sect (e.g., the question of the origin of evil—whence comes evil—and of whether God's body is like a human's—the Christian doctrine that humanity is made in God's image, 3.7.12), and resolves them. Being and goodness are correlative realities, and evil is not some infinite substantial being, but precisely the lack of being, the privation of what ought to exist in things (7.13.19). And it is the human soul, the animating principle of the body, not the human body, that bears the image of God (7.9.15). Not only do the writings of the Platonists resolve those puzzles for him, but they bring him to conceive rightly the nature of God as immaterial spirit, as Truth that is transcendent, immutable, eternal.

By the beginning of Book Eight, Augustine has been freed from the two concupiscences that had held him captive since Books Three and Four. The concupiscence of the mind, "a frivolous, avid curiosity," has been replaced by the vision of the Truth, and he is no longer "fired by ambition," though he still reluctantly treads the path.[28] His spirit no longer magnetized by the desire for worldly fame and fortune, and his mind no longer clouded by the teachings of Mani, he rejoices: "Concerning your eternal life I was now quite certain.... What I now longed for was not greater certainty about you, but a more steadfast abiding in you.... I was attracted to the Way, which is our Savior himself, but the narrowness of the path daunted me, and I still could not walk in it" (8.1.1). He is still held tightly—and has been since Book Two—by the concupiscence of the flesh, by the power of his sexual appetite. He refers to this in the opening sentence of Book Eight, speaking of his intention to give thanks to God for breaking the chains that bound him. And he returns to the same image later: "Now I will relate how you set me free from a craving for sexual gratification which fettered me like a tight-drawn chain, and from my enslavement to worldly affairs" (8.6.13). It is not reading philosophers or listening to Ambrose that finally turns his way of life around, or even reading St. Paul, but the experience of hearing God speak directly to his situation, to his heart's dilemma. Perhaps one could borrow John Henry Newman's terminology and say that by the end of Book Seven he has a notional assent to Christianity but not a real assent.[29] By the end of Book Eight the last of the bonds, of the concupiscences that chained him, is gone, and he can open Book Nine with a prayer of thanksgiving: "You burst my bonds asunder" (9.1.1).

The stages of Augustine's sequential bondage and liberation are told in books thus symmetrically centered around Book Five: Two corresponds to Eight, Three corresponds to Seven, Four corresponds to Six. This chiasmic narrative structure not only reinforces the perception of Five as the center of the narrative books, but displays it as the center of a descent into sin and isolation (he sails, apparently alone, for Rome in the center of the center book), and an ascent into graced freedom and community with God and his friends.[30]

Book Five and Books One through Nine

There is one more sign of the partition of the narrative around Book Five that is simple and evident, but easy to overlook. It is that in the earlier books, Augustine does not mention the names of any of the people he knows personally (with one exception). He uses the names of such figures as Virgil and Cicero and Aristotle, of Dido and Aeneas, of Christ and Adam and Abraham, and of the contemporary orator Hierius, to whom he dedicates his book on beauty (and carefully adds, "I did not know him personally," 4.14.21).

But in Books One to Four, he does not name his mother or father, or the boyhood friend who dies, or his common-law wife or son, or his friend and student Alypius, or Vindicianus (the physician who tried to disenchant him from astrology), all of whom are named in the books after Five. Only in Book Five do we begin to learn the names of people he encountered: Faustus the Manichean bishop and Ambrose the Catholic bishop, Elpidius who disputed with the Manichees (Augustine heard him back in Carthage, but only mentions him by name now), and Symmachus, who recommends Augustine for the post as orator in Milan. Each of the succeeding narrative books adds more names, but it is not until the last lines of Book Nine that his mother and father are named, just as he finishes his story.[31]

What do those named have in common, considering that some others are never named, e.g., his common-law wife of fifteen years, or any of his Manichean companions in Carthage and Rome? It would appear that all of those who are named were instrumental in assisting Augustine's turning and journey toward the true God, whether unintentionally (e.g., Faustus and Symmachus) or intentionally (e.g., Ambrose and Simplicianus). Faustus disillusions him with the teaching of Mani and so begins to turn him around, while Symmachus unknowingly sends him on his way to Ambrose. In contrast, his unnamed common-law wife and Manichean friends were obstacles on that path.

It was noted above that there is one exception to this partition in the naming: it occurs in Book Four when the there-unnamed Vindicianus (recalled and named in 7.6.8) and Nebridius (also recalled there) are trying to dissuade Augustine from consulting astrologers (4.6.5–6). After having described the criticism of Vindicianus, Augustine writes: "Yet at the time neither he nor my very dear friend, Nebridius, a fine and extremely sensible young man who ridiculed the whole business of divination, was able to persuade me." Why this singular instance in Books One to Four of naming someone Augustine knew personally?

Perhaps the first thing to say in response to that question, before trying to answer it, is to remark that its singularity implies that there is a deliberate pattern. As the saying goes, the exception proves the rule, shows that there is a rule. (Perhaps the saying should be that the [apparent] exception presses us either to reformulate the rule to include the exception or to explain why the apparent exception does not fit under it.) And the pattern seems too consistent not to be intentional. So why name only Nebridius in the first half and not, for example, Alypius, also close to Augustine's heart and converted with him in the garden?

Assuming that it was not a slip or oversight—unlikely, given the consistency—one can only speculate on why Augustine would have made an exception. Of various conceivable reasons, perhaps the likeliest is that by the time the *Confessions* is written, his "dear" friend (as he always refers to him) had died seven years earlier, and that naming him before all of the others is a commemoration of his friend and companion (who may, indeed, have been the comrade with whom he sailed to Rome).

Conclusion

Although it is certainly fair to say that the scene in the garden is the dramatic climax of his story, we have argued that telling that long dramatic story of the journey away from and returning to God is not the primary purpose of the *Confessions*. Anyone who is converted, turned about, toward faith in the God of the Bible, even if that conversion is dramatic and memorable, if they reflect on the nature of the God they have come to have faith in, will be led to recognize God's hand in the earlier course of the journey. And frequently, if not always, they will notice the hitherto unnoticed events, decisions, encounters, etc., that now show themselves to have been important steps on the way.

Already in his early treatise *The Usefulness of Believing*, written six years or so before the *Confessions*, Augustine had commented on this dimension of the search for true wisdom or true religiousness:

> When religion is the object of our quest, God alone can provide a solution. . . . We ought not to be seeking true religion unless we believe that God is, and that he brings help to human minds. . . . If the providence of God does not preside over human affairs, there is no need to worry about religion.[32]

The passage just cited contrasts with teachings about how the individual can make his own way toward the absolute, the unchanging and abiding—for example, the teachings of Plotinus and the "Platonists," and also those of Buddhism. In these teachings, it is up to the individual to realize the situation he is in and take measures to escape from or free one's self from this situation. The soul can, through coming to know the way, through right conduct and meditation, arise to union with the One (Plotinus) or with what is "Unborn, Unbecome, Uncreated" (Buddha). One can be told about the situation and the path, but one must act for one's self. As the famous last line of the *Enneads* of Plotinus puts it, it is "the flight of the alone to the Alone." But Augustine, like Cicero, thinks of religion as the offering of prayers and sacrifices to a superior being called divine, and the seeking of his help in making one's way. Prayers and sacrifices imply our need for assistance in that journey.

If the providence of God does preside over human affairs, and God cares about whether we come to him or not, then events that perhaps did not appear important to us at the time may now show evidence of that hidden providence. If the God we seek does not know of our seeking or is unable to help us, then that is not the God we should seek.

An important philosophical and theological issue arises here. It is the issue of whether there is a meaning in the sequence of events in our lives—or, more broadly, also in the lives of nations and empires. The *Confessions*, from this point of view, deals with the same issue as the *City of God* that Augustine will write toward the end of his life. For classical philosophy, the course of events could indeed be partially intelligible, could be something for our reason to understand in part, but only as illustrating or instantiating universal laws or tendencies in a particular context. So, for example, Plato outlines in the *Republic* a sequence of political constitutions, arguing that one form of constitution (e.g., oligarchy) naturally evolves into another (e.g., democracy), and that naturally into another and so on. Analogously, the "lifestyle" of a typical oligarchic citizen naturally evolves toward the way of life of a typical democratic citizen. These law-like progressions are the patterns through which contemporary Athens, for example, could be understood. Thucydides, writing about the war between Athens and Sparta, says that his history will be instructive for later generations, because such encounters between dominant opposing states as he is describing tend to repeat themselves in later eras.

But Augustine thinks of individuals (and nations) as singular, as having a life history that may indeed exhibit typical kinds of patterns of development, but which has a comprehensive, linear, noncyclic history, a history under God's providence. It is the *Confessions* that articulates that vision for his own life, and implicitly for the life of every individual. He wants all of his readers to understand his life not as unique in this regard, but to be able to think about the role of God's hidden providence in their lives.

Of course, all individuals (and nations) can look back at their past and see, in retrospect, an additional dimension of meaning in those past events, a meaning of which they were unconscious at the time. This is true simply because when looking back, and now being aware of the then-unknown consequences of those events, the events take on a different significance for us. We now see, in retrospect, an importance (or unimportance) in what happened then of which we were unsuspecting at the time. The ever-widening horizon of subsequent events, of history, constantly changes—enlarges or diminishes—the significance of those anterior happenings. And that changing is in principle never-ending.

Augustine's perspective in the *Confessions* is fundamentally different, for at least two reasons. The first is that looking back he now sees some earlier events as intentionally aimed (although not by him) at bringing about the later events that give those earlier events their new dimension of meaning—intentionally planned by God's "hidden providence." (For example, his going from Rome to Milan.) And the second reason is that the perspective he is now endowed with will not itself fundamentally change with the passing of time, because he now shares, to some tiny extent, God's understanding of those occurrences. The viewpoint from which he writes the *Confessions* is that attained by the climax of the narrative, the understanding sown in the garden. For that event is not a chance event whose significance may be changed by what occurs later in his life.

This can be clarified perhaps by reflecting on the experience he has in the garden of picking up the Scriptures, God's Word, and reading those words addressed exactly to his life situation. But he has earlier been told by Vindicianus (4.3.5) that the common practice of picking up and opening some standard text and randomly reading the first excerpt one's eye falls upon will indeed sometimes find a relevant passage, but that will be due to chance. In that time it was usual to employ Virgil's poetry in this way (in our day perhaps Nostradamus). How is Augustine's experience different? Couldn't his relevant passage found by simply picking up the letters of St. Paul and opening them at random also be a matter of chance?

What makes the difference in the two readings is the understanding of the universe and all that is in it and all that happens in it as under God's providence, as his creation. God not only brought the world into being long ago, but continues to preserve it in existence along with all of its coming-and-going creatures. This conception of creation is the ontological context for the affirmation of God's providential design for us. So it is very different if I, on my own initiative, pick up a book and open it at random and find a meaningful text, or, on the other hand, if God moves me to pick up a book that describes itself as presenting the Word of God and, opening it, find God speaking to me. Only the foundation of the doctrine of creation allows apparently random events to take on the status of being integrated into God's foresighted plan for all things. If God were not the creator of all events as well as of creatures, then what happens to me could be simply a chance event. It would be a chance event that I happened randomly to open, say, Virgil's *Aeneid* to just this page. And as Vindicianus tells Augustine, it would then only be by chance, coincidence, that I found some passage significant for my situation at the moment I did that. No one intended that significance. But as he writes at the end of Books Eleven to Thirteen, where he reflects deeply on God's relation to creation, "We, therefore, see these things you have made, because they exist, but for you it is different: they exist because you see them" (13.38.53). What God foresees comes about in his timelessly creating the world, moment by moment, to put it paradoxically.

This conception of how meaning can be found in one's life is exemplified for the reader of the *Confessions* by the way in which Augustine describes how he discovered that providence in his own life. It is another example of the fruitfulness of the maxim that guides Augustine's theological reflection from the beginning to the end of his life as a Catholic Christian: unless you believe, you will not understand. Unless you believe in God, the creator and sustainer who calls to each of us, you will not understand those crucial aspects of your life that are part of God's "hidden providence."

Our argument has been that there are many indications, when you take note of them, that the central axis of the "autobiographical" narrative of Books One to Nine is in the center of those books, in fact in the center of the center book, Book Five. Many of those indications are easy to pass over, not to notice, but that is part of Augustine's intention. He wants us to discover the hidden signs of God's providence, just as those were hidden to Augustine himself until he recalled, with the eyes of faith, what led up to the moment in the garden. So writing, he will give glory to God for his farsighted mercy (5.1.1).

That argument does not claim exclusivity for Book Five as a central book. There is yet another problem, another dimension of the *Confessions* that first begins to come into view at the end of Book Seven. There he arrives, thanks to reading the Platonists, at a correct conception of God as transcendent Truth, as pure spirit, as immutable, infinite Being. But there he is also reading the New Testament, especially St. Paul, and he finds things in the latter which have no counterpart in the Platonists. He finds that that pure spirit, that immutable, infinite, transcendent Being calls to us, acts in time, can have a narrative told about him—just what Augustine had come to think impossible for the Platonist God/ One. This problem needs to be addressed, but not in terms of the narrative of what happened ten years ago. It needs to be addressed by Augustine's reflections in the interim and now at the time of writing. So more books are needed. And that is why Books Eleven to Thirteen were included along with the narrative books, to address the question of the relation between God's eternity and our temporality, and how a narrative like the opening of Genesis can be told about the immutable God.

CHAPTER THREE

Show and Tell

The Concept of Teaching in St. Augustine's *De Magistro*

It is worth remarking that only one of the two dozen or so writings which Augustine had completed by the time he wrote the *Confessions* is mentioned in that work: the philosophical dialogue with his son, Adeodatus, which he entitled *De Magistro*.[1] The reference to the latter work is indirect: it occurs in the course of recounting Augustine's return to Milan in order to prepare for baptism. Alypius, converted with him in the garden, also resolved to be born again. When Augustine comes to mention his son, he is moved to praise the qualities with which God had endowed the boy, and this leads him to refer to the dialogue.

> We also joined to ourselves the boy Adeodatus, born of me in the flesh out of my sin. You had made him well; he was about fifteen years old but in power of intellect he surpassed many grave and learned men . . . That he was raised by us in your discipline, to that You inspired us. Your gifts do I confess to you. There is a book of ours, entitled On the Teacher: in it he speaks with me. You know that all the ideas expressed there as from the persona of the one speaking with me really were his when he was in his sixteenth year.[2]

It is clear from this passage and others in the *Confessions* that, writing a decade later, Augustine was still strongly moved by the memory of his son. Remembering his natural gifts and the intellectual and spiritual formation which Augustine imparted before the boy's early death, he reminds his readers (and himself) of the dialogue. In that dialogue, he implies, some of the talents which God gave to Adeodatus are exhibited. The dialogue is a literary memento for his son, whether deliberately written as such at the time or not.

Several other useful inferences may be drawn from this passage. First are the chronological data. Adeodatus was about fifteen in the early Spring of 387, when they went to Milan to be inscribed for Easter baptism (which was in April). Depending on whether his fifteenth birthday occurred shortly before or not long after going to Milan, we may infer that, if it came after, he would have reached the age of sixteen somewhere before the middle of 388, and that his seventeenth birthday (if he reached it) could then have come, at the latest, before the middle of 389. Conversely, if his fifteenth birthday had come in late 386, his sixteenth birthday could have come as early as the Fall of 387 and his seventeenth as early as the Fall of 388.

This means that the conversations in which Adeodatus expressed the opinions later put in the mouth of his persona in the dialogue, if they occurred when he was sixteen, must have occurred between late 387 and the middle of 389. (We do not know when he died: in the passage of the *Confessions* cited above, Augustine only says, "cito de terra abstulit vitam eius.")

When did the actual conversation take place? In the Fall of 387, Augustine and his companions including Monica and Adeodatus went to Ostia to await a ship to Africa. There his mother died, and the voyage was deferred until August–September of 388.[3] On his return to Africa, Augustine stopped briefly in Carthage and then settled in his natal town of Thagaste, establishing a small community of like-minded servants of God. It is in this period of residence in Thagaste (388–391) that he completes the *De musica*, writes the *De Genesi contra Manichaeos*, and, as he then tells us in the *Retractationes*,

At the same time, I wrote a book whose title is De Magistro; in which we dispute and inquire and discover that there is no teacher who teaches knowledge except God, according as it is written in the Gospels: "One is your Teacher, Christ."[4]

If Augustine arrived in Thagaste in late 388, established and organized the community in the paternal residence (now his property), completed two treatises and then wrote the *De Magistro*, it is unlikely that the last could have been written before sometime in the first half of 389.[5]

And now we can pose the critical question: what is the relation between the statement from the *Confessions*, "illius esse sensa omnia," and the text of the dialogue? Many commentators have taken the statement that all of the ideas expressed by the persona of Adeodatus in the dialogue really were his when he was sixteen to mean that the text of the *De Magistro* is, in part or in whole, essentially a stenographic record of an actual conversation which Augustine held with Adeodatus.

G. Wijdeveld,[6] who held this view of at least the first part of the dialogue, takes it to mean that the conversation was held in Thagaste, and so that Adeodatus was still alive and had not yet reached his seventeenth birthday in the first half of 389. This is not impossible, although it requires the corollary that he did not reach his fifteenth birthday until a corresponding date in 387. In defense of the stenographic thesis, Wijdeveld cites, among other evidence, the "rather uncertain and confused progress of the discussion."[7] This is, as will be noted subsequently, a not uncommon position: that the irregular construction, the "sophisms," and the apparent confusion of the dialogue all tend to confirm the supposition that the text is essentially a stenographic record of an actual conversation.

But the strength of this argument rests on the premise that the course of the exchanges in the dialogue is in fact as spontaneous, digressive, and unplanned as is asserted. Two considerations give one pause in accepting that premise. The first is that it belongs to the very nature of the philosophical dialogue, as a mimesis of a conversation, to possess a sense of spontaneity and apparent impulsiveness.[8] Indeed, the greater the appearance of its being a genuine conversation, the less it can seem to be planned in advance to move toward a pre-set conclusion. But *ars est celare artem*: everything depends on whether or not in fact the appearance hides a careful structure. And that is the second consideration that gives pause: the possibility that the *De Magistro* does possess a carefully organized structure.

It is a hypothesis of the analysis of the dialogue which follows that the *De Magistro* is in fact very carefully organized, not only in the *oratio perpetua* but throughout the whole. That hypothesis is, I believe, amply confirmed by the logical sequence and interconnections of the parts of the discussion, even to significant details such as beginning each of the three parts with the same word (*consideremus*). Indeed, Augustine indicates early in the text (1.1) that he already has conclusions in mind which will be arrived at in the course of their discussion:

> But I think that there is a quite reasonable kind of teaching by re-minding, which will be shown in the course of the discussion.[9]

What is the relation of this interpretation of the text to the "critical question" raised above? Is this interpretation at variance with the assertion of the *Confessions* that the ideas expressed by the persona of Adeodatus really were his—and so must have been expressed in actual conversation? Not at all, so long as we think of those ideas as the raw material for the textual dialogue (and Augustine does not say that the words were those of Adeodatus, but only the *sensa*). Nor does this interpretation exclude the possibility that there was (or were, if several discussions had been recorded) a stenographic record of such a conversation with Adeodatus (although I am inclined to doubt it). What it does seem to exclude is that the received text is essentially, in whole or in part, such a record.

How then should we think of the relation of the textual conversation with the unquestionably historical conversation(s) to which the *Confessions* implicitly refers?

Here we touch on the larger and much-disputed question of the historicity of the early (Cassiciacum) dialogues.[10] B. Voss posed the issue of the literary character of the dialogues in terms of two extremes: Postmas, who held them to be historical records, and O'Meara, who maintains that they are to be explicated in terms of their literary genre.[11] G. Madec, after a long and careful consideration of the arguments, concludes that the truth lies in the middle, but on the side of the historical:

> Les *Dialogues* de Cassiciacum sont historiques: leur conformité au genre litteraire n'est que relative et ne fait, du reste, pas obstacle à cette conviction; [...] Dument enregistrés, les entretiens n'ont eu à subir qu'une operation de *rewriting* pour être intégrés dans les

Dialogues tels que nous les lisons. Je ne crois pas que le caractère litteraire qu'ils ont ainsi acquis, porte prejudice a leur valeur documentaire.[12]

One seems to be here in the realm of the more or less in making such judgments. It does not seem possible to exclude the possibility of a stenographic transcript, but even assuming such a document (for some of the dialogues), it remains difficult to assess exactly in what the "documentary value" of the extant dialogues consists. That assessment would seem to depend, to a large extent, on how extensive the "rewriting" has been. That there was an actual trial of Socrates, that he made a speech in his defense, seems unreasonable to doubt. But whether much (or any) of that speech has been incorporated into Plato's *Apology* or Xenephon's *Defense* remains dubious. Even if the narrator mentions such a record, or asserts that he was an eyewitness of the proceedings he is going to relate, we do not necessarily escape from the *mos dialogorum* (cf. *Phaedrus, Phaedo, Symposium, De natura deorum, Dialogues Concerning Natural Religion*, etc.).

In these circumstances, it would seem that the word "rewriting" may suggest too little change from a presumed transcript. It seems more prudent to think of any transcript as being more like raw material which has to be "reworked," reshaped, in order to take on the carefully structured form which seems to be present in the dialogues.

In the case of the *De Magistro*, the distance of the received text from any actual transcript is reinforced by the generally acknowledged difference of the third part, the *oratio perpetua*. Why does the dialogue conclude with a long section in which there is no dialogue? Why, all the more, since that section incorporates potential dialogical exchanges which could easily have been put into the mouth of the persona of Adeodatus?[13] The most likely answer to that would seem to be that Augustine and his son never had a conversation which incorporated his thoughts about the Divine Teacher.

But this suggestion clearly implies that the two previous parts did, as the *Confessions* relates, express ideas which Adeodatus and his father discussed when he was in his sixteenth year. So clearly there is a historical basis for those two parts, whether or not there was a transcript of any (one or several) discussion(s). However, once again it seems difficult to assess the "documentary value" of those first two parts. How extensively did Augustine rework them, reshape them, in integrating them into a unitary whole with a third part which seems to have no historical basis? My own inclination is more toward O'Meara's position. One ought not to appeal to a transcript or to a historical conversation to explain or account for the progress (or apparent lack of it) of a dialogue, unless (as in this case) there is some independent ground for assuming a historical conversation. And even then, explaining apparent irregularities in the text by such an appeal should only be an absolutely last resort.[14]

If we return now to the dating of the conversation(s) and the text, on the basis of the above remarks, it is plausible to decline the late date assigned to the conversations by Wijdeveld on the basis of his assumption of the historical character of the text. Granted that the composition of the dialogue is, on the testimony of the *Retractationes*, to be assigned to the period of residence in Thagaste, the occasion for its composition and the dating of the conversation(s) remains open. E. Schadel[15] notes that there is a passage in the text which tends to confirm its being written in Africa—and, one infers, of the actual conversation(s) having taken place there. In explicating the word "ex" in the line from Vergil, Adeodatus says "sicut ex urbe Roma dicimus esse negotiatores in Africa,"[16] which certainly seems appropriate to being said in Africa—but which might not be inappropriate to a conversation between two travellers in Rome waiting to go to Africa. On the other hand, G. Bardy and G. Bonner both suggest that the conversation(s) took place in Italy, during the year's residence in Rome before the departure for Africa, and that the dialogue was composed in Africa after the death of Adeodatus as a memorial to him.[17]

On the basis of the passage from the *Confessions* from which we began, which bears witness to the memories and emotions of a father a decade after his son's early death, and which unusually—in the context of the *Confessions*—goes on to mention the writing in which he appears, one is inclined to concur that the *De Magistro* was probably written in 389 as a memorial to Adeodatus shortly after his death, that it was written in Thagaste but drew upon tutorial conversations from the past (most likely in Rome), and which were now shaped to lead toward an original discourse (the *oratio perpetua*) on how *intelligibilia* are taught.

Perhaps Augustine's germinating conception of the dialogue can be approximated in the following way. The issue to which the discussion will be addressed is, how indispensable is the role of signs, especially words, in teaching someone what a word signifies? How much can words, in particular, contribute toward *showing* what is signified, rather than merely deferring that showing by giving other words in order to explain what a word signifies. Only such showing is truly teaching; only such showing gives the thing itself. Well, there are three different cases to be distinguished: 1) in the case of some words, namely those which signify other words symmetrically and reflexively, the words themselves can show what they signify; 2) in the case of some extra-linguistic things, namely human actions, neither words nor signs are essential in showing what the words for those things signify; 3) in the case of other extra-linguistic things, in particular the *intelligibilia*, it is beyond human power to *show* them. All that we can do is use words to draw the attention of the learner to what is shown to him by a supra-human Teacher.

Now our assumption is that Augustine has had tutorial conversations with his son on the first two cases, conversations about the syntax and grammar which included 1) discussion of ways in which some words show themselves by signifying other words symmetrically, and 2) discussion about how some extra-linguistic things can be shown by a teacher and why the knowledge of extra-linguistic things is to be preferred to their signs. What must be done then is to shape those conversations— whether recalled or recorded—so that they lead logically to a discussion of the third case. Then Adeodatus must fall silent, if the dialogue is to show what he himself really thought and said. But the reader will be led, with his assistance, from the liberal arts to a glimpse of those regions "ubi beata vita est" (8.21).

All that remains, then, is to shape from those tutorial conversations a prologue in which the uncritical notion that learning comes about through words, through hearing the words of someone explaining, is shown to be problematic.

I

The text has not always been well served by its commentators, for a variety of reasons: the reader may think he already knows what the argument is, or the reader may think that Augustine doesn't know as much as the reader does (about semantics, logic, epistemology . . .), or the reader may simply not read the text carefully enough. In each case, one of the consequences of the misreading is that the structure of the dialogue is distorted: divisions and transitions are made where they ought not to be or not made where they ought to be. As Plato's Eleatic Stranger says in the *Statesman*, cuts ought to be made at the joints if we want to divide properly. Some examples of each of these cases of misreading may be helpful in removing obstacles to the analysis of the text.

First, the reader thinks that he already knows what the argument is. How can this be "already" guessed or known? One way derives from the fact that the work stands in a long tradition, has been read and summarized many times. So, it is often said that the thesis of *On the Teacher* is that there is only one teacher, namely, the Interior Light. For example, R. A. Markus writes that the argument is devoted to showing that:

> . . . this Interior Teacher is the source of all truth and knowledge; that he is the invisible light "which we confessedly consult in regard to visible things, that it may manifest them to us to the extent that we are able to perceive them."[18]

In the case of Augustine's writings, there is another possible source for "knowing already" what a particular work is about. At the end of his life, Augustine wrote a long review of work which he had published over his lifetime, the *Retractationes*, in which he reconsidered things which he had then written. In a very brief paragraph on the *De Magistro*, he described it as a book in which

> we discuss and inquire and discover that there is no teacher who teaches man knowledge [*scientiam*] [*sic*] except God.[19]

A number of interpreters have explicitly used this description to divide the text of the *De Magistro* into two fundamental parts: first, everything preceding the section where this thesis is stated for the first time (1.1. to 10.37), and second, everything following (10.38 to 14.46).[20]

Second, the reader may think that Augustine makes a number of sophistical errors, perhaps because he does not know as much as the reader does about logic and semantics. Naturally enough, if this belief is wrong, it will lead the reader to miss what Augustine is saying. Sometimes this is coupled with the belief that the text is a kind of transcript of a conversation between Augustine and his son Adeodatus. If this is so, one may excuse what seem to be discontinuities and disorder in the discussion. For example:

> Cast in the form of a dialogue, it is a report of an actual conversation with his son Adeodatus [...] Like most conversations, *The Teacher* is spontaneous in expression and irregular in construction [...] arguments sometimes become specious and tenuous.[21]

The belief that the dialogue is a transcript is based on a reference to it in the *Confessions*, where Augustine is telling of the early death of Adeodatus:

> There is a book of ours, entitled *The Teacher*; in it he converses with me. Thou knowest that all the thoughts expressed in the person of the one discussing with me are his own, although he was only sixteen years of age . . .[22]

But Augustine does not say that the work is a record or transcript: he says that the thoughts expressed by his interlocutor in it actually were opinions [*sensa*] of Adeodatus. In fact, in the *Retractationes*, he says, "At the same time [in which he wrote the *De Musica*] I wrote a book whose title is *De Magistro* . . ."[23]

The first division of the subject matter of the book is concerned with signs which signify signs: "word" (*verbum*), "name" (*nomen*), etc. At the beginning of the second division, Augustine deals with words taken materially, i.e., as sounds. Markus comments on this as follows:

> This [second] part begins with the long overdue distinction between use and mention [...] To solve the puzzles which arise from neglecting this distinction Adeodatus points out that "the things we speak of, we signify; and what comes forth from the mouth of the speaker is not the reality signified but the sign by which it is signi-

fied." […] Neither of the speakers seem to be aware of the relevance of this observation to the first part of the discussion.[24]

But as Mary Sirridge has pointed out, the distinction between using a word to signify and talking about the word as a word *has* been made previously, in the first part of the discussion.[25]

The first division is not primarily about the words '*verbum*' and '*nomen*' and '*signum*' as mentioned; it is about what they signify. To imply that Augustine is there dealing with, e.g., '*verbum*' as a token of itself (material supposition) is incorrect. Some modern philosophers have indeed held that mention of a word excludes using it. But the convention of double quotes (as distinguished from single quotes) is a convention for using a word by mentioning it: it is a way of referring to the meaning of the word, a way of *naming* its meaning.[26]

Third, the reader may not read the text carefully enough because the reader does not expect the text to bear careful reading. Of course, this source of misreading is not necessarily independent of the first two reasons. But it can have a distinct basis: the prejudgment that Augustine was not a careful writer. The noted scholar Henri-Irénée Marrou wrote in the first edition of his *Saint Augustin et la fin de la culture antique* that Augustine "composes badly because the ancients generally did not give to composition the attention that we do."[27] This view has been widely held about other works as well, in particular, the *Confessions*, to the detriment of understanding that profound reflection on being and time.

But whatever be the reasons for it, the *De Magistro* has not always been read carefully enough. The following analysis does not purport to resolve all of its puzzles, but at least to determine its basic structure, the logic of its argument, and some of its philosophically interesting conclusions.

II

A classical dialogue is not a treatise. It does not usually begin by stating the fundamental issue to be addressed, which may not emerge for some time. One of the reasons for this is that for it to be the representation of a conversation, the interlocutors must be represented as talking to each other in the way that a more knowledgeable person talks to a less knowledgeable one. And this means that the level of address must take into account the capacity of the addressee to understand, as well as the context or stage of discussion which has been reached. This principle of reading the text does not have to be imported or inferred. Augustine himself says to Adeodatus toward the end of the conversation:

> . . . if I were to ask you whether it is true that nothing can be taught by means of words—the very topic we are now discussing—you would at first think the question absurd, because you could not see the problem in its entirety. Then I should have to question you in a way adapted to your capacity for hearing that Teacher within you.[28]

So there is an introductory exchange, in which indeed Augustine asks questions which have in view the long approach to the core issues, but in which those issues are not yet grasped clearly and firmly. He leads Adeodatus to claim that we speak in order to teach or to remind others or ourselves, and that we use words as signs in doing this (1.1–2). Augustine then elicits his agreement that if words are signs because they signify, Adeodatus should be able to indicate to him what it is that the words in a line of Vergil signify, what they are signs of. The line is shrewdly chosen: *Si nihil ex tanta superis placet urbe relinqui*, because two of the first three words are syncategoremmatic, and that means that there is no possibility of Adeodatus responding by showing, i.e., by exhibiting, what they signify. Of course '*nihil*' has similar difficulties.

Augustine begins the exercise by asking Adeodatus to "*tell* me what the individual words signify" (*Dic mihi quod singula verba significent*, 2.3). So Adeodatus responds, naturally enough, by telling: i.e., by using other words to define and describe. His response exemplifies the position of Derrida and other contemporaries that, in discourse about things, the word never delivers the thing itself, but only points to other words. We move only in the universe of signifiers unless something extra-linguistic shows itself. This leads to the next impasse: Augustine now protests that he wants to be *shown* the things signified, not given more words.

... you [Adeodatus] can readily see that you have explained words by words—that is, signs by signs—and what is quite familiar by what is equally familiar. But I would like you to show, if you can, the things themselves of which these are signs.[29]

Adeodatus is dubious about whether this is possible without using *some* kind of signs (e.g., gestures), but Augustine gets him to agree that perhaps some actions, under certain conditions, can be shown in response to a "what is . . ." question. For example, provided one is not walking when asked the question "what is walking," can't one show what the sign signifies without using any signs, just by walking?[30] It seems so.

With this tentative agreement, the introductory part of the dialogue ends, and Augustine now gathers together the fragments and states the *tripartita distributione* which is to structure the remainder of the dialogue. The question is, how does one person teach another what it is that a sign signifies?

[1] When, therefore, certain signs are asked about, [those] signs can be shown by signs

[2] But when [signs signifying] things which are not signs are asked about, [they can be taught]

[2a] either by doing them after being asked, if they can be enacted,

[2b] or by giving signs by which attention can be directed to them.[31]

There are three possible cases, divided into two genera. If we are asked about certain signs, they can be shown by signs; if on the other hand we are asked about things which are not signs, either they can be shown by doing them after being asked, if they are the sort of things which can be performed, or (if they are not) they can be explained by giving signs which direct attention to the things. The remainder of the discussion takes up successively the three cases: in his very next sentence after giving the threefold division, Augustine says, "Let's consider first, if you please, the case of signs shown by signs" (*prius illud consideremus, si placet, quod signis signa monstrantur*).[32]

It is important to emphasize the structural significance of this threefold division.[33] The more common interpretation has been to acknowledge it but to let its importance be overridden by a two-part organization based on the appearance of the thesis of the Interior Teacher, or of Augustine's monologue in the last third of the text. But this leads to attempts to find a threefold division in the earlier part of the text, which is difficult to do convincingly.[34] I shall try to show that the threefold division structures all of the rest of the dialogue.

First, then, if certain signs are asked about, they can be shown by signs.[35] This part of the dialogue has often been passed over as "an exercise in pure dialectic to very little purpose except as an exercise."[36] Markus says that it is "a bewildering and often sophistical discussion of the ways in which 'speech also signifies itself along with other things.'"[37] It may seem trivial or bewildering if we do not ask ourselves why the proposed discussion about signs signifying signs turns out to be almost wholly about signs which are symmetrical and hence reflexive, i.e., which signify themselves along with other things (4.7–10) and which, taken in pairs, signify each other mutually (5.11–6.18). Why isn't the discussion about signs that are signified by signs directed to what Adeodatus has been doing (explaining some signs by other signs) or directed to signs which signify other signs, like "conjunction"? We use words like "conjunction," "exclamation," "adjective," etc., to talk about signs: why does Augustine merely mention this category (signs which signify other signs but not themselves) in order to discriminate his thematic category (signs which signify other signs mutually and therefore also themselves)?

The interchange here between Augustine and Adeodatus deals with two subtopics: first, showing that there are such signs, i.e., signs which signify mutually: '*signum*,' '*nomen*' and '*verbum*' are given as examples. Second, they discover that these words are alike in signifying each other mutually, but that they differ in three ways: there are three species of mutually signifying signs, which, together with the first genus mentioned, make four categories. Since we are dealing with the signifying relation, we can characterize them by the logical properties of the relation. Following Adeodatus' summary (7.20), we have:

SIGNS SIGNIFYING OTHER SIGNS:

A. signs which cannot themselves be signified by the signs which
    they signify: non-symmetrical (and irreflexive) (e.g., "conjunc-
    tion")
B. signs which can signify each other mutually:
    1) but differing in extension (e.g., "word" and "sign")
    2) symmetrical, same extension, but differing in meaning (e.g.,
       "word" and "name")[38]
    3) symmetrical, same extension, same meaning (e.g., "name"
       and "*onoma*")[39]

The quick-witted Adeodatus, having summarized these results of
the discussion thus far, remarks that all of the signs in the second class
are reflexive: they signify themselves as well as other signs. Why has this
been important to establish?

If no sign which signifies other signs signified itself, i.e., if no signs
were symmetrical and reflexive, if they were all like "conjunction," then
signs could not *show* signs, they could only tell—remind—of other signs.
We would have to already know what the sign signified was in order for
the signifying sign to be able to direct our attention to it. On the other
hand, if a sign which signifies itself along with other signs is presented
to me, it cannot find me completely ignorant of that of which it is a sign:
it "shows itself," so to speak. Or better: it shows what it signifies.

But it is not simply reflexivity which Augustine wants: his definitions of *signum* in both *De Dialectica* (5.7) and *De Doctrina christiana*
(2.1.1) require that signs show something beyond themselves. So he
reaches the category of reflexive signs—those that signify themselves—
by means of the category of mutually signifying signs.

After the elegant recapitulation by Adeodatus, Augustine remarks
that his son cannot yet see the larger relevance and importance of this
discussion about signs signifying signs, but that he should be patient.
One of the themes to which it will be relevant is the topic of the third
division, in which signs (of things in the world) which cannot show
what they signify will be treated. We can anticipate a bit by saying that

the argument is *not that signs can never show what they signify*—these words we have been considering can do that—*but that signs of things cannot show what they signify.* This means that there will be—is—a kind of epistemological gap in the latter case between the reality signified and its sign, which does not exist here because of the closure effected by the reflexive signs of language.

Augustine now turns (8.22) to the second part—what has been designated above as [2a]—of the threefold division: "let us now consider (*consideremus*) that part in which signs signify not other signs, but those things which we call signifiables."[40] First (*primum*) he says, tell me *utrum homo homo sit* (whether man is man). The puzzle that lies in this simple question takes some time (8.22–24) to get clear about and to deal with. Apart from the use of signs to signify signs and their use to signify things, there is a way of speaking words which is not a signifying way at all, but which merely exhibits the sound, the syllables of the word. In this use, the question asked above could be construed as something like: tell me whether these two syllables "ho" and "mo" are the two syllables "ho" and "mo"?[41] Clearly, all sorts of sophisms can enter into our conversations if we regularly allow this construal. Sometimes whether it is so intended by the speaker is indicated by the context: perhaps we are discussing phonemes, or the questioner asks, "Tell me whether man has one or two syllables?"

Even if the context does not disambiguate such questions (or statements), there is a rule of speech (*regula loquendi*) which naturally prevails in discourse unless explicitly contraindicated, namely, that our attention is spontaneously directed to what is signified rather than to the sign (8.24). Signs are naturally self-effacing, so to speak: they do not draw our attention to themselves, but to what is signified.

Why does the attention to this way of construing signs arise only here, with the beginning of the second alternative? Markus finds this puzzling, since what he describes as the "distinction between use and mention" seems to him to be even more relevant to the first part of the dialogue (on signs showing signs) than here.[42] That Adeodatus explicitly denies the relevance of the distinction increases the puzzlement, or the suspicion that Augustine does not understand the semantics involved. What Adeodatus says is:

The things we speak of, we signify; and what comes forth from the mouth of the speaker is not the reality signified, but the sign by which it is signified. *The exception is when it is the signs themselves that are signified, a class we treated a little while ago.* [emphasis mine][43]

That is, in the consideration of the first division, the sign and the signified were the same, and so the possibility of *either* the sign *or* the signified being exclusively intended did not arise.

This possible ambiguity having been noted and set aside, Augustine continues the inquiry into the second alternative, i.e., [2a]. Recall that we are considering the alternative where signs do not signify other signs, but rather where signs signify signifiables; more specifically, we are considering how the latter can be shown. He says that he now (9.25) wants Adeodatus to understand (*jam ego intelligas volo*) that the knowledge of things signified is always to be ranked (*pendendas*) above signs, because signs exist for the sake of knowing the things and not vice versa. For example, we do not teach in order to speak (signify), but we speak in order to teach. If this is the case, then if it should be that we can show (teach) without signs, so much the better. Signs will be only a regular but not a necessary condition of teaching.

Can we in fact teach anything without using signs? It is only at the end of 9.28 that the discussion reaches this core of the inquiry into the second part of the threefold division. Augustine's language makes it clear that we are not beginning a new division[44] but proceeding along the same path:

Wherefore let us discuss further that class of things which we said can be shown by themselves, without the use of signs . . .[45]

The tentative summary (10.31) recapitulates the conclusions of this part[46] of the discussion: 1) nothing is taught without signs, the result reached in 10.29–30; 2) knowledge of things is better than signs, even if 3) not always better than the things themselves (9.25–28). As at the end of the first part, after the summary Augustine adds some reflections. This time, he remarks on the danger in an inquiry where we are criticizing and rejecting opinions previously held: the danger that one may fall into a distrust of even the most clearly manifest truth. For now he leads Adeodatus to see that what the latter had agreed to before, namely, that nothing can be taught (shown) without signs, is false. Not only can men exhibit certain actions in response to a question about these actions—given sufficient intelligence in the listener—but God and nature show us (*ostendit*) thousands of things without using any signs.[47]

Taken as a whole, then, the second part diminishes the importance of signs, first by showing that there is a natural *regula loquendi* which impels us to ignore the sign itself in favor of what is signified (8.22–24); second, by showing that the knowledge of the thing signified is more important than the sign (9.25–28); third, that in fact signs are not always necessary for teaching: there are some things man can teach by showing, without using signs (10.29–32).

The third part of the threefold division, [2b]—"or by giving signs by which attention can be directed to them [signifiables]" (*aut signa dando per quae animadverti queant*)—begins with 10.33 (the *oratio continua*). The first two parts began with the words "let us consider" (*consideremus*): the third and last occurrence of this word comes at the beginning of 10.33.

This section begins with the thesis that nothing is taught (i.e., shown) by its proper sign (*sua signa*), its *nomen*.[48] Even in the case of pointing, which he considers briefly and then dismisses, what is pointed to is not shown in the strict sense of being made manifest or present. What is pointed to must already be there, but perhaps not attended to. In any case, the gesture of pointing is not a proper sign of the thing pointed to: it is rather a sign of the directing of attention, like saying "Ecce" (10.34).

But Augustine's main concern here is with words: '*signum*' does not occur in the third and final part of the dialogue (after 10.34),[49] because the argument of the last part is about the incapacity of those signs which we call words to teach anything. And the reason for this is that the knowledge of the thing (the signifiable) is not only independent of its word-sign (it is not shown by its sign, as was the case with *nomen, verbum*, etc.), but the knowledge of the thing signified is necessarily prior to the knowledge that the word is a sign, i.e., a sound that signifies. If we do not know what the word signifies, we do not know the word as a sign. Words are not pointers—they are not like the gesture of pointing—they are tokens whose value depends on already knowing what they are tokens of.

Augustine goes on to remind us how men can use words, if we already know their meaning, to draw our attention to things perceptually present or remembered. As he has already remarked (in 1.1), this is a *kind* of teaching, and indeed an important kind, which consists in reminding: using words to call to mind in another something that he could in principle already have taken note of. So we can be taught, in this sense, to know (*scire*), but this kind of teaching and knowing is only of external things, of individual kinds of things in the world. Moreover, for this kind of teaching, there is no reference to the Interior Teacher.[50]

> But concerning everything which we understand (*intelligimus*), it is not a speaking which sounds exteriorly that we consult, but that truth which presides over the mind within, though perhaps the words admonish us to do that.[51]

When it comes to understanding (*intelligere*) the truth of the universal essential relations of things signified, neither can man exhibit these by his actions nor are they shown by God and nature in the world. We can indeed by our words sometimes succeed in directing the attention of the learner's mind to such significations, but only because they have been shown, disclosed, by an inner light, by the light of truth which is beyond our capacity to produce, but in which, by the gift of God, we live. For *intelligibilia* there are no natural signs; no meaningful gestures like pointing are available. It is beyond our power and beyond the power of physical nature to show or exhibit or manifest the truths which are disclosed to the mind.

Still, even here, there is something which our words about things can show, can accomplish by themselves. We cannot always succeed in directing the mind of our hearer to the things which we have in mind—the failure of words to communicate what we intend is all too common[52]—but under favorable conditions, one can at least learn what the speaker is thinking. Our thoughts can be exhibited by our words.[53] Augustine's comment on this is that even if it is possible, that's not what we call teaching or learning.

For who is so stupidly curious as to send his son to school to learn what the teacher thinks?[54]

Once again, the discussion of this part [2b] of the threefold division is terminated by a summary. This time it is Adeodatus who, upon the end of the uninterrupted discourse of Augustine (10.33–14.45) and the latter's invitation to comment, summarizes what he has learned (been admonished by Augustine's words to see for himself), thanks to the interior oracle.[55] And again, as in the previous divisions, there is a reflection on the meaning of what he has learned, in words which recall the then enigmatic statement of Augustine in 8.22 about God as the goal of their inquiry into signs.

III

I have argued that the *De Magistro* is divided clearly and logically into three parts (after the introduction), following the threefold division of 4.7. The central question is this: if we are asked, as Adeodatus was, to explain or teach the meaning of word-signs, then

[1] when the question is about certain signs which signify each other mutually, we can do that by showing because the sign itself can show what it signifies (4.7–8.21);

and

[2] when the question is about signs which signify things that are not signs, then
[2a] for some sensible things, we can show them by doing them without using any signs (8.22–10.32)
[2b] and for other sensible things, we can draw attention to them by giving signs (10.32–37);
but for intelligible things we can only use words to try to draw attention to them (10.38–14.46).[56] There is no other way to show them or to point to them. Words do not make present what they signify.

Clearly, then, there are two different ways of responding to someone's desire to know, two quite different ways of teaching; and Augustine holds that only one of these is teaching in the proper sense of the term:

Only he teaches me something who presents to the eyes, or another sense organ, or to the mind itself, that which I want to know.[57]

To teach is to bring it about that something shows itself to someone who desires to know. There is another, secondary, sense of teaching, in which the teacher does not exhibit or make manifest what is to be known, but rather uses signs to tell the learner where or how to look in order to see. In this second sense, the teacher does not make present what is to be learned, but relies on its having been made present by some other source. In this second sense, then, we can say that the teacher tells the learner of what is there to be seen if you look in the right way: telling or reminding presupposes what is already there.

In terms of these two sorts of teaching (showing and telling), the argument of the dialogue may be summarized as follows: first, for some kinds of signs, human beings can both show and tell what they signify because the telling is the showing; second, for signs about some kinds of signifiable things, we can show what they signify; third, for other kinds of sensible signifiables, we can never show but only tell or remind. And in the case of signifiables which are not sensed but are understood by the mind, words are necessary but limping aides, because they neither deliver (show) nor can point to what they signify. Some power greater than ours is necessary to make such intelligible things manifest, and that power is the true Teacher of what we understand.[58]

There are a number of philosophically interesting issues which are involved in the inquiry of the dialogue and which deserve to be explored. I should like to comment briefly on a few of them.

1) Although the thesis of the Interior Teacher clearly is a central doctrine of the dialogue, it does not obliterate or imply the denial of the human capacity to teach, in the paradigmatic sense of that word. Contrary to what is often said, the inquiry does not conclude that Christ is the only true teacher. In each of the three sections, the conclusion is reached that there is something which man can teach, i.e., show, as distinct from his ability to teach in the secondary and analogous sense

which consists in reminding, or calling to mind by words. In each case, *it is what man himself brings into being that he can show*: in [1] it is signs; in [2a] it is actions such as walking, bird-catching, sitting, lying down, etc.; in [2b] it is thoughts, the "thinkings" of the speaker.

This making-something-present which constitutes human teaching in the primary sense is, in each case, a form of what may be called "ontological causality," in which the effect (speaking, walking, thinking) exists only so long as I continue to bring it about. In this respect it is analogous to God's causality in bringing creation into existence. So we can say that there are three different regions of being, three different regions of origin for meaning, three different regions in which something can show itself: the mind (the intentionality of signs), the world (human actions and the things of nature), and the intelligibles.

That the things brought into being by human action are transient does not mean that they cannot be defined, that there is not something for the mind to grasp. Aristotle, for example, says that there is no definition except for natural essences, but this only means that any "definition" of transient things will not be a "real," i.e., eternal, natural kind of definition. So Adeodatus says in his last speech in the dialogue (before the conclusion) that "si enim sit bene intelligens [...] totum quid sit ambulare cognoscet" (10.32).

All of these forms of human teaching are of course negligible compared to that teaching which enables one to understand the timeless truths and which leads toward the *vita beata*, knowing and loving God (14.45; cf. 8.21); nonetheless they reflect the unique status of man as himself a teacher in the primary sense.[59]

2) Why does Augustine think of teaching by words (the secondary form of teaching) as a kind of reminding, which seems to imply that learning is a kind of remembering? Is this simply the weight of the Platonic tradition, in which coming to know is often described as or likened to recollection, *anamnesis*?

The first thing to notice is that it is not learning as remembering which is the focus of his account: it is rather teaching as reminding. And what does "reminding" mean? The sense we need to keep in mind here is the sense in which one says, "May I remind you that I am your commanding officer," or "Remember man that thou art dust [...] (*memento homo quia pulvis est* . . .)." In these cases, the speaker is not asking the hearer to recollect something which has been forgotten. Rather, the speaker wants to draw the attention of the hearer to something of which the hearer is not ignorant but which he has "lost sight of," something to which he is not paying attention.

One who teaches us about intelligible things, about things which we *understand* (*intelligimus*) (10.38), does not ask us to recollect something which we have known previously and forgotten, but rather to attend to something which is already accessible to us, although unnoticed. The field of awareness in general, not merely in sense perception, is structured into focal and marginal regions.[60] The marginal or background region is not absent, it is simply not salient, we do not integrate it into the focal gestalt. By asking questions, we induce the learner to draw from the background elements which are relevant to the focal theme to relate those elements to the focal gestalt, to make them parts of the focal whole.

So the content of *memoria* for Augustine includes not only images of events perceived in the past but also those objects of understanding which are present in the mind's field of awareness, but which are in the background of that field. Like the images of sense memory, the objects of understanding before we are reminded of them have a characteristic quality of presence-absence, and the language of "reminding" serves to characterize both those cases where we need to recollect something which we have known previously and those cases where we have simply not paid attention to elements which lie within our field of awareness, but only in an implicit or marginal way. For objects of understanding, it's not that knowing them now is a re-cognizing of them, a knowing of what we have known previously, but that their presence-absence is like that which we experience in sense memory.

The epistemological similarity, of course, is distinct from their ontological difference: the sense memory image is of what no longer *is*, while the object of understanding is unaffected by temporal difference. In the language of the *Confessions*, the images of sense memory are present, but not the thing or event which they represent, while in the case of intelligible things, it is the thing itself which is present when we know it.

So neither does the language of teaching as reminding entail a commitment to a theory of recollection (nor a fortiori to the pre-existence of the soul), nor does that seem to be any part of Augustine's intention in developing the conception of teaching as reminding in the last part of the *De Magistro*.

3) We remarked earlier that the question of whether any things can be shown without signs is one on which Adeodatus goes back and forth: first no, then yes, then no again, and finally yes. Indeed one cannot avoid the impression that, since Augustine knows from the start that yes is the final and correct answer, he deliberately induces these dialectical reversals in Adeodatus' opinion. Augustine's reflections at the end of the second section (10.31) enable us to see why he has done this. He tells his son:

> It is extremely difficult not to be perturbed when those opinions which we hold easily and readily are made to totter by contrary arguments, and, as it were, twisted from our hands. That is why, just as it is right to yield to arguments that have been thoroughly investigated and weighed, so it is hazardous to consider as known what is not known. Since things which we presume are going to stand firmly and endure are frequently undermined, there is the danger of our falling into such a great dislike or distrust of reason that we might decide not to place confidence even in evident truth.[61]

But granted the rightness of such a warning to a novice in dialectic, can we give any reason for greater confidence in the last answer that Adeodatus has come to? Augustine returns to this in explaining why they have had to follow such a long and winding path in investigating the role of signs in showing and telling.

> It often happens that one denies something when he is asked about it, but is brought around by further questions to affirm it. The reason for this is the weakness of his vision; he is unable to see the matter as a whole by that [inner] light. He is led to bring the problem part by part into the light as questions are put regarding those same parts that constitute the whole, which originally he was not able to see in its entirety.[62]

That is, reversals in our opinions are made more likely when we form a judgment about something without seeing its connections to related issues in the whole topic. We don't see all that is implied by our judgment or what is implied about it by other judgments. Conversely, as the larger problem comes into view, we can see that the issue about which we have formed an opinion is, in fact, a part of a more comprehensive whole. As the whole comes into view, our corrected judgment about the part is "anchored" by seeing its proper place in the whole, its relations to other parts and how it matches the various facets of the question. (Recall how Augustine said that he couldn't have asked Adeodatus at the start whether it is true that nothing is taught by means of words, because the latter would not have grasped the whole problem and so, not having perceived the segmentary nature of the question properly, would find the question absurd.)

The firmness of *scientiam* [*sic*], which is the terminus of inquiry, rests upon the fact that the judgment arrived at is not isolated. It is very important to stress that for Augustine *scientiam* [*sic*] does not come about simply by some inner light illuminating an intelligible object. That would be a simplistic picture, and a misleading one. Rather, his conception of firmly grounded knowledge, like that of Aristotle's *episteme*, requires that the interconnections of judgments be seen, that the entailments and reasons become visible. And for that, discursive ratiocination is required, which the dialogue exemplifies.

Understanding, *intelligere*, as Augustine indicates both here and in the *Confessions*, requires the bringing together, the bringing into relation, of isolated elements of knowledge. Understanding is not the same as knowing some isolated intelligible thing: it depends upon integration into a gestalt which has a sufficient wholeness and unity. *Intelligere* is not so much *intus legere*, to read within, as *inter legere*, to bring together:

> . . . to learn such things [...] is just this: by acts of thought to gather together and collect as it were things that memory contained here and there without any order . . . they must be brought together (*cogenda*) so that they may be known. That is, they must be collected together (*colligenda*) as it were out of a sort of scattered state.[63]

"Gestalting" elements, integrating them into an understandable whole, is something which the learner must do for himself, though admonished to do so by the questions of the teacher. This is why understanding cannot be taught, and why the simplistic picture of a light shining on monadic forms in the mind is far from Augustine's conception of learning. Even if I could, in some way, lead you to see the Form of Virtue in your mind's eye, that would not be understanding or *scientiam* [*sic*].[64]

4) The relation of the human teacher to the Interior Teacher. At the end of the dialogue, Augustine asserts that *he* hasn't taught Adeodatus that the Interior Teacher is a necessary condition of intellectual understanding, for "I am unable to teach at all" (*nunquam possum docere*) (14.46). Socrates, of course, could have said (and did sometimes say) as much. But it sounds more paradoxical coming at the end of a long uninterrupted discourse. If Augustine hasn't been teaching, what in heaven's name has he been doing?

Of course, Augustine has from the very beginning (1.1) asserted that there is a kind of teaching, and indeed very reasonably so called (*magnum sane*), which consists in "reminding" (*commemorationem*). But this teaching by telling or by asking questions is, in the noetic realm, not an easy task. Augustine goes into some detail in enumerating various ways in which communication may fail, and often does.[65] Words are not, like the gesture of pointing, in the same cognitive field as the signifiables to which they seek to draw attention.[66] Words which signify things do not, unlike the reflexive signs of part [1] and the enactments of part [2a], show what they signify. How do we cross the gap from signs to signified things?

One of the things that makes it possible is that the interiority of the "interior man" is not closed. It is all too easy for us moderns to read Augustine in the light of the subjectivity discovered by Descartes and his successors.[67] But for the classics, it is body, not mind, that is private. Through noesis, we share a common world of intelligibles. Modern philosophy assimilated mind or consciousness to the body, and conceived both as private, in contrast to the represented common world. In contrast, Augustine thinks of the light of Truth as above—not in—the mind, of the mind as open to what lies above it.

But one of the things that makes teaching by words, by telling or reminding, difficult is that there is no pre-programmed one-to-one correspondence of signs and signifiables. If there were, Adeodatus would

not have needed this long dialectic. Making the right connection between words and signified takes pedagogical skill; because words are not
ostensive, they can't point to what they mean.[68]

For a more appropriate analogy, think of how a teacher of checkers
or chess might try to teach us what the "style of play" means in a match
we are watching. Every game instantiates the rules for moving pieces
and exhibits more or less foresight in its moves, but one player plays
aggressively, another defensively, one boldly, another timidly. No single
move or set of moves represents aggressive play. There is no simple thing
that can be pointed to, even though the style of play is not hidden to one
while visible to another.[69] To discern it, we must learn to integrate a
number of phenomena, to see their interconnections and their relative
importance. Just so, teaching by reminding, by giving signs which seek
to draw attention to what is there to be seen, requires a complex art of
discerning the capacities of the learner at any given time and knowing
how to draw attention to what otherwise is passed over unnoticed. It
may require a long dialogical path before the learner comes to see for
himself what has been at least obscurely present in the awareness of the
teacher from the beginning.[70]

Nevertheless, when that moment of insight occurs, Augustine is
convinced that the external teacher has only been a secondary cause of
the learning because he is himself incapable of exhibiting, showing, what
is then grasped by the learner directly. Heteronomy has a part, but teaching would remain on the level of merely believing the teacher unless the
moment of autonomy ensued. But the central topic of the dialogue is
not the role of autonomy, however important that is: indeed, Adeodatus
may have been capable of seeing that at the start, or early on in their
discussion.

The central theme of the dialogue is the necessity of something
showing itself, if we are to escape from the self-referential network of
signifiers which constitutes language. If there is not a kind of teaching
through which we go beyond words to encounter what is real, then
teaching is only telling and learning is only mastering the interrelationships of words.

What Adeodatus comes to see is that there is never seeing without
a showing that discloses, reveals, what otherwise remains inaccessible.

Some third thing, as Socrates says in the *Republic*, is necessary as a condition of accessibility to insight.[71] Just as man is the source of showing—teaching in the primary sense—for the things which he originates, so in the space of intellectual signifiables, Augustine follows Scripture in confessing, the primary teacher is the originating source of the signifiables, that Light from Light which is Christ.

Perhaps this is why the mode of discourse in the last part of the dialogue becomes that of a lecture, if an informal one: Adeodatus cannot, in principle, be brought to see by dialogue that the interior light is Christ. Hence Augustine must assert this and Adeodatus can only believe it. Believing it, he can now see what his father was hinting at in his remarks at the end of the first section about God being the end of their enquiry.

So it is not that human teaching about timeless truths is impossible but that it is not a self-sufficient dyadic relation of speaker and hearer. I do not show you the moon, as if it were not there to be seen before I draw your attention to it by words or signs. I do not show you the difference between knowing and believing, as if the meanings were not discernible before I spoke. But I can draw your attention to the difference only because the two of us stand together under a Light which opens up all truth to our understanding.

CHAPTER FOUR

Philosophy and Belief

Perhaps the most fundamental difference between classical and early Christian thought is the role allotted to belief in the pursuit of understanding. Not only do thinkers such as St. Augustine reconceptualize the relation of belief to knowing in that pursuit, but there are significant consequences for the human community in the reevaluation. There are indeed other fundamental differences or shifts that involve new perspectives on the human situation—e.g., creation, providence, sin, and evil—but all of these would appear to trace their roots to religious belief.

Classical love of wisdom sought understanding through what showed itself to be true or false, what was evident, or was evidently implied by what is known. In the pursuit of that goal, all opinions, traditions, hearsay, conventional beliefs, and values are bracketed, to be subjected to examination. Although there are opinions that are de facto true opinions, they are not anchored by insight and so, for those capable of it, they are always to be replaced by knowledge, where possible. As Socrates says in the *Phaedrus* when asked a question about what actions are pleasing to the gods, "I can tell you what I've heard from our ancestors. Whether it's true or not, I don't know. But if we could find out the truth for ourselves, should we still bother about human opinions?"[1] "A ridiculous question!" Phaedrus responds.

Christianity confronts this conception of the way to wisdom with the assertion that "the folly of God is wiser than human wisdom."[2]

(Erasmus will later write *In Praise of Folly*, at almost the same time that Machiavelli is writing *The Prince*, that searing critique of the folly of ideals in the real world). It is necessary, in order to be a follower of Christian religiousness, to believe things that have been hidden since the foundation of the world, but are now revealed by the life and doctrine of Jesus. Flesh and blood, human wisdom, cannot discover the whole truth, although it may be able to come to know of the invisible God.[3] So although some steps toward the whole truth can be taken by reason, ultimately faith—belief in God and what he has revealed—is the only means of accessing the critical truths and the Tao, the right Way. (Jesus said, "I am the Way," I am the Tao.)

One may adopt and adapt, as Aquinas does, Aristotle's comment about the appropriateness of a learner's believing and defer the knowing until we are face to face with God. But Aquinas is also insistent that the content of revelation is in principle beyond our capacity to reason to in this life. In fact, we could define revelation in just that way, as truths that are inaccessible to human reason except by believing.

I propose to explore this issue by thinking about an early work of Augustine, *De utilitate credendi*, written about 391 to a longtime friend, Honoratus, who had been, together with him, a hearer in the Manichean sect, but who had remained a Manichee. It is five years or so since Augustine's conversion to Catholic Christianity, and he wants to remove possible philosophical obstacles to his friend's reasonably considering the claims of the church in his search for true religiousness. So the work is not theological or religious in the sense of utilizing premises from Scripture; it does not argue for the truth of Catholic Christianity, but rather considers from a philosophical angle the subjects of reading and of believing in the context of searching for true wisdom, which may be true religiousness. However, the work also bears the character of personal testimony, of a person who has traveled the road of thought that he maps out.

The title has been variously translated: the usefulness of believing, the benefit of believing, the advantage of believing, the profit of believing. If the meaning of *"utilitate"* could be stretched, perhaps "The Indispensability of Believing" would describe the argument of the text. Like many works of Augustine, especially from his early writings, its worth has been deprecated. A recent writer dismisses it as "dreadful . . . unconvincing, lamely argued, poorly organized."[4] I disagree with that judgment, as will become evident.

The work is marked by the insertion, precisely in the center of the text, of a brief autobiographical section that divides the argument into two parts. It is striking that the autobiographical details in this section come up to the end of the middle book of the first part of *Confessions*, book 5. That is, they deal with Augustine's search for true wisdom and religiousness and hence with his joining the Manichees, their criticism of the Old Testament, his increasing doubts about their teaching, the coming of Faustus, the Manichean bishop, Augustine's going to Milan and learning from Saint Ambrose that the church did not read the Scriptures in the way that the Manichees asserted it did, and finally his decision to remain a catechumen in the church. Now it is just these issues that the first half of *De utilitate credendi* addresses: the criticisms by the Manichees, how to read the Scriptures and the need to find a teacher of how to read and of the true way.

One of the things which this autobiographical passage in *De utilitate credendi* suggests is that five years after his conversion and five years before the *Confessions*, Augustine is already thinking about the episodes of his life as having the unity of a narrative. Following Augustine's division, I shall consider these two parts of the work—before and after the "autobiography"—serially. First, some general observations.

The first half of the discussion is about reading texts of all kinds, but especially those which may embody true wisdom, and the need to have a teacher who can *show* us how to read texts (including religious texts), *show* us the different ways in which texts may have to be read in order to be rightly understood, or *teach* us true wisdom.[5] The second half is about finding a wise person who can be our guide on the path to true wisdom. In the first part, the terms "believing" and "authority" play no part, because it is about a teacher *showing* us the different ways of construing texts. But the second part *is* about believing an authority, a guru. The historical Christ is discussed, but he is never referred to there (or elsewhere in Augustine's writings) as a teacher, and he is never described as *showing* us the truth. Rather, he is called a *preceptor*, who instructs us concerning true religiousness. (At the close of Augustine's presenting of his case to his friend, he urges him to commit himself in faith and charity to "good preceptors of Catholic Christianity."[6]

So, in Augustine's view the historical human being Christ is *not* a teacher, because he does not *show* us that what he says is true—because he cannot. We have to simply believe Him.

Recall from the *Confessions* that the Manichees ridiculed the superstitious Christian position that belief comes first, and they promised instead to provide reasons for all of their teaching. They did not, and that was one of the things that finally turned Augustine away from their sect. He wants his friend to think about the difference between believing God—faith—and *seeing* the reasons for something being so.

I

We are writing to Honoratus because we know that he joined the Manichees in search of true religiousness, and we want to help him continue that quest by removing certain difficulties that tend to prevent him from considering other alternatives, particularly Catholic Christianity. All we need to know for the moment about Manichean teaching is that they rip to shreds (*discerpentes et dilaniantes* 2.4) the Old Testament and ridicule the Catholic Church for accepting it, and second that they promise that their hearers will not have to *believe* their teaching but that reasons will be given for all of it, whereas Catholic Christians, they say, are dominated by a superstitious fear and commanded to believe without reasons being given (*superstitione terreri et fidem . . . ante rationem imperari* 1.2).

There is a special problem that arises when, in the search for true wisdom, true religiousness, a religious group under examination has a sacred text that is alleged to contain revealed doctrine. There can of course be a kind of sacred text or texts without the latter claim. Buddhism, for example, and Hinduism (at least in its Advaita form) have texts that teach how to achieve certain states of realization, but the belief required here is more like that of Aristotle's learner—in principle, the disciple can ultimately verify for himself that the teaching is true. They do not require faith in the sense earlier specified.

But there is a problem common to all such texts, and that is the problem of reading them rightly. Thus, Augustine says, consider the possibility that the Scriptures are misread by the Manichees, and that there is a different and more appropriate way to read them, one that discloses their hidden meaning (*secretam significationem* 7.17). We need to consider that the many read texts without considering that the surface meanings may hide a latent meaning, one accessible to the few who ponder them.

So, we have to think about the ways in which all kinds of texts can be misread, readings that are the occasion for errors in understanding. And in particular we need to think about the ways in which texts containing revealed truth would have to be read, ways to which Augustine was introduced by Ambrose and which he now recapitulates and explains for Honoratus. Among other things, the historical situation of the events related in such texts would have to be considered essential, unlike philosophical texts that deal with timeless or tenseless knowledge, because the alleged revelation occurs at or through a particular time and place and to particular persons. We do not have time here to examine these matters in any detail; I would like to comment on only one issue, one with implications for revealed texts.

After analyzing the various kinds of errors that can occur in reading, Augustine says that the best situation is where the writer understands something true and to his profit (it is good to understand what is so) and the reader also understands the writer and so understands the same truth to his profit. But then he remarks that although this is the ideal and does occur, we can never *know* such concurrence to be the case. We can only believe it. A fortiori is this the case if the writer is dead or absent and the text stands by itself; but even if the author were present, Augustine says, he might have honorable reasons for not disclosing his thoughts beyond the written text (5.11).

In approaching any genre of text for the first time, we need the help of a teacher to learn how to read below the surface meaning, to discern the author's implied meaning, if one is present. In the case of what may be a revealed text, we not only need such authoritative hermeneutic help—since the text is presented as God's word and so crucial to understand rightly—but even in being willing to regard it as revealed, we first of all believe those who bring it to us as such a text. What leads us to do that? Well, the character of the community that conveys the text to the world, that, so to speak, bears witness to its alleged revealed character. As Augustine will later write, "I would not believe the Gospels unless the authority of the Catholic Church moved me to do so."[7]

This issue leads us to the second topic discussed in the first half of *De utilitate credendi*, after the nature of reading rightly, namely, how to begin to search for a teacher of true religiousness. Suppose, he says, we have never heard any teacher of religion. How should we go about deciding to whom to listen? If it is wisdom about religiousness we seek, it might seem that since the many are not wise, then a priori we ought not to look for a large religious sect. But what if the few who understand the truth are able by their authority to guide the multitude? "Granted that the truest and most sincere worship of God is likely to be found among a few, if to them the multitude rally, despite their passions and their lack of deep understanding . . . should we respond that we were deterred by the many?" (7.16). It is true, after all, that with respect to numerous genuine goods of human life, many seek what few exemplify with any accomplishment (for example, skill in rhetoric).

II

The second half of our work is concerned with the need for belief, and is directed against the Manichean scorn for faith and their promise to give reasons for their teaching. Much of it is written in incipient dialogue form, with the questions and objections of a fictive Manichee and an imagined Honoratus being responded to by Augustine.

So, is it not desirable, we might ask, to be given reasons when asked to assent to some proposition? Generally, yes, Augustine responds, but in some cases, no. Nor is this unreasonable, as we shall see. As he writes later to a friend, "Let no one think that God hates in us that faculty by which he made us superior to all other living things. Let no one think that we should believe in such a way as not to accept or to seek a reason for our belief, since we could not even believe if we did not have rational souls."[8]

But there can be at least two simple grounds for believing something without being given reasons. One is Aristotle's, the pedagogical ground that we may have to accept a number of things on the authority of our teachers for some time before we come to see the reasons for ourselves. Perhaps for some subject matters we will never be in a position to see for ourselves. Indeed, all of us believe things our teachers told us, things that we either could not demonstrate or that would take years of training and observation to verify, such as that the earth spins rapidly on its axis, although we feel no such motion.

The other case is logically simple: we must believe without reasons when what we are asked to believe is in principle beyond any human capacity to demonstrate. In such circumstances, what makes faith the potentially valuable thing that Augustine thinks it is is that it can enable us to go beyond all possible proof. That does not mean we cannot still ask whether it is reasonable so to believe.

We might ask (as Augustine's interlocutor does here) whether such a position does not seem to commend credulousness or credulity. But not all believing without prior reasons is credulous. Indeed the question of whether something is credible is logically prior to whether it can reasonably be believed. So with our learner, or with us who say we "know" that the earth revolves, relying on the scientific community. But how can we evaluate doctrine in a case where no human being can claim to know? Some of the effort of medieval theology was directed toward a partial answer to that, namely to try to show that no logical inconsistency was involved in the credal formulations.

Before going on to think about this last question, consider two objections to what has been said so far.

The first derives from Kierkegaard's *Philosophical Fragments*, written by an assumed persona or author (Johannes Climacus). The nonreligious author proposes an anti-Socratic thought experiment. Suppose—this is his hypothesis—that there were some truths that were, in principle, inaccessible to human inquiry—no matter how many grants we won or how many generations pursued them. And suppose those truths were important, crucial for understanding our lives. How could we come to learn them? Well, only by believing, believing someone who told us about those truths. The time, the moment, when that opportunity opened up to us would be crucial, because our hypothesis is that those truths were eternally, in principle, inaccessible to the human mind's powers. Kierkegaard draws out several other interesting implications of the thought experiment, but I will mention only one. Suppose we hear that some man, long ago, announced such truths, proclaimed them on his own authority, and we are invited to believe these truths, to believe him. Is that not contrary to our hypothesis—which is that such truths are, in principle, inaccessible to the human mind, so no human being *could* know them?

Well, there is a way to remain consistent with the hypothesis, but it adds to what we have to believe—we would have to believe something about the identity of that human being, of who that human being really was in order to be able to tell us about those truths, without his having heard them from someone else. You would have to believe something really paradoxical, Kierkegaard says—a kind of absolute paradox.

The second question derives from Thomas Hobbes, who says in *Leviathan* that when someone believes that the Scriptures are the word of God, unless they have some special revelation from God, they in fact believe human beings, believe the ones from whom they learned of the Scriptures, namely parents and pastors.[9] So when we say we believe the preceptor, but have never seen him or heard him preach, we in fact believe those human beings who are intermediaries in telling us of him. They are the object of our belief, of our faith.

Indeed, when he wrote *On the Advantages of Believing*, Augustine accepted something close to that analysis, although with the proviso that what *he* believed was the church, which Christ had instituted to be the vehicle of that revelation. Ten years later, however, when he wrote the *Confessions*, he was able, on the basis of his reflections over those years about the course of his life, to add a foundation to that analysis. For now he had come to see that God could—and did—speak directly to him through the words of his creatures, that God could speak to him in the voice of a child playing, could speak directly to him in real time, on line, in the words of Scripture. Thus, the hearing through which his faith came was indeed a hearkening to *God's* calling him.

What makes that position distinctive can be seen by contrasting it with the practice he discusses earlier in the *Confessions*, of some people, in Augustine's time and in our own, who open up randomly the pages of some ancient book (Vergil's *Aeneid* was popular in Augustine's time, perhaps Nostradamus in ours) and find sentences that seem to have current import for us. Augustine's mentor at the time told him that that is just chance, like the predictions of astrology occasionally being relevant. His experience in the garden of picking up and opening the Scriptures, seemingly at random, and finding a passage aimed straight to his heart, right to his situation, may seem like the practice with Vergil or Nostradamus. Augustine does not understand it to be chance, though, not only because the book he seizes is one that presents itself as the word of God, but because he has learned that God causes the existence of all events, that all is under his providence. It is not chance that just those words addressed him at that point in his life.

III

A broader response to the question of how to assess a doctrine in a case where no human being can claim to know can be found in William James' *Varieties of Religious Experience*,[10] which I introduce here only because I think Augustine employs these same metrics. James says that there are three questions to ask when examining a religion. First, is its teaching illuminating, does it help us to understand our lives and the human condition, does it offer accounts that explain things? Second, is it consistent with what we know to be the case about the way things are, do we have to surrender any of what we know in order to believe? And third, what are its fruits, what kinds of changes does it effect in the lives of its adherents? Augustine uses all three of these standards in his reflections on true religiousness. Indeed the second—consistency with what we otherwise know—was one of the major factors in his abandonment of Manicheanism, namely, its incompatibility with what he knew about astronomy.[11]

On the basis of his analysis and arguments thus far, Augustine now turns the table on his antagonists, the Manichees, and contends that no one promising reasons for everything they teach *should* be listened to. In fact, the Manichee preachers did not deliver on their promise, and we know enough of the struggle of philosophers toward wisdom to say that no religion can reasonably make such a promise. Beyond that, human life as we experience it depends on people believing things that cannot be known in the strong sense of that term. (Here again, we deal with arguments repeated in the sixth book of the *Confessions*.) We would have no friends if we did not believe that such persons are not merely pretending to be our friends. If one did not believe on their word who one's parents were, the love and care that bonds children and parents would be groundless. We believe many things about the past which are beyond the capacity of anyone living today to know—things that contribute to our sense of identity and that explain much in the present. So, the Christian religion is hardly unique in proposing belief without giving compelling reasons; it is, rather, arguably reasonable in doing so.

Belief (as distinguished from opinion) requires someone to believe; it requires an authority in whom we believe. Thus, the question reappears of how to look for such an authority, and Augustine argues conceptually and empirically. Conceptually he claims that unless the providence of God presides over human affairs, religion is otiose, and if there is such providence one can reasonably hope that—given the human situation as presented—God will provide or has already provided such an authority.[12] If God does not know that we are searching, or is unable to help us, then that is not the God we seek. Empirically he cites the church's continuous tradition, the spread of its teaching, and its effect on the moral ideals and lives of ordinary people.[13]

But I want to go back to James' first criterion, whether the doctrine is illuminating. I want to look at this issue in terms of a maxim that appears already in *De libero arbitrio* and runs throughout his writings. It is the maxim from the Septuagint version of Isaiah, "Unless you believe, you will not understand." Although he does not quote it in *De utilitate credendi*, Augustine clearly refers to it several times (e.g., 9.21). The maxim may sound alright at first, but it can seem puzzling upon reflection. Does it mean that if you do believe, you will understand? Would that not be paradoxical, if faith means believing something that no human being can see to be true? Does it mean that if you believe a proposition, you will come to understand its meaning?

Norman Kretzmann has argued that it would be ridiculous to take the maxim to mean that you have to believe a proposition in order to understand it.[14] Surely we can know what a proposition means without having to believe it. Nor does it seem that "understanding" could mean that having some kind of evidence for a proposition requires already believing it, and then continuing to *believe* it. So he suggests construing "believe" as referring to the "way of faith," a way of life, and "understand" as the heavenly reward of that way of life, the vision of God.

I think that part of the problem here is that Kretzmann thinks of "understanding" a proposition as supplanting, rather than supplementing, belief, so that if you have understanding you no longer have to—indeed no longer can—simply believe it. That is why he has to find another construal of the maxim. Yet, the puzzle raises broader issues about the sense of "know" and "understand" in Augustine's thought.

I want to argue that understanding, *intelligere*, is coextensive with knowing, *scire*, in the strong sense of the latter term. There is evidence for this in a number of texts—interestingly, in Augustine's own comments on *De utilitate credendi* in the *Retractations*.[15] There he writes, quoting himself from the text, "What we know [*scimus*] we owe to reason, what we believe to authority." But the text itself says, "What we understand [*intelligimus*] we owe to reason, what we believe to authority." The text itself adds, "everyone who understands also believes . . . [but] not everyone who believes also understands." He goes on in the *Retractations* to say that in a looser sense of the term "know" it is permissible to say we know what we perceive with the senses, or what we believe on the testimony of trustworthy witnesses. And in *De magistro* he says, "All that I understand I know, but I do not know all that I believe."[16]

Therefore, sense perception is not knowledge, strictly speaking, because knowledge requires reason, and reason is what comes into play in understanding. As Augustine argues in *De magistro* and elsewhere, understanding is not having some single thing—a form, a proposition, an idea—in the mind's eye; it is rather a "gestalting" of elements of knowledge; it is making connections, seeing how things fit together and affect each other's understanding. He says in the *Confessions*: "[T]o learn such things . . . is just this: by acts of thought to gather together and collect, as it were, things that memory contained here and there without any order. . . . they must be brought together [*cogenda*] so that they may be known. That is, they must be collected together [*colligenda*] as it were out of a scattered state."[17] There are the elements and there is the gestalting, and only as these come together do we approach *scientiam*, the fullness of knowledge. If we have only the elements, then we "know" only in a weak sense of the term. Myles Burnyeat has a nice example of the relationship: "[If someone says] 'The only part of modern physics I *understand* is the formula $E = mc^2$,'" [that] is nonsense. [But] 'The only part of modern physics I *know* is the formula $E = mc^2$,' is merely sad."[18]

Now let us return to our maxim ("Unless you believe . . ."). I want to suggest that, as a maxim for guiding religious reflection, the object of the term "believe" is plural. That is, the term picks out a whole set of propositions from Scripture and tradition that can illuminate each other. If we believe, that is, bring that set into play in our reflection, we will begin to understand their relationship to each other. Although in this case the elements are believed, rather than given as evident, gestalting them can articulate their meaning in ways that elemental contemplation never could. One might say unless you believe a whole set of propositions, you will not understand this proposition.

IV

Hence, there can be something more involved in faith than *simply* the assent to truths beyond reason's power to know, something that can possibly validate a role for human understanding (and so possibly a role in education). I want, in the last part of these reflections, to identify three ways in which the maxim we are discussing with Augustine—unless you believe, you will not understand—can be understood.

The first way is its personal dimension, the one that is embodied in the *Confessions* and intensely felt by Augustine. He says to his friend (as I have mentioned before), that "if the providence of God does not preside over human things, then there is no purpose in bothering about religion." But if we believe that God cares about whether we find the Tao, the Way home, then we might expect to find signs of that care in the events of our lives—if we look for them. Looking back over his life until now, Augustine discovers the hand of God in what befell him. The quest for understanding can be directed not only upward, toward the eternal Truth and truths, but it can also be directed, through memory, toward the meaning of the narrative that our life enacts.

The second way in which "unless you believe you will not understand" can be understood has already been indicated, namely, that reflection on the content of revelation as a whole can elucidate the meaning of particular propositions, sayings, and narratives by the mutual light they can cast on each other. Philosophy or human wisdom plays an important part here, as John Paul II underlined in his encyclical, *Faith and Reason*. First, with respect to the *hearing* of what is proposed to faith, the understanding of what is being declared, philosophy's treasure-trove of reflections on language, meaning, logic, and what is is indispensable in unfolding the proper meaning of the words of Scripture and tradition. Second, with respect to the elaboration of those proper meanings into a coherent doctrine, a coherent understanding of the faith—which takes the name of theology—human reason is indispensable.

At every step of this way, of this *fides quaerens intellectum*, this faith seeking understanding, there are human inferences to be justified, human arguments to be made, texts to be interpreted. Remember the first half of Augustine's *De utilitate credendi*, which is devoted to finding a *teacher* to *show* us how to read texts. My reason for reminding is to draw attention to the fact that there is something in this enterprise that can be taught. So, theology is like the hypothetical method of the *Phaedo*, or like what Aristotle calls dialectic; it tries to find out what reasonably follows from or is implied by the premises we begin from. And that is to say that there is something in theology that can have a place in liberal education, if we bring reason and revelation together.

A third way of understanding our Augustinian maxim is the opposite of the second: it is about what revelation can do for philosophy. It certainly cannot replace philosophy, as is already evident, but perhaps faith can cast a light on the problems of philosophy that can point philosophers toward insights that might otherwise be overlooked. I like to call this, tongue in cheek, the "Galileo principle," because Salviati, in the *Dialogue on the Two World Systems*, asserts that "[knowing] that a conclusion is certain assists not a little in the discovery of its proof."[19]

Faith cannot enter into the *reasons* for affirming a philosophical thesis, but it can lead—and I think historically has led—philosophers to look at the data in a certain way, to gestalt the problem being explored in a different way, even to discover a problem. So the concept of "person" entered philosophy through the theological attempts to clarify the notions of the Trinity and of the Incarnation. Another example concerns the notion that human beings are made in the image of God. In what does that image consist? The Biblical tradition is that that image of God becomes visible "in the communion of persons" and that God is near to each of us, is *with* us. I think it is not accidental that Gabriel Marcel and Martin Buber (and other so-called "personalist" philosophers) have been influenced by Scripture in drawing attention to the issues involved in the notion of "I and Thou," of the "Absolute Thou," and to the essentially interpersonal character of personhood.

Augustine states in the *De trinitate* that "faith seeks and understanding finds."[20] Kretzmann has reservations about that, on the not unreasonable grounds that seeking of that sort more often goes not with believing but with being in doubt about a proposition. As Charles Sanders Peirce said, it is the "irritation of doubt" that tends to give rise to inquiry.[21] I think that is true, but it is also true that belief or faith is not a terminally satisfying state either, precisely because it affirms a proposition in the absence of evidence, of *seeing* that what is affirmed is true. It is therefore not odd that theology should have been characterized as *fides quaerens intellectum*, faith seeking understanding, or that faith should be defined by Aquinas, following Augustine, as "thinking and assenting," or perhaps, "thinking while assenting."[22] "To believe," Augustine said toward the end of his life, "is nothing other than to think, to ponder, while assenting. One can think without believing, and often people think in order not to believe. But whoever believes, thinks—both thinks in believing and believes in thinking. . . . If faith does not think, it is nothing."[23]

"Understanding is the reward of faith,"[24] Augustine says in his commentary on John. Understanding alleviates, without dissolving, the unsatisfying nature of faith. Faith seeks that alleviation because we were made to see.

CHAPTER FIVE

Cicero and the Philosophy of Religion

I

Choosing Cicero as a representative of classical thought about religion (or indeed any philosophical topic) may invite a raised eyebrow or two, and so warrants some observations about the reasons for taking him as a significant figure. Two kinds of reasons may be mentioned.

The first is simply stated: in Cicero's trilogy (*On the Nature of the Gods, On Divination,* and *On Fate*)[1] the basic themes of the philosophy of religion which had emerged over the previous centuries are brought together for the first time and critically examined. Those themes involve the distinction and consideration of the various kinds of possible grounds—pro and con—relevant to the reasonable justification of religious belief and practice.

The affirmative grounds can be represented schematically as follows:

1. Personal or inward evidence
2. Regular order in the course of natural events
3. Marvelous disorder or discontinuities in the regular course of natural events
   a) manifestly marvelous
   b) latently marvelous

The first category is represented in Cicero's discourses by two proposed examples: a universally observed inclination to acknowledge the existence of gods and reported experiences of the inward manifestation of gods.[2] But of course this category can be expanded to include all such reported inward experiences—for example, reports of gods appearing in dreams or the sense of the presence of the divine in religious and mystical experience.

The second category is represented in *On the Nature of the Gods* by the Stoic spokesman Balbus, who argues, as many had before this time, that the comprehensive regularities in natural processes provide a reason for inferring the existence of some agent with powers and intelligence superior to man. This seems to be the oldest of explicitly formulated arguments for divine existence, appearing already in Plato and Aristotle and continuing down to modern times in the so-called argument from design.

The third category complements rather than replaces the second. While one might argue that the order that we find in nature is beneficial for human life (providing food, warmth, materials for clothing, shelter, etc.),[3] the specific care that the gods have for humans—what comes to be called special or particular providence as distinguished from the original or general providence allegedly displayed in nature[4]—is exhibited in specific events. Balbus mentions two kinds of these: theophanies or manifestations of gods and presagings of future events.[5] The first kind, extraordinary appearances of divine or preternatural beings, are for the interlocutors of the dialogue (and for us readers) hearsay accounts, reported or repeated by others whom we believe (or disbelieve). The second kind is different, because although as in the first kind the events may be seen by many, the futural and religious significance of the phenomena have to be interpreted. The significance is not evident to the untutored eye or ear: it is latent rather than manifest, and the skill or gift of a hermeneut is required. It was this second kind of marvelous event which played an important part in Roman religious practice in the form of the interpretation of auspices and prodigies. And once again, one can expand the second kind of category to include prophetic interpretation of various events or phenomena (Joseph's interpretation of the Pharoah's dream, Daniel's interpretation of the writing on the wall), oracular responses to questions (as at Delphi), and so forth.[6]

The critical or negative grounds for denying the reasonableness of religion include the following:

1. The argument from evil against divine concern with human affairs
2. Denial that the course of nature provides ground for such inference
   a) because chance and necessity can explain the order
   b) because natural things have internal principles of order
3. The claims for extraordinary events are superstitious

Here again, these points are not only argued in *De Natura Deorum* (DND) but instantiated in later discussions—for example, evolution as alternate account of order, the problem of evil, and the critique of miracles in Hume and others.

It is relevant to note also that Cicero's inquiry into natural theology or the philosophy of divinity does not for him exhaust the range of philosophical reflection about religion, as it often seems to do today.[7] For Cicero the questions about the existence and nature of the gods arise out of the practices which he finds in his world and address the problem of whether there are rational grounds to affirm the existence of the kind of superior nature addressed or intended in such practices. This is why he adds the two dialogues on divination (are there omens or messages from the gods?) and fate (is the notion of foreknowing and predicting the future reasonable?). Conversely, it is possible that a validated assertion of divinity could provide a ground for distinguishing between genuine religiousness and superstition.[8] Hence for him, and properly so, the philosophy of religion moves between two foci: religiousness (communal doings and sayings) and the intended superior nature.

A second reason for examining the work of Cicero is that his writings are slighted today, apparently because he is not perceived to be a significant figure. Two examples: a widely used standard history of philosophy uses a comment of Cicero's (that he only translates other philosophers) to downplay his significance.[9] Similarly, the *Great Books of the Western World* published by Encyclopedia Britannica (1952, 1990) has no writings of Cicero, although it includes texts of writers whose works are less central by its own standards. Ironically, the principle of selection enunciated by Robert Hutchins in his introductory essay to the collection, "The Great Conversation," is that the great books are almost self-selected: they are the books (and authors) that the subsequent writers have read and which the latter discuss in order to amplify, modify, or oppose.[10] But on that principle it is hard to see how Cicero could have been left out. It is certainly arguable that Cicero and Vergil divide Roman culture between them and are the main bearers of it into the Western tradition.

Augustine considered Cicero the originator and the exemplar of Roman philosophy,[11] Aquinas cited him more than any other Latin writer, and modern philosophers like Locke and Hume admired him, studied his works, used his categories, and imitated his writings. Indeed it would be hard to find a writer more continuously respected and cited down through the centuries.[12] Not without reason: he has a sense of humor, of style, of irony, and of what is important. He wrote for the general reader, as wrote Aristotle in his dialogues, his so-called "exoteric" writings, but he is quite capable of close analyis of complex issues like fate and free will, as the parts of the *De Fato* show.[13]

Some think that the change began when Theodore Mommsen published his *Römische Geschichte* in the middle of the nineteenth century and declared Cicero to be a mere transcriber whose writings were useful only as compilations of Hellenistic philosophers. Of course Hegel had already passed judgment on Cicero as one who did not understand the march of history (of "Geist"), one who still thought the individual's choices and moral responsibility to be decisive. In any case, by the time Windelband wrote his influential *Geschichte der Philosophie* at the turn of the century [nineteenth to twentieth], Cicero was demoted from the ranks of significant thinkers and has remained so to this day.

Why should the depreciation of Cicero have occurred? Partly, no doubt, because of his method of addressing philosophical questions in dialogue. This method, carefully traced out from his predecessors and appropriated by Cicero, involved recapitulating the various historical positions which had been articulated on any question and subjecting them to criticism. This meant drawing extensively on the writings of earlier thinkers who had developed the classical or paradigmatic positions—that is, the various schools of philosophy. And so it became possible for later (nineteenth century) scholars to regard his philo-sophical works as a kind of "cut and paste" philosophizing, to treat them as sourcebooks of "fragments" of the writings of his Greek and Hellenic predecessors.[14]

Strikingly enough, the philosophical dialogues of Cicero are the first ones since those of Plato to come down to us. Although Aristotle wrote dialogues, he seems to have abandoned that genre eventually, and there is not much evidence that dialogues were written by the Helle-nistic philosophers of the intervening period.[15] And Cicero's dialogical model seems to have been most influenced by Aristotle's method, both in the latter's (now lost) dialogues and in his treatises. One way to con-trast Plato's dialogues and Aristotle's dialogues and treatises in regard to the way they approach philosophical issues is to observe that Plato's Socratic dialogues advance by Socrates challenging some proposition, leading to its reformulation which is again challenged, and so on. In the early "aporetic" dialogues, this process is exhausted in the *elenchus*, the successive exhibitions by Socrates that no proffered formulation is ac-ceptable.[16] Aristotle on the other hand approaches a topic by laying out alternative views which have already been advanced, and then criticizing these.[17] In the treatises, he then treats the results as a means toward the formulation of his own position.[18]

To understand why Cicero revived Aristotle's dialogue form rather than Plato's, the best place to begin is with Aristotle and his characteri-zation of dialectic (*dialektike*). In the *Topics*, he contrasts demonstrative and dialectical reasoning in terms of the premises from which they begin:

> A syllogism is demonstrative (*apodeixis*) when it proceeds from premises that are true and primary . . . ; it is dialectical (*dialektikos*) when it reasons from beliefs that are generally accepted (*endoxa*) . . . those beliefs are "generally accepted" which seem true to everyone or to the majority or to the wise (*sophoi*).[19]

Given that characterization, it is easy to see why rhetoric, which must begin its argument from premises shared by its audience, is related to dialectical reasoning.

[R]hetoric is the counterpart of dialectic: both are concerned with the sorts of things that are generally known and do not belong to any specific science. . . . In fact, rhetoric is a branch of dialectic and similar to it. . . . Neither of them is a science that deals with the nature of any definite subject: both are skillful capacities for providing arguments.[20]

Just as dialectic is the skill of deriving arguments from given premises (*endoxa*) and so testing those premises by showing what follows from them, so rhetoric is the skill of finding the means of persuading by showing, for example, what course of action is implied by given premises. (Part of the reason for Cicero's abiding concern with methodical argument also comes into view here: it is no accident that the bulk of his life's work is composed of orations on the one hand and of philosophical dialogues on the other, since like Aristotle he saw a commonality in the skills necessary for each.)[21]

But it is the differences that need to be delineated: rhetoric aims at persuasion and is addressed to public audiences, and so must draw for its premises on "notions possessed by everybody."[22] In contrast, as the description quoted above notes, one can begin from *endoxa* which seem to the *sophoi* to be true, and that ultimately implies for both Aristotle and Cicero the incorporation of the history of philosophy into the on-going process of philosophical inquiry. The critical examination of *endoxa* that have been held by the *sophoi* is thus for both Aristotle and Cicero not a separate historical discipline (as the "history of philosophy" is often thought of today) but an integral part of philosophical inquiry. Dialectical reasoning, Aristotle says, is useful for the philosophical sciences because like rhetoric it can draw opposite conclusions[23] and

the ability to raise searching difficulties on both sides of a subject will make us detect more easily the truth and error about the different points that arise.[24]

When Cicero resurrects the dialogue form for philosophical inquiry after almost three centuries, he follows and adapts Aristotle rather than Plato as his model. This means, first, that instead of the conversation focusing on some topic unfolded and challenged sentence by sentence, he presents us with a dialogue between two positions (or one position and its critique) which brings into view the differing conceptual frameworks of the interlocutors.[25] Second, it means that, unlike Plato, Cicero places himself as a persona in the dialogue, and indeed like Aristotle takes the principal part for himself.[26] Third, it means that—by the very nature of the dialogue/dramatic form—he conceals his own views.[27] Fourth, it means that the presentation and critique of positions is not an integral preparation for a resolution of the question, as in Aristotle's treatises,[28] but is itself the substance of the work, as it apparently was in Aristotle's dialogues.

There is no inconsistency between the second and third points. There are at least three ways in which an author can "hide himself" or his views in a dialogue. One: by not appearing as a participant, which is Plato's way.[29] Two: by appearing as a listener, which Cicero adopts for dialogues placed in a historical time when he was too young to participate (e.g., De Oratore). Three: by speaking only in criticism of positions defended by others, and this is his practice in all but one of the seven philosophical dialogues he wrote as a set toward the end of his life.[30]

But the first point mentioned above in which he follows Aristotle's dialogue model is the most important for the understanding of how Cicero's philosophical dialogues came to be depreciated.

For Cicero, as for us, philosophy comes into view as subject matter divided into schools, each of which has articulated and defended a perspective, a way of approaching philosophizing. Unlike, say, Descartes, Cicero thinks of that pluralism as part of the human situation, not something that can be definitively overcome by some new method. Indeed, although he follows Aristotle in wanting to incorporate the differing perspectives into the exercise of inquiry, he differs from Aristotle who thinks that one may finally leave the *endoxa* behind and attain some primary premises from which demonstrative knowledge may be developed. For Cicero there is no philosophical *episteme*: philosophy lives in the disputed questions of the schools and the best it can hope for is to eliminate some positions as untenable and reach those more probable. In order to do that, we need to confront each school just in the language in which it articulates its own proper position—so in what is likely to be its best formulation—with the critique of that position and, if possible, the presentation of alternatives. Even if we cannot present fleshed-out alternatives, there is or can be advance in hearing the criticism and weighing the results. And then we will be able to judge—after adding up the pros and cons—which seems the closest to the truth.[31]

As he says in the *Tusculan Disputations*,

> These considerations always led me to prefer the rule of the Peripatetics and the Academy of discussing both sides of every question, not only for the reason that in no other way did I think it possible for the probable truth to be discovered (*veri simile esset inveniri*) in each particular problem, but also because I found it gave the best practice in discourse (*dicendi*). Aristotle first employed this method and later those who followed him.[32]

It has been argued that Aristotle's practice of reviewing the various positions that had been formulated on a question (the "doxographic" preliminary) was used after him to support a skeptical or Academic position in philosophy, leading not to the resolution of an issue but to an epoche or suspension of judgment. However that may be, Cicero's method of reviewing and critically analyzing the positions of the various schools he regularly declares (as in the last quotation) to be in the service of discovering the truth or the closest possible approximation to it remains.[33]

So, far from it being a proper criticism of Cicero that he incorporates the arguments of others and relies upon their texts, it is not only his conception of philosophical inquiry through dialogue that dictates such incorporation, it is fairness to the others' positions that dictates that he stay close to their formulations. If he did not do so, his doxography might be like that of Velleius, the Epicurean in *De Natura Deorum* whose account of the history of philosopher's views on the gods betrays no sympathy or understanding for any views but his own. Cicero's method is neither simply objective recording of other's positions nor assimilation of them to his own: it is rather to create a dialogue by incorporating enough of the conceptual framework of the respective claims to rise to the level of disagreement (as distinguished from mutual misunderstanding). But the price for such a dialogical method of philo-sophical inquiry is the possibility of being dismissed as a compiler and translator.

Even if he did no more than compile and translate, it would still be true that the result is not a simple eclecticism: the position developed through the dialogues is not a composite doctrine, like a collage.[34] Even if he did no more than that, one reading through the philosophical writings comes away with a recognizable philosophical position, one which indeed has been recognized by many of the first-rate philo-sophical minds mentioned above. This may seem, if not inconsistent with, at least in some kind of tension with the suggestion already made that Cicero hides his own opinion by adopting the dialogue form. But there need be no inconsistency in offering only critique and no judg-ment of one's own, and yet letting a position come into view.[35]

There are at least two ways in which this is possible. One is that a critique inevitably implies or points toward some alternative position merely by the principles from which it argues and the paths which it closes off. And the other is that Cicero places the position which he finds more probable or cogent at the end of the exchange.[36] Normally in his philosophical dialogues this means also in the mouth of his persona, since (as has been noted) he gives the principal part to himself. This raises a problem of interpretation, as will be seen, for *De Natura Deorum*.

II

Toward the end of his life, when the Roman Republic was reaching its end along with Cicero's place in it, the leisure which the situation al-lowed or forced upon him led to his conception of another way to make a contribution to the common good of Rome: to write a series of philo-sophical works that would make philosophy a part of the intellectual culture of Romans.[37] Until that time, philosophy had remained a visitor: it was still being written in Greek, and although Greek was a second language widely possessed by educated Roman citizens, philosophy had remained, if not alien to "Romanitas," at least not domesticated. Between 45 and 44 B.C., Cicero composed a series of philosophical dialogues which he enumerates and characterizes at the beginning of the second book of *De Divinatione* (DD).[38]

In all of these dialogues, following the practice cited above, he reserves for himself (i.e., the Cicero persona in the dialogue) the principal part (with one exception: the work on the nature of the gods, *De Natura Deorum*, where the main speaker is Gaius Cotta, like Cicero a follower of the skeptical Academic school). Four of these seven dialogues deal with questions about the need for philosophy, about what can be known, and about basic issues of ethics and of human happiness. The last three, the ones in view here, deal with the nature of the gods, the practice of divination, and the foretelling of the future as exhibited, for example, in astonishing happenings or in appeals to the pages of the Sibylline books.[39]

This threefold division reflects the statements in *De Natura Deorum* and elsewhere that Roman religion is composed of three parts, or two main parts and one additional part:

> The religion of the Roman people comprises ritual, auspices, and the third additional division consisting of all such prophetic warnings [*praedictionis*] as the interpreters of the Sibyl or the soothsayers have derived from portents and prodigies.[40]

"Ritual" [*sacra*] refers to the ceremonies and sacrifices supervised by the college of priests [*pontifices*]; "auspices" [*auspicia*] to the interpretation of ordinary events or things (e.g., flights of birds) as signs of divine attitude toward human plans, supervised by the college of augurs of which Cicero was a member;[41] and "prophetic warnings" to the prediction or foreshadowing of the future by extraordinary signs, whose interpretation was supervised by the college of fifteen [*quindecimviri*] and the haruspices.[42]

These practices constituted the religion of the Roman community: there was no creed or doctrine or dogma in addition to them to which one had to subscribe. There was not even any need to attend the ceremonies and sacrifices: what was important was that the rituals and divinations be carried out on a regular basis, as the tradition prescribed. To that end, the colleges of priests and augurs, etc., had been established and charged with the responsibility. One might think that such an "establishment of religion" with no required attendance would run the risk of becoming a marginal affair. But aside from the fact that many of the ceremonies were holidays[43] and grand public affairs, the institution as a whole was integrated into the political life of Rome by the fact that membership in the various priestly colleges was restricted to those in public life.

In an address to the college of pontiffs or priests, Cicero began by noting this:

> Among the many divinely-inspired expedients of government established by our ancestors, there is none more striking than that whereby they expressed their intention that the worship of the gods and the interests of the state should be entrusted to the direction of the same individuals, to the end that citizens of the highest distinction and the brightest fame might achieve the welfare of religion by a wise administration of the state [*rem publicam*] and of the state by a sage interpretation of religion.[44]

Part of the reason for which Cicero praises the ancestors [*maiores*] is that they saw how important religion was to the health of the political community. Indeed this is the context for the inquiry into the nature of the gods in the dialogue of that name.

Since there was no creed or doctrinal definition about the gods—rather the most strict supervision and concern was directed toward the careful performance of the rituals and divinations—philosophers were free to speculate about their being and nature. But the philosophy of religion, for Cicero, arises not from reflection on the abstract question of whether anything divine exists but from reflection on these practices. It thus takes the general form of whether divinities such as those addressed or hearkened to (prayed and sacrificed to, attended to in divinations) could reasonably be said to exist.

What sorts of beings would they have to be? Well, they would have to be able to hear and respond to our prayers and sacrifices, to care enough about our collective fate and to have enough power to be able to do something which men found beyond their power to reliably bring about, and to protect us from misfortunes over which we have no or inadequate control. They would have to be able to speak to us in some form, to warn us of dangers, and to alert us to missteps—not by personal appearance, perhaps, but through some hermeneutic medium which we could interpret. So the question for philosophy of religion as Cicero addresses it in these dialogues is not so much whether anything divine exists but rather the question of the nature of the gods: do gods possessing the characteristics presupposed by religious practice exist? Although the dialogue touches the broader, more general, question occasionally, it remains in the background.[45]

As an instance of a divine being not accessible to religious concerns, one could think of Aristotle's prime mover. This divine, immaterial, living substance is wholly self-sufficient. Its capacity to know is exhausted by its self-knowledge, so that it faces, so to speak, away from the universe—and in particular, from the affairs of human beings.[46] It does have a fundamental causal role in the order of the universe, namely, as the "omega-point" of attraction for all moving, changing things, so that the motion of the heavenly bodies such as the sun, and its influence on the life-cycles of living things on earth, and their role in the life of the human community are all ultimately polarized by the universal attraction exercised by the prime mover. But that attraction is exercised unconsciously, as it were, by the very nature of its dynamic actuality. It does not respond to prayers because it is ignorant of them, and its causality is not effected by agency, by doing anything voluntarily, but simply by being what it is.

Cicero's concern with the philosophy of religion is not only speculative, and it is not simply the question of whether gods who exemplify the required properties exist. As he remarks in the opening prologue to *De Natura Deorum*, it is also a question with practical consequences, especially if we answer it negatively.

> Piety, like the other virtues, cannot long exist in mere appearance and pretence, and with it reverence and religion must go; these taken away, life itself becomes disorderly and confused, and I hardly know whether, piety toward the gods being removed, fidelity and social bonds will not disappear, and even justice, the greatest virtue.[47]

But piety and reverence and religion

> are tributes which it is our duty to render in purity and holiness to the divine powers solely on the assumption that they take notice of them, and that some service has been rendered by the immortal gods to the race of men.[48]

So, he says in the prologue, don't ask my opinion: come and listen to the evidence, try the case, and come to your own conclusion. Even among those of great learning, there is wide diversity of opinion about this question of the immortal gods, a question that is important for the guiding of religious practice and also for understanding the human soul.[49] And with that invitation to the reader to be the judge, he introduces the dramatic setting of the dialogue.

III

As a younger man (about thirty) he was once a listener at a conversation about the nature and existence of the gods carried on among an Epicurean, Velleius, a Stoic, Balbus, and an Academic, Cotta, which Cicero proceeds to relate.[50] The account of that conversation occupies three books, but takes place continuously on the same day.

It begins with (what turns out to be) the weakest defense of the gods' existence, that of the Epicurean position.

Epicureans were materialists who held that the only enduring, permanent things that exist are (microscopic) atoms and the space or void in which they move. The motion of the atoms brings some of them into clusters, aggregations which can take all kinds of transient shapes. Such clusters are formed by chance collisions, and so no explanation is possible of why the things we see around us have the "nature" they have. There are no natural kinds of (macroscopic) things, only different sizes and weights of (microscopic) atoms. Some sorting of atoms by weight and size occurs as they rise or sink, and it just so happened that some atoms came together in this or that shape. The world exhibits no programmed order, if we understand its genesis properly: no god or "deus ex machina" is necessary to plan it or put it together, and no design brings about events in nature. Indeed, far from its being unusual and needing explanation, Velleius says, such "worlds" as ours are constantly coming into being elsewhere and passing away (like galaxies).[51]

At first such an account sounds outlandish, so impressive does the order and regularity of nature seem.[52] To make it more plausible, one has to add several postulates or clarifications. First, that there was no beginning to the existence of atoms or of their colliding and clustering: this has gone on for an infinite time. Second, that the number of atoms in *this* world which we are trying to account for is finite. Third, that in an infinite time a finite number of randomly moving atoms will assume all possible configurations—including this one, the world we inhabit—just as any given finite series of numbers will appear in an infinite random sequence of integers.

Now one might wonder how someone who thinks that the world does not and cannot exhibit any genuine sign of design, of purpose or teleology, could find grounds for a reasonable assent to the existence of divinity. But this problem has recurred regularly in the history of philosophy. Descartes encounters it as a result of denying the relevance of final cause or "why" questions about the course of nature; William James encounters it as a result of the general consensus by the end of the nineteenth century that evolution forecloses teleological claims. Both of them, like Velleius, turn inward to experience, the experience of innate ideas or of a numinous presence.[53]

According to Velleius, what needs explanation is not merely the apparent order of nature but the universal religiousness of human beings.[54] And to account for that, since it cannot be based on the world, he contends that human beings have certain "preconceptions," one of which is that of divine beings. There is what may be called an "innate" possession of an idea of divine beings, although in fact it arises from mental impressions which begin at birth and continue throughout our lives. Such beings have never of course been encountered in perception—they inhabit the spaces between the worlds—but we are nevertheless inclined by the subtle impressions we receive to acknowledge their existence.[55]

Given this foundation, Velleius draws another consequence: the gods "appear" (in our experience of their images) as having human form, as having "quasi-human" bodies. This is why the familiar gods and god-desses of Greece and Rome are anthropomorphic deities. (He declares also that they are perceived through these preconceptions as happy and eternally existing, a consequence which seems less intuitive.)

And now we can make sense of something that comes before this argument in the dialogue and that has been found a puzzling part of Velleius' discourse—a long doxography or "history of philosophy" listing the opinions of previous philosophers about the gods, from Thales to the Stoics. The doxography is, to begin with, rather unepicurean. The founder of the school and his followers were notorious in antiquity for their inward-facing exegesis and their ignoring of other philosophical traditions.[56] And although the doxography has been mined by those searching for fragments of other thinkers, the account of previous non-epicurean views is so unsympathetic and uncomprehending that it verges on parody. Indeed it does seem that Cicero wanted to make fun of the Epicureans' ignoring of others and implicitly to contrast his own presentation of views with which he disagrees, a presentation that tries to be fair and faithful to them.

But if the doxography makes an implicit point by having the Epicurean spokesman present a caricature, it also has some structure and significance for the discussion as a whole. First, one may wonder about the principle of selection for the twenty-seven philosophers who are named, since some philosophers who are mentioned elsewhere in *De Natura Deorum*—for example, Heraclitus—are not included. The clearest principle of selection would seem to be that which Cotta mentions later in his critical remarks—namely, that all of them thought that gods can exist in other than human form (DND 1.32.91). So the catalogue of errors is a catalogue of those who espoused or allowed non-anthropomorphic deities.[57]

Second, it is only here in the whole dialogue that any reference is made to the idea of an immaterial (*asomatos, sine corpore*) divinity. Plato is said to have held that god is incorporeal,[58] a position that Velleius finds incomprehensible since without a body there can be no cognition, no practical wisdom, and no pleasure—things which are entailed in our notion of gods and their happiness. Aristotle is said to have made the same erroneous claim. Indeed it may seem strange to us modern readers that both of the theologies treated *ex professo* in the dialogue—

Epicurean and Stoic—assume the materiality of divinity, and that only in passing is any (critical) reference made to the idea of an immaterial god. We will come back to this later.

In the Epicurean argument, the gods must have bodies in order to be capable of reason and virtue and pleasure and so of happiness, which consists in tranquility of mind and exemption from any tasks or re-sponsibilities to others (DND 1.20.53). If the gods were creators or governors of the world, if they had clients to whose prayers they had to respond, they would have to be concerned with the way things were going, with keeping order, etc.—a supposition incompatible with the tranquility necessary for happiness.

In his critique, Cotta has little difficulty in finding fundamental inconsistencies in the Epicurean position, first in its view of the uni-verse as the product of chance and then in its conception of the gods. If the gods have (humanlike) bodies, then since all macroscopic bodies are transient clusters of atoms, the gods cannot be immortal. Moreover, what would be the use of bodies if they engage in no action, live in-between any worlds, do not eat, etc. One suspects that the Epicurean gods are simply the paradigm for the Epicurean conception of human happiness—namely, withdrawal from public life and the cultivation of personal happiness.[59] Indeed, since even if the Epicurean teaching on the gods were true they would be religiously irrelevant, one may suspect, Cotta says, that Epicurus was really simply protecting himself from the charge of atheism in such a teaching. For gods who do nothing, who know nothing of our prayers and sacrifices, who send no signs by means of natural events, and who indeed have no care of or power over the course of events, are no gods at all, but only fairy tales.[60] Book One of *De Natura Deorum* ends with this conclusion by Cotta, and Velleius defers any response until some later time—a deferral repeated at the end of the day's discussion, so that no response to the critique is ever given.

IV

The second theology discussed is that of the Stoics (represented in the dialogue by the senator Quintus Lucilius Balbus) to which the whole of Book Two is devoted.

Like Epicureanism, Stoicism's analysis of the nature of knowledge and of the world was in the service of determining the right way to live, and it is indeed best known for its disciples like Marcus Aurelius and Epictetus who taught and exemplified a practical wisdom. But unlike Epicureanism, Stoicism provided a conception of the divine which seemed to be able to support the practices of popular religion. The god or gods of Stoicism were responsible for the ordered course of the universe and so were, in principle, able to respond to prayer and sacrifice; they exercised a watchful providence (*pronoia*) over the future course of things and so were, in principle, able to give signs, through divination and portents, of what was to come.

Before sketching the Stoic position, it is pertinent to note that, in contrast to Epicureanism, the Stoic position developed and changed over the course of two and a half centuries, and to speak of "the" Stoic position is a little like speaking of "the" scholastic position. (The term "scholasticism," after all, designates a current of thinking that ranged over four or five hundred years, and no one set of doctrines could characterize all of its phases.) The focus here will be on the Stoic position as it is articulated by Balbus, which is in fact largely consistent with the collections of fragments from Stoic writers and the contemporary reconstructions of Stoicism based on those fragments—many of which come from Cicero's writings.[61]

If one were to try to identify the basic intuitions that lie near the base of the Stoic position, one might find the sense that only that is real which can act on other things or be affected by other things—and that leads one to the view that only material bodies exist. Macbeth's dagger can't be clutched because it isn't real, it's only an unsubstantial illusion. A second intuition that is fundamental is that of the resplendent pattern of beauty and order which the universe presents to our vision. Borrowing from Aristotle's lost dialogue *On Philosophy*, Balbus exclaims that the glorious spectacle of the earth and the sky, of the regularity and majesty of the sun and the stars, compels our wonder and admiration and leads anyone to think that gods exist and are responsible for this harmonious order (DND 2.37.95. Cf. 2.2.4, 5.15, 21.56). This presentiment of order underlies the reflective elaboration of the argument from design which played a central role in Stoic physics. A third intuition is the sense that what is animate has warmth within it, has some kind of fire within it, as the breath and the body do.

The position to which the Stoics were led by thinking about these intuitions and their interconnections was that the divinely produced regularity which the world exhibits is the result of a fire-like immanent divinity pervading the universe and producing order everywhere as the soul produces order in the body's processes and behavior (DND 2.9.23–24). Just as the life of the body unifies it and harmonizes all of its processes, so the divine ruling principle (*hegemonikon*, DND 2.11.29) makes the universe and its parts cohere in an ordered unity. So the universe can be called the greatest and most excellent of things, can even be called divine if we keep in mind that what is truly divine and immortal is the vital warmth that moves and pervades it. For the manifest physical form of the universe is composed of other elements as well, ordinary fire and earth and air and water, and these together with the bodies that they make up are periodically destroyed in a great conflagration in which everything except the creative fire itself is consumed and then remade, reformed by that divine breath.[62]

The passage from this pervasive living cosmic principle to the pantheon of the many gods and goddesses proceeds in several steps. First, the astronomical division between the fixed and wandering (planetary) heavenly bodies entails their separate motions and suggests separate (immanent, divine) principles of movement: Saturn and Mars, Venus and Apollo, but also the sphere of the fixed stars and their constellations (DND 2.19.49, 20.51, 21.54). Next, following the ways of the Greeks and ancient Romans, whatever had great benefit for human beings was considered a divine gift and called by the name of a god, "so we speak of corn as Ceres, of wine as Liber," and then any powerful influence in human affairs, as witness "the temples of Wealth, Safety, Concord, Liberty, and Victory" as well as negative forces which can overpower human nature such as "Desire, Pleasure, and Venus Lubentina" (DND 2.23.60–61). But as Balbus goes on detailing the etymologies and legends that accrue to all these deities, he reaches a point where his benevolent accomodation toward popular religiousness breaks off, and he denounces the way superstition overpowers the reasonable discoveries of natural science and creates imaginary and fictive gods.[63]

But though repudiating these fables with contempt, nevertheless the divinities pertaining to the elements of nature can be understood by the names custom has given them and to them we owe veneration and worship. (DND 2.28.71)

What is at issue here is the accommodation of a pervasive divine presence to popular polytheism, a problem familiar in Advaita Hinduism and indeed wherever the One is affirmed and the Many demoted, as in Hegel's contrast between the figurative thinking of religion and the conceptual knowing of philosophy.[64]

For the Stoics, then, there is a divine ruling principle in things: alive, intelligent (as the order of things shows), immortal, and providential. This god is not a creator, even in the sense of the demiurge in Plato's *Timaeus*, for this god does not look to a pattern laid up in heaven by which to form the world but is itself the pattern unfolded in space and time.[65] Immanent agency avoids the problems associated with the idea of a finite material agent or agents bringing about something as massive and intricately ordered as the cosmos. As Velleius says in referring to Plato's demiurge making the world:

What method of engineering was employed? What tools and levers and derricks? What agents carried out so vast an undertaking? And how did it come about that air, fire, water and earth obeyed and executed the will of the architect?[66]

(Of course, Velleius also has slashing arguments against the Stoic conception of god as embodied: DND 1.10.23–24, 14.36–15.41.)

In his presentation of the Stoic position, Balbus divides it into four parts: the existence of the gods, their nature, their providence over the universe, and their providential care for man. He begins the discussion of the first point by saying that it is so evident that argument for it is unnecessary, but nonetheless he discusses four kinds of grounds for affirming gods' existence. First is the order of the heavens; second is the consensus of mankind; third is reports of the appearances of gods and fauns, and of prodigious events and portents; fourth is the evidence of divination and prophecies of future events.

When Cotta resumes his role of critic in Book Three, he responds to each of these claims. Acknowledging the order of the heavens and earth, he argues that we don't need to infer a divinity to account for that: it is sufficient to recognize that things have a nature, an intrinsic principle of movement.

> [N]ot all things, Balbus, that have fixed and regular courses are to be accredited to a god rather than to nature . . . [the universe's] coherence and persistence is due to the powers of nature, not of god . . . the greater [nature's] innate power, the less one need posit a divine reason.[67]

To Velleius' appeal to universal consensus about the gods as evidence for their existence, Cotta had replied by challenging the empirical basis for such an assertion (how could you know that gods were acknowledged always and everywhere), asserting his own belief that not every society had or acknowledged the gods, and citing as evidence the names of philosophers well known for their atheism. To Balbus' appeal to universal consensus, Cotta responds by commenting that the opinions of the foolish should not be decisive and by questioning its relevance: the question to be asked is not whether some peoples believe that the gods exist; the question is whether the gods exist or don't exist (DND 3.4.11, 7.17). (Of course the explanations for the alleged universal consensus offered by Epicureans and Stoics are quite different—namely, "innate" impressions for the former and spontaneous reaction to perceived order for the latter.)

Some commentators think that Cicero himself accepted an argument from consensus, similar to the Stoic one.[68] He does mention such arguments in the *Tusculan Disputations* (1.13.30, 16.36) and acknowledges that there are such beliefs—mentioning also the widespread belief in some kind of survival of the soul—but it does not appear that he infers the fact from the belief (i.e., that he accepts consensus as an argument rather than simply as an alleged datum).

The third argument of Balbus for the existence of gods is the many reports of extraordinary events such as portents and theophanies, reported appearances, for example, of Castor and Pollux on the battlefield at Lake Regillus. Cotta waves away such stories as hearsay (rumor) instead of reasoned argument. Balbus has, after all, undertaken to provide philosophical arguments for the existence of the gods.[69]

The fourth argument is based on the Roman practice of divination, including the practice of augury and of predictions of the future based on signs (soothsaying, *haruspicum*). The first involved seeking a reading of the approval or disapproval of the gods, regarding some action or enterprise to be undertaken, by examining the entrails of sacrificed animals or watching for flights of birds, etc. The second involved interpreting the meaning of some extraordinary event or consulting the pages of the book of Sibylline oracles.

Balbus laments that the practice of augury has become rote, the lore lost or forgotten, and the lively confidence that once gave it authority has waned. But his argument rests on the claim that its once-flourishing practice shows that there were indeed signs which the gods gave and which influenced the great Roman statesmen. About soothsaying, the interpretation of signs to foretell the future, he says very little, merely endorsing it as an art of the divine.

Some part of Cotta's response seems to be lost, but in his brief comments he raises two of the central points which are alluded to by Velleius (DND 1.20.55) and are developed at length by Cicero in the subsequent dialogues *On Divination* and *On Fate*. One is how the signs, which are quite ordinary and everyday occurrences—for example, a cleft in the liver of the sacrificed animal, or a raven croaking—came to have the meaning given them. The "alphabet" seems to be rather arbitrary and to be sometimes meaningful, sometimes not.[70] The other point is that if divinely inspired foretelling of the future did occur then it would seem to entail that the future is already determined by chains of causes begun in the past (hence the gods can know what will come about), and that seems to be incompatible with human freedom and responsibility. Moreover it would be singularly unhelpful information if we can do nothing to change it.

After the discussion of the existence and nature of the gods, Balbus goes on to assert the general providence which is exercised over the heavens and the earth as manifested in the order of nature, and then the particular providence which is directed toward the good of human beings. Under the latter heading, he rehearses observations about the earth and its creatures serving the needs of mankind, appeals again to divination and to theophanies as signs of the gods' care for us, and ends with a brief defense of what is implied by the claim of particular providence—namely, that what happens is for our good.

A major difficulty here of course is the problem of evil: if all that happens is divinely controlled, and if the gods intend our welfare, why do bad things happen to good people and good things to bad people? Balbus addresses this question in a mere eight lines at the very end of his defense of particular providence and limits himself to two points. One seems to concede that bad things happen, but it nullifies the possible anti-religious consequences of that admission by saying that the gods are too busy with major issues to take care of small ones (*magna di curant, parva neglegunt*). The other response seems to take back what is implicitly conceded in the first—that bad things do happen—by arguing with Socrates that no harm can come to the good person in this life or the next,[71] or that virtue and the happiness that goes with it are independent of what happens to us.

Cotta, obviously perceiving this as a weak part of the Stoic defense of divine existence and providence, spends at least a fourth of his critique on it.[72] All of his arguments have appeared over and over again in discussions of theodicy through the centuries. His main points are as follows.

First, it is no excuse to claim that the evil we see around us is due not to the gods but to human beings. If human reason is arguably employed as much or more in pursuit of selfish advantage and in wrongdoing as in seeking what is right, one may wonder why god didn't make us incapable of doing wrong, instead of empowering us to devise ways to take advantage of others (DND 3.31.76).

Second, after reminding us of notorious examples of evil men who enjoyed wealth and health and good fortune—and conceding that a good or bad conscience can be a powerful sanction for some, quite independently of any divine punishment or reward—Cotta argues that just as no political society exists if there is no law enforced by punishment for transgressions, so no divine governance of the world exists if it makes no distinction between the fortunes of the good and the wicked

(DND 3.35.85). We praise persons of outstanding virtue, because we take that to be something they achieve themselves and not to be simply a gift of a god, but we pray to the gods for health and victory and good fortune. If prosperity and good fortune go to the wicked as well as the good, it is hard to believe that the gods care (DND 3.36.87–88).

Third, the claim that the gods only care for major things and not the concerns of individuals not only is belied by the destruction of cities and of whole peoples (misfortunes are not simply individual) but it undermines the religiousness which finds expression in an individual's prayers and vows and sacrifices.[73]

Finally, Cotta draws these criticisms together in formulating what has become a classical dilemma (or trilemma): given all this counter-evidence to a benevolent divine providence, it seems necessary to conclude that

either god has no knowledge of what goes on in human affairs
or god has no power to change what goes on
or god does not care. (DND 3.39.92–93)

V

By the end of the third and final book of the dialogue, there seem to be no admissible grounds remaining for claiming that gods exist: consensus, natural order, prodigious happenings, and divination are all rejected without concession or qualification. Polite things are said at the ends of the critiques of Velleius and Balbus about their responding to Cotta, but this response is deferred until some other time. We are left, as Cicero's brother Quintus says about the third book of De Natura Deorum, with an argument that seems utterly to nullify the gods, despite his (Cotta's) repeated protestations that that is not his intention.[74]

But it must be said at once that there are disagreements about how the ending of the dialogue is to be understood and about what Cicero's own thoughts on the subject were. As noted earlier, the Cicero persona in the dialogue is a listener, not a participant in the discussion. He speaks only twice (once to Cotta and once to Velleius), although as the narrator he addresses the reader in the prologue and in the last sentence. And it is the last sentence that has given rise to different readings and so to different assessments concerning what Cicero the author thought about the whole discussion.

After Cotta has finished his critique of the Stoic theology, Balbus says he would like to respond on another day and defend the Roman religion. Cotta protests that he has not wanted to do away with any conception of divinity but rather to show how difficult the question is. He adds that he is sure that Balbus will easily refute him, a likelihood on which Velleius comments sarcastically. And then the voice of the narrator, the Cicero persona, returns:

> Here the conversation ended, and we parted, Velleius thinking Cotta's discourse to be the truer, while to me that of Balbus appeared closer to what looks like the truth.[75]

This last comment may seem curious on several grounds. It has seemed to some strange that the young Cicero could find the discourse of Balbus more probable after Cotta's extended criticism without any response.[76] It has seemed strange that after saying in the prologue that curiosity about his own opinion was unreasonable and that in any case his opinion was irrelevant to the issue (DND 1.5.10) he should end by volunteering his opinion. It has seemed strange that he could seem to side with the very Stoic position which in his own name he subjects to such unrelenting stricture in *On Divination* and *On Fate*.

Three categories of interpretations have tried to address this anomaly of the last sentence. First, that Cicero himself, the Roman author, did not believe what his persona here says. Second, that he did believe it because he accepted at least significant parts of the Stoic case. Third, that as an Academic he neither accepted nor rejected any of the positions discussed, but was simply being descriptive (suspending judgment and reporting the various schools' arguments without taking sides) and so is here separating himself from the position of Cotta the Academic interlocutor in order to show his neutrality.[77]

The determining issue in choosing among these interpretations, since the last sentence itself does not settle the question, is what Cicero himself thought about the existence and nature of the gods, as far as that can be inferred from this and other writings. But even apart from the dialogue form of his philosophical works (which inherently hides the author, as we have remarked), one must remember that his statements about religion are never wholly separated from his deep concerns about the place of religion in human society. Part of the genius of the Roman constitution, in his eyes, was its placing the same kind of public-spirited citizens in both political and religious office.[78]

In the prologue to *De Natura Deorum*, in a passage cited earlier, Cicero expresses the concern that if religious practice is subverted and robbed of its reasonableness—as seems to him the implication of the Epicurean philosophy—the social and political consequences will be profound. Stoicism has at least the merit that if its teachings were true they would provide some philosophical support for the three parts of Roman *religio*. But, as we have seen, serious questions can be and have been raised about the truth of its claims (DND 1.2.3–4).

So what did Cicero himself think about the Stoic doctrines? Some have argued that he could vote for Balbus at the end of the discussion because he accepted some of the Stoic case—namely, the argument from consensus and the design argument.[79] But in the passages cited in support of this, Cicero's language is clearly cautious. Thus, regarding the "argument from consensus," the Cicero persona in the *Tusculan Disputations*[80] says:

> this seems to be offered (*adferri videtur*) as the surest basis for our believing the gods to exist, that there is no race so uncivilized, no one in the world so barbarous whose mind has no inkling of a belief about gods (*deorum opinio*).

However wrong or distorted their conception of the divine nature may be, "in every matter the consensus of all peoples is to be regarded as a law of nature."

That is, if there is truly such a consensus, it's not accidental. I take "law of nature" here to mean no more than he says later: "that gods exist we believe by nature, what they are we apprehend by reason."[81] "By nature" simply means that there is a human inclination, based on what he calls the suggestions of nature (*admonente natura*), to believe in the existence of some numinous beings, such as come into view in the apparitions of our dreams (*Tusculan Disputations* 1.13.29). But to observe that there seems to be such a natural inclination is not to construe it as an argument, or to draw the conclusion that what is believed is therefore true (as Velleius and Balbus seem to do). One might simply inquire why people hold such a belief. (It might, as he says in the beginning of *De Natura Deorum*, tell us a lot about the human psyche.) Indeed, in this same context, Cicero cites the widespread belief in the survival of the soul, which makes people fear death. But the conclusion of his argument in the book is that whether the soul survives or not is finally irrelevant: death is not an evil in either case.[82]

Similarly, in the prologue to *De Divinatione* (1.1.2) he declares, in his own name, that he knows of no people who do not believe that signs are given of the future and that such signs can be interpreted by some persons. But this dialogue is notorious for its no-holds-barred critique and explicit rejection of divination by Cicero.[83] So it hardly seems that Cicero took alleged universal consensus as an argument—that is, as more than a generalization about what people believe. (If I am not mistaken, in formulating the claim that people are naturally inclined to admit the existence of gods, he nowhere formulates it in the first person singular. Nor does Cotta anywhere in *De Natura Deorum* affirm any philosophical argument for the existence of gods, but only a belief based on tradition.)

Moderns like Hume and Freud look for psychological reasons for the origin of such beliefs. But Cicero seems to trace the natural belief in god to a spontaneous reaction to the perception of order in nature, especially in the heavens.

> [T]he beauty of the world and the order of heavenly things impel us to admit some great and eternal nature (*aliquam aeternamque naturam*) to exist, which human beings look up to and reverence. (DD 2.42.148)

A long and lyrical passage from Aristotle's lost dialogue *De Philosophia* is quoted by Balbus in the course of making the Stoic argument.

As a passage which clearly influenced Cicero, it bears at least partial quotation.

> So Aristotle says brilliantly: "If there were beings who had always lived beneath the earth, in comfortable, well-lit dwellings . . . and who though they had never come forth above the ground had learnt by report and by hearsay (*fama et auditione*) of the existence of certain deities or divine powers; and then if at some time the jaws of the earth were opened and they were able to escape from their hidden abode and to come forth into the regions which we inhabit; when they suddenly had sight of the earth and the seas and the sky . . . and beheld the sun and realized not only its size and beauty but also its potency in causing the day . . . then saw the whole sky spangled and adorned with stars and the . . . moon's light, now waxing and waning, and the risings and settings of all these heavenly bodies and their courses fixed and changeless throughout all eternity—when they saw these things, surely they would think that the gods exist and such great works are of the gods (*et esse deos et haec tanta opera deorum esse*)." (2.37.95)

There are similar statements earlier in *De Natura Deorum* and in *Tusculan Disputations*. It is worth remarking that in none of them does the language suggest that the universe is made by the "great and eternal nature."[84] And the reason for that may be that Cicero knows that Aristotle, the author of this striking passage, did not think that the universe was made but rather that it was eternal, and that he thought that the divine substance (the unmoved mover) was indeed the cause of the order of nature, but only as a final cause, as the "omega point" of attraction for bodily natures. Thus, in *Tusculan Disputations* after sketching again the impression of the splendor and order of nature, Cicero says:

> when we behold all these things and countless others, can we doubt that some being is over them, or some author, if these things have had a beginning, as Plato holds, or if they have always existed, as Aristotle thinks, some governor of such a great service and work?[85]

Despite most translations suggesting otherwise, Cicero's language in stating this natural inclination of human beings to believe that gods exist because of the order of nature is careful to describe it simply as the belief that there is some divine source of the order. The natural inclination does not lead to the belief that the universe is made, or that any particular gods exist or respond to prayers and sacrifices, etc. If, as in the passage attributed to Aristotle above, people have heard stories about certain gods or powers, then this natural inclination will tend to strengthen the credibility of those stories. It is only on reflection that questions about the nature of the gods will be raised: "that gods exist we believe by nature, what they are we apprehend by reason."

Moreover, the involuntary inclination to pass from the perception of order to the belief in the existence of gods is not irrevocable. In the dialogue *On the Nature of the Gods*, doubts about whether any gods at all exist are expressed by Cotta, and there are several references to philosophers who became atheists (DND 1.22.61, 23.62). What may happen is that on critical reflection it becomes difficult to find any reasonable grounds for asserting the existence of gods who can perform the roles which religious practice presupposes.

I conclude that the ancient and traditional reading of the last sentence of *De Natura Deorum* is the most plausible: that Cicero is not there expressing his own view, but protecting himself (and the Academic school) from the censure implied by the words which he himself puts into the mouth of Quintus in *De Divinatione*.[86] Cotta, declares Quintus, says indeed that he is not intending to destroy men's religiousness, "yet it seems to me that in his eagerness to refute the Stoics, he utterly destroys the gods" (DD 1.5.8). Certainly Cotta presents no positive alternative to the doctrines of the Epicureans or Stoics, which is of course consistent with his stance as an Academic skeptic.

What should a responsible person who finds himself in the position of Cotta at the end of the dialogue think about religion? As Cicero says in the prologue, it may be that none of the many philosophical schools' views about the nature of the gods are true. As the dialogue unfolds, it turns out that neither of the two schools examined are free of serious difficulties. That does not entail that no conceivable views could be true: perhaps some yet-undeveloped notion of the divine nature could be consistent with religious practice. What to do in the meanwhile (or even if we never find one), particularly if one is, like Cotta and Cicero, a holder of religious office with political responsibilities?

Cotta is explicit in his response to this question: believe the "founding fathers," the *maiores*, follow the practices which they instituted.[87] First, because we don't have rational grounds for surrendering our practices if we only have negative evidence—that is, if we so far lack rationally compelling arguments for the existence of gods with appropriate natures. That is why it is consistent for Cotta not to put forward any positive position of his own on the gods. It is not necessary to do so because, he says, authority—the authority of tradition of the *maiores*—does not require or offer logical reasons. It is the Stoics who "condemn authority" and undertake to give reasons for the beliefs which they are willing to accept.[88] Only if we could show by some argument that the very notion of a divine nature is logically inconsistent and impossible (like a square circle) would we have positive evidence for atheism. Short of that, we can logically only have difficulties (like the argument from bad things happening to good people).

Second, because we can see the good which such beliefs have for society and forsee the bad consequences which would follow their loss. In *De Divinatione*, Cicero says:

> because of both the beliefs of the people and their great service to the commonwealth, we maintain the augural practices, religious rites and laws, and the authority of the college of augurs.[89]

And at the end of the dialogue *De Divinatione*, he asserts that "it is the part of wisdom to preserve the institutions of the founding fathers by preserving their sacred rites and ceremonies."[90] Cicero never allows his critical examination of religion to be sundered from the awareness of its political office, as the prologue to *De Natura Deorum* makes clear by linking piety to justice.

In the opening sentence of *De Natura Deorum*, Cicero declares that the question to be discussed is, for all its difficulty, most important for the understanding of the human soul and also for the regulating of religious practice. (Even if there are no gods answering to the presuppositions of religious practice, the discussion could still inform us about both of these topics.) Perhaps one may conclude that the dialogue and its two sequels offer us insights into the roots of the natural inclination to believe in gods, into the weakness of the philosophers' explanations of divine existence, and into the human and political role of such beliefs, as well as into how *religio* tends to well over into a superstition that needs to be criticized and pruned.

VI

One topic that is not addressed in the discussion but only mentioned in passing is the conception of the divine as incorporeal, *asomatos*. As we noted, Velleius cites as part of the confused teaching of Plato and Aristotle that they sometimes attributed incorporeality (or mentioned the possibility of it) to divine beings. But the possibility of such a way of thinking about god or gods is never explored or even seriously mentioned. Both of the theologies examined—Epicurean and Stoic—assume that the gods are material, whether made of finer atoms or of a fiery element.

This may seem strange to us modern readers, accustomed to talk about God as a spirit, as without matter or spatial dimensions. But the philosophical problems connected to such a notion were perceived as of major difficulty, at least if one wanted to retain a conception of the nature of god which supported religious practice and its implicit beliefs.

One basic problem is alluded to by Velleius in a text cited above: if one believes that the gods are responsible for the universe, for its order and for bringing about things prayed for, two things seem to be required. The first is that the gods be material beings. How else could they act on and bring about the elements and bodies that come together to form the universe and the events we imprecate? How could an immaterial thing act on or have an effect on a material body? Aristotle had analyzed at length in the seventh book of the *Physics* the necessity for the mover (efficient cause) to be in contact with what is moved, in all the kinds of change or motion, and showed that as a result such causes must occupy space (i.e., must be bodies).[91] The second thing required is that the agent cause have a power and instrumental means commensurate with the effects brought about. As Velleius suggests, when you look at the universe and think of its constituent elements, it seems ridiculous to imagine some finite material agent—especially an anthropomorphic Olympian god—wrestling with the constellations or summoning dispersed air and water and earth to form the sublunar world.

The Epicurean solution to this problem, as we have seen, is to deny that any maker is responsible for the universe: it comes about by chance, and the gods have better things to do with their time. The Stoics indeed taught that the universe is a result of divine causality and that the cause is material, but it is immanent to the world and its processes, so the divine is not a distinct efficient causal agent. It acts the way the principle of life acts in the organism: assimilating, growing, organizing, moving, and assuring, so to speak, the common good of the organism and its diverse parts.

A third solution was known to Cicero: that of Aristotle, whose universe is eternal, without beginning, and whose unmoved mover is certainly *asomatos* and is called divine. But this first mover is without material magnitude and so is incapable of contact. Aristotle's alternative explanation for the role of god as governor of the universe is that the divine substance produces order among natures by being the object of desire (i.e., as a final cause, not as an efficient or agent cause). The price one has to pay for that is to remove such a being from religious accessibility. Though living, the unmoved mover is pure act, it has no possible capacity to be acted upon by outside things, and it is beyond change of any kind, including coming to know what happens to human beings.

The more one reflects on this problem of the nature of the gods, the more one can see how intractable it seemed to ancient philosophy. (Of course mythology had no such problems, since it had no need to respond to the sorts of questions that philosophers bothered themselves with.) Descartes struggled unsuccessfully with an analogous difficulty when he tried to conceive of the soul as an immaterial thing distinct from the body: how then to explain the action of the soul on the body? And, in terms of this analogy, one can see how the Stoic conception of the divine was more like Aristotle's hylomorphic conception of the soul and body: the soul is not a separate thing but the internal principle of life and organization and movement of the living body, so there is no problem of how it acts on, or rather with, the body. There may be other problems with those conceptions of Aristotle and the Stoics, but at least they escape the difficulties associated with the conception of the gods as separate finite material causal agents.

The only other developed philosophical theory in the ancient world which tried to give an account of how an immaterial reality could be the source of the world was that of the third-century A.D. Alexandrian thinker Plotinus. In his teaching, the One—ineffable, transcendent, and indivisible—in its plenitude "overflows" and produces something distinct from (and therefore less than) itself by a necessary and "natural" process of generation. That second reality, the Nous, in its turn produces a third and finally the material world is emanated. Without entering into the many subtleties and explanations of the processes of generation and emanation, it can be seen how such a conception of the relation between an immaterial origin and the spatio-temporal world attempts to avoid the kind of difficulties that the notion of corporeal causal agents presented. But again there is a religious price to pay. Like Aristotle's divine substance, the One has no knowledge of our prayers and sacrifices and no providential governance over the world. Plotinus indeed was reported to have experienced a kind of ecstatic, mystical union with the One, but such an ascent was from below, so to speak. It was through the ascetic efforts of the individual that such an ascent might be made, not by a gracious assistance from above. (In this, the means and the union sought by Plotinus resemble the ways of yoga in Hinduism and of the eightfold path in Buddhism.)

Looking back, one can see why Cicero titled his dialogue *On the Nature of the Gods*, because his discussion rose out of reflection on religion as a practice, and his focal question was not whether some god or gods exist(s)—though that question occupies a large part of the work—but whether there are reasonable grounds to affirm the existence of the gods presupposed by that practice. Such a god would have to be able to hear our prayers and care enough about us to respond to them, to be able to communicate with us in some form, and to have providential foresight over the course of what is to happen. His position, as represented by the three dialogues on philosophy of religion, can perhaps be summarized as follows.

1. Neither of the most developed philosophical schools offers a tenable doctrine about the nature of the gods: the Epicurean gods would be

religiously irrelevant even if the conception of their nature were logically consistent, leading to the suspicion that Epicurus was only seeking to avoid the opprobrium of atheism in speaking of gods at all. The Stoic position, if true, would be supportive of religion, but its arguments are not compelling and it has no response to the problem of evil (a problem for any religiously relevant conception of gods).

2. No philosophically acceptable account of the nature of the gods is found that does not entail that religiousness is irrational, for neither has the idea of a god been shown to be logically inconsistent or impossible. So it is not unreasonable to recommend that people believe what has been handed down from long ago, especially when we see that for many people at least religion is a natural good (i.e., leads them toward virtue and justice).[92] This conclusion rests on the evidence of long experience of Roman practice, and so does not endorse novel religious teachers or teaching, or emotional religiosity.

3. However, one aspect of religion is absolutely unacceptable in Cicero's eyes: any practice that assumes that the future can be predicted. In *De Divinatione* he argues that divination, defined as foresight and knowledge (*scientiam*) of future events (1.1.1), is superstitious, is impossible, and ought to be purged from Roman religion (2.72.148). For if foreknowledge of future contingent events were possible, human freedom—and so responsibility and virtue—would be impossible. Augury, which does not entail prediction of the future (2.33.70), can be maintained. Perhaps one could say that for religion to look for meaning by taking events as signs is simply to suppose that the world and what happens in it is intelligible—an assumption which science also makes. Then Cicero's conclusion in *De Divinatione* and *De Fato* is that the notion that events can be signs is not unacceptable so long as the gods who give those signs are in the present as we are—that is, without knowledge of the future or the ability to predict it.

4. Never in these dialogues does Cicero even mention the idea that religion might take an individual out of the community, might conceivably set a person against the surrounding society, or might foster inwardness. (Even the so-called mystery religions such as Mithraism, so prevalent during the Empire, only bonded the initiate into a smaller group without setting them over against the political society.) Religion, we might say, paraphrasing his definitions, is a communal pattern of saying

and doing, of offering prayer and sacrifice and service to a superior nature which men call divine. It is a form of justice, through which we offer
to the gods what is due to them for the benefits conferred upon us.[93]

Through seven hundred years of ancient philosophy's examination
of religion, no articles of peace seem to have been signed. Plato's quarrel
with poetry, laid out in the *Republic*, was largely a quarrel with the gods
of the poets and of the myths. Aristotle's conception of a divine unmoved mover was intellectually breathtaking but inaccessible to religion.
Epicurus made religious hopes and fears irrelevant by removing the gods
from earthly cares and denying any afterlife for us. The Stoics came
closest to making philosophy and religion compatible, and they deserved
the greater attention which Cicero gave to them. Plotinus conceived,
like Aristotle, an extraordinarily lofty Absolute, but like him, one so far
above us as to be beyond the reach of religion. It was the coming of
Christianity that metamorphosed the relation between religious belief
and natural reason, between faith and philosophy.

CHAPTER SIX

Newman and Augustine

The Narrative of Conversion

Two of the enduring classics of Western literature are the *Confessions* of St. Augustine and the *Apologia* of Cardinal Newman. Both are the recounting, many years later, of the events which led to becoming a Catholic Christian. Neither of them is a mere chronicle: the telling involves a shaping of the past, a putting of the events into an order which manifests various kinds of connection between them. The artfulness of rhetoric, we may say, draws mere chronicle toward narrative—which need not be history or autobiography.

I want to reflect on the way in which these two works—these two lives as presented in the stories—structure the narrative in order to achieve their purpose. To mention only one obvious and yet significant instance: neither of them has any hesitation about ignoring chronological order if it serves another, more artful and more important order. So Augustine ends Book Four of the *Confessions* by reporting on his reading of Aristotle, although he explicitly tells us that he had read it seven years prior to the events which he has just finished relating in Book Four. Similarly Newman describes at length the writing of Tract 90 and the storm that broke upon it in Chapter Two, although the Tract was published in 1841 and Chapter Two is entitled "History of My Religious Opinions from 1833 to 1839." Why, in recounting a history, would one depart from the order in which things happened?

I

One thing that distinguishes the class to which our two retrospective narratives belong is that two levels of meaning, two patterns of intelligibility are discerned and folded into the story by the authors. For Augustine, not only is there a meaning in the things which I intentionally brought about, but there is a meaning in everything which happens to me, which cuts across my path: the meaning intended by God in His providential care of me. Indeed in the case of St. Augustine we have to formulate it more strongly than that: not just what happens to me, but my own intentions as well are under God's providence, are used by Him to guide me toward Himself. Thus Augustine tells us that he left Carthage for Rome because he had heard that the teaching conditions were better there. But having said that, having explained satisfactorily why he took the boat for Rome, he adds another explanation: God was leading him toward Milan, toward Ambrose, who will open up the Scriptures to him. The second explanation of why he left Carthage does not abrogate the first. God is not a cause in the sequence of temporal causes; His causality does not replace or expunge that of Augustine. It is simply that there are two intentional patterns here, complementary and equally efficacious. Only in retrospect, of course, does Augustine become aware of this second level. Prior to that time, he was simply unaware that there was another meaning to the things that he is narrating. Looking back, he remarks:

> Why I went from the one place and went to the other, you knew, O God, but you did not reveal it to me or to my mother . . .

> All unknowing, I was led to [Ambrose] by you, so that through him I might be led, while fully knowing it, to you.[1]

Newman is equally clear that some of the things happening to him had a significance of which he was ignorant at the time. I cite several examples:

It [his article "The State of Religious Parties"] may now be read as my parting address and valediction, made to my friends. I little knew it at the time.[2]

... [referring to Tract 90] while I was thus speaking of the future of the Movement, I was in truth winding up my accounts with it, little dreaming that it was so to be; (89)

From the end of 1841, I was on my deathbed, as regards my membership with the Anglican Church, though at the time I became aware of it only by degrees. (121)

But I want to draw attention here to an apparent difference between Augustine and Newman in regard to the duality of levels of meaning. Augustine is perfectly explicit that God was guiding his footsteps all the way, although Augustine was unaware of it at the time. Newman's references to a second dimension of meaning in his life, of which the quotes above are typical, can be read as simply expressing the wider view which the later time (the present time of writing) has over the earlier (the past). That is, looking back we can often see things differently, in a way which was impossible for us at the time, because we now know things about the circumstances which we didn't know then, or because we now know what the consequences of some action were which were unforeseen at the time. That's clearly not the kind of wider view which Augustine has in mind.

Before turning to the structures of the two works, it might be interesting to note a number of coincidences in their narrated lives, some of which are surely simply accidental parallels, some of which may be elements in some typical paradigm of the process of religious conversion.

They both tell of two visits to Rome; for both of them the second visit comes at the end of their narration, by which time they have each become a Catholic Christian. Each of them is sent off to school by the parents to become a lawyer, but each is turned away from the practical world to become a teacher. Each of them is deeply influenced early on by a book which marks their thinking permanently. (For Augustine, this is Cicero's *Hortensius*; for Newman it is Butler's *Analogy of Religion*.) Each of them experiences a climatic moment of reversal and abandonment when their religious convictions are overturned and there seems nowhere to go.[3] For each, there is a slow illumination of the ascending path to be followed, an illumination provided by an intense study of the writings of classical thinkers: for Augustine, the Platonists, for Newman, the Patristic writers. Finally, there is a time which each describes in the language of (spiritual) death and rebirth, the last part of the journey.

Perhaps some of these (and other) coincidences are not merely coincidences, because of course Newman himself had read the *Confessions* and indeed in 1835 published an essay entitled "Conversion of Augustine."[4] In that essay he discusses at some length the death of Augustine's friend, and the role of Ambrose, Simplician, and (the story of) St. Anthony in the saint's conversion. Moreover, he leaves no doubt that he sometimes saw his own situation in the light of Augustine's story. Thus, seeking to explain to the reader the powerful resonance which the Augustinian maxim *Securus judicat orbis terrarium* set up in his mind, he likens it to the "*Tolle, lege*" which Augustine hears in the garden and which crystallizes the latter's incipient faith in the Christ of Catholic Christianity (99).

Augustine, of course, takes those words to be a divine command, to be God speaking to him; does Newman mean us by this reference to understand his hearing the words—which his friend "repeated again and again"—in the same way? Notice here again that it is in the time of the narrating and not the time narrated that Newman makes the comparison. Although he does describe the powerful effect which the "*Securus . . .*" had on him at the time ("By those great words . . . the theory of the *Via Media* was absolutely pulverized"), the comparison with the "*Tolle, lege*" only occurs to him now:

> . . . the words of St. Augustine struck me with a power which I had never felt from any words before. To take a familiar instance, they were like the "Turn again Whittington" of the chime; or, to take a more serious one, they were like the "Tolle, lege,—Tolle, lege" of the child, which converted St. Augustine himself.[5]

And of course the "*Securus . . .*" does not have the same direct consequences for Newman as for Augustine. Rather than providing certainty, it subverted that confidence which the hard-won justification of the *Via Media* had provided.

II

The main thing I want to do is to compare the structures of the two narratives and to see how the telling of the events has shaped their meaning.

Let me begin with Augustine. I note just four features. All but one need to be argued for at length, but I shall not do that here.[6]

First, his work is not an autobiography, although it is often called that. Not only does it not tell us things we would expect to find in an autobiography (e.g., we learn only in passing in the ninth book that he has a brother, Navigius), its purpose is to exhibit God's saving action in his life and to reflect on how such providence is possible (hence Books Ten through Thirteen).

Second, the overall structure of the story is divided into a narrative part (Books One through Nine) and a reflective part which speaks of the present mind of the narrator. There is a gap in years between the one and the other, which need not be recounted because his religious position has not changed since the time of the narrative's end.

Third, the narrative books divide neatly in half around an axial event (the encounter with Faustus) which makes Augustine realize that there is no place for him in the Manichean church. The first half details his increasing estrangement from God and from his family and friends, a descent into successive stages of sin and isolation.[7] But the second half describes his ascent toward God and toward the community of the Church.

Moreover, the descent of the first half of the narrative is marked off in three stages, corresponding to the three concupiscences: of the flesh (Book Two), of the eyes (Book Three), and of worldly ambition (Book Four). The ascent of the latter half of the narrative tells of Augustine's liberation from these three in reverse order, so that the overall structure is that of a chiasm.

Fourth, between his Manichean years (Books Three to Five) and his conversion (Book Eight), there is a period of drift, beginning with his thinking that the skeptic's counsel that we should suspend judgment is wise.[8] Yet he decides to return to being a catechumen "until such time as something certain (*certi*) should become clear, by which I might steer my course."[9] Slowly he comes to realize that the intellectual objections which he had to the doctrines of the Catholic Church were mistaken. At that point, it is not further understanding which he needs, but certitude. And that is how he describes himself after the experience of the "*Tolle, lege*": "as if before a peaceful light streaming into my heart, all the dark shadows of doubt fled away."[10]

The telling of his story discloses the pattern—in fact a chiasmic structure—but not because he has shaped the story in order to make it edifying or to fit it to some dramatic form. Rather he is led by his faith—seeking understanding—to look for and to find in his remembered life a second level of meaning which is the evidence of God's providential care for him. The wider horizon of perspective which is provided simply by historical retrospect (alluded to earlier) could not suffice to reveal the dimension of divine providence. Yet having encountered in the garden the call of a transcendent God who acts in the world, Augustine now comes to see that what he had lived through as a search was a journey in which he had been guided at every step. He did not find God: God came to get him. The truest and deepest origination of his actions was not his seeking the true God: rather God was drawing him to an encounter.

If we turn now to the *Apologia*, it is not difficult to draw the parallels.

First, it is not an autobiography (despite having often been so described),[11] not even of the years narrated. Not only does it omit much of what one would look for in an autobiography, that is simply not his purpose. It is not even an intellectual autobiography, but rather, as he entitled it, a "History of my Religious Opinions."

Second, it is divided into a group of narrative chapters (One to Four) and a non-narrative chapter (Five) which deals with his present situation and thoughts. It omits, like Augustine, telling of the years intervening between the end of the narrative and the time of writing.

Third, the four narrative chapters are divided neatly in two. The division is not strictly chronological, but is dictated by his intent to structure his story around "the blow" which came down upon him (70), an axial point which marks the limit of his effort to find himself at home in the Anglican Church and also the limit of his distance—so it seemed—from Rome. The axial point which Newman chooses[12] is the publication of Tract 90, although this raises the problem about chronology to which I alluded earlier and to which I shall return. His attempt at a vindication of a Catholic interpretation of the Thirty-nine Articles climaxes the story of what seemed to him at the time an ascending Movement (*Exoriare aliquis!*), but which by a dramatic peripeteia turned out to disclose an unsuspected Achilles' heel.[13]

Moreover, it appears to me that, like the *Confessions*, Newman's narrative also has a chiasmic structure. Three successive ties incorporate and bind him to the Anglican Church. The first is his ecclesiastical office (pastor of St. Mary's), which he assumes in 1828 and clearly takes very seriously: as late as 1845, he writes to a correspondent, "I have never said, nor attempted to say, that any one in office in the English Church, whether Bishop or incumbent, could be otherwise than in hostility to the Church of Rome" (127). The second tie is his participation in the Tractarian Movement from 1833, during which he feels himself in the seven years of plenty, truly at home, "the happiest time of my life" (69). The third is the intellectual foundation of his life in those happy days, the *Via Media*, which he first elaborated in *The Prophetical office of the Church viewed relatively to Romanism and Popular Protestantism*, published in 1837.[14] These three ties are severed in reverse order, in 1839, 1841, and 1843 respectively.

Fourth, like Augustine, Newman has to tell of an interim period in which he is neither firmly in the one camp nor the other. Even after the storm over Tract 90 broke, he writes:

I had not less confidence in the power and prospects of the Apostolical movement than before; not less confidence than before in the grievousness of what I called the "dominant errors" of Rome: but how was I any more to have absolute confidence in my present confidence? how was I to be sure that I should always think as I thought now? (79)[15]

Like Augustine before him, the loss of confidence in his previous convictions and yet the "fact, however it is to be accounted for, that Rome has added to the creed" (95) left him spiritually adrift. Like Augustine, whose doubts about Manicheism did not lead him immediately to abandon the network of Manichean believers, Newman did not contemplate, at the end of 1841, leaving the Church of England.[16]

To summarize, four basic similarities in the narratives can be specified: 1) neither story is autobiography; 2) the works are divided into a narrative section about the past and a terminal section about the present situation; 3) the narratives are organized around an axial event (and in fact structured as chiasmic); 4) the original and final religious positions are separated by a period of uncertainty and drift. My thesis is that these similarities are not coincidental, but derive from the kind of story each man is trying to tell.

III

So let me try to state in general terms what that kind of story is and is not.

First, it is not and does not pretend to be an autobiography. Apart from other internal evidence of that, the gap of decades between the events related and the time of writing should be sufficient to show that the writer has a more limited purpose in view.

Second, it is not centered around the actual entry into the Catholic Church—in neither story does this take up more than half a page—nor even the decisive moment when that action is resolved upon. This is perhaps easy to see in Newman's account; in Augustine's, much misunderstanding has come about by focusing on the garden scene as the axial moment.[17] It is indeed a dramatic scene, but what it marks is not the axis of the narrative but the moment when Augustine's consciousness catches up with the action. To focus on the garden scene is not only to miss the real axis of the narrative, it is thereby to miss the author's intention.

Third, the years-removed point of view of the narrator means that the narration of the earlier time is based on a reflective thinking-back, on a reading of the events of those years, an emplotment of them and not a mere chronicling. One might say, with some confidence, that if the story had been written immediately or soon after the events, the point of view which the narrator now possesses would not have been formative. That seems obvious enough, but to make it a useful observation we have to try to infer what the point of view—and so of emplotment—is.

So fourth—still trying to state the general characteristics of a type—looking back beyond the moment where it all "came together," where the last doubts had been removed and what to do was at last certain, one can discern a crucial moment of turning which was the real beginning of the moment of coalescence. It is this characteristic which not only marks the way in which Newman and Augustine structure their narratives, but which, on reflection, one can see to be implicit in any religious encounter with the God of history. And in a story of religious conversion, it will be God's hand that is discerned in that axial moment.

Fifth and finally, God's hand will be all the more surely discerned if that axial moment was one contrary to one's own thoughts and intentions at the time. If it came down as "a blow" (Newman) or as the disappointment of "intense longings" (Augustine), it could not be merely the next step in one's search. It is this, I believe, which makes such a moment salient to the retrospective vision of the narrator.

Moreover, it is related to this facet of the narrative that the result is a period of doubt, even of skepticism, of wandering "in the desert" (127). And all the more will this period be lengthened if the previous state had been one which set the person at enmity with the community of journey's end. Critical here is the passion for firmness in the truth, the inability to "close one eye" to counterevidence, which both motivates the departure and postpones the arrival.

So it is that, detached by time and reflection from the earlier years, Augustine and Newman each perceives a certain period of his life to have a decisive significance. That perception is the result of a certain way of reading the past, which is expressed in the emplotment of their narratives. To put one's past into a narrative is to understand it in a particular way, whether one is conscious of that or not—and Augustine and Newman unmistakably are.

IV

The *Apologia* and the *Confessions*, I have argued, have a similar fundamental structure, one deriving from the kind of account that each set
out to give. Before going on to remark on some differences between the
two, I want to deal with two questions about the rhetorical organization
of the *Apologia*.

First, why is it the story of Tract 90 that is chronologically displaced
to Chapter Two? (Newman also deals with it, more briefly, in its proper
place at the end of Chapter Three.) Why is this moved to the center of
the narrative chapters? And second, why, since Chapter Four is by far
the longest chapter and is in fact subdivided into two numbered parts,
was it not divided into two chapters? (This is not unrelated to the first
question, since if Four had been subdivided, Chapter Three would have
become the center.)

To take the second question first: Walter Houghton wrote that
"Judged as a rational account of Newman's final steps, [Chapter Four] is
confused and disorganized. We do not see any progress."[18] Now, I can
sympathize with that reaction. Chapter Four is not only the longest
chapter by far, it is subdivided only by a numeral '2' without any subtitle
or immediate indication of the reason for the division. Moreover, it is
dense with quotations from letters. In Chapter One, Newman quotes
from one letter; in Chapter Two from four of his letters; in Chapter
Three from thirteen of his letters; and in Chapter Four from fifty-one
of his letters.[19] Since letters have a conversational style and tone, this
profusion of quotations can indeed be a little confusing at times—e.g.,
keeping track of who is being addressed (if indeed they have been
identified).

But that the chapter itself is confused and disorganized seems to me
wrong. The reason, of course, for the letters is that during these years
(1841–1845) Newman published very little in the way of books or peri-
odical literature from which he could quote to trace the development of
his opinions.[20] Despite that handicap, the progress of his account seems
clear. The subdivision marks the autumn of the year 1843, by which time
he says there was no more change in his ideas to relate (157).

I had one final advance of mind to accomplish, and one final step to take. That further advance of the mind was to be able honestly to say that I was *certain* of the conclusions at which I had already arrived. That further step, imperative when such certitude was attained, was my *submission* to the Catholic Church. (167)

He does have still to recount the actions to which his opinions led him, namely, the public retraction of his verbal attacks on Rome[21] and the resignation from St. Mary's. Since the chapters mark off generic changes (so to speak) in his religious opinions, the actions of 1843–1845 do not require a separate chapter, and so Newman gives them a subdivision status.

Now to the first question: why is the account of Tract 90 in Chapter Two? Houghton, following F. L. Cross, thinks that:

> . . . the drama is staged to show an intellectual development from the summer of 1839 to October 1845, leading Newman slowly but logically to Rome, whereas in matter of fact the real turning point, according to Cross, was in 1841 with the hostile reception of Tract 90. That was followed by a growing sense of isolation, rejection and resentment, which finally led to conversion as an act of revenge.[22]

Passing over the concluding psychological comment, if it were the case that Newman wanted to make it look like a steady intellectual development from '39 to '45, why would he focus attention on Tract 90 by changing its chronological place and locating it at the end of a chapter which does not speak of any difficulties with Anglicanism?

Newman titles, and then subtitles (in subsequent editions), the work "A History of His Religious Opinions." It is a story of the significant changes in his religious opinions, and Houghton is right to suggest that there is the tracing of an intellectual development (almost in Newman's sense of the word) through those years. It is certainly more linear than circular or erratic, and we can mark it off stage by stage.[23] But Cross contrasts this as artificial foreground with the real world of Tract 90 and its hostile reception. What he ignores, it seems to me, is the historical character of Newman's religious ideas.

Newman is not wrestling with metaphysical questions (like whether God exists), which might be thought independent of historical circumstances and change, or with the kind of "religiousness" exemplified by a deist or a Buddhist. His thoughts about religion are thoughts about a historical community, the Catholic Church, and those thoughts cannot be independent of his historical situation. His goal is to be a member of the Apostolic church, if he can tell which community among those known to him is that church. His religious opinions are about, in effect, how to identify a community which began long ago, whose continuity—and so whose identity—has been obscured by events, so that he has, so to speak, only a description of the properties which marked it long ago. How to find that true community among the jostling churches?

The answer clearly is that he has to "try spirits, whether they be of God." He has to test whether this particular community is the one for which he searches. Tract 90 is that test.[24] That the patient reacts violently to the test, that the immunological system rejects his test as foreign, reveals to him that he is incorporated in the wrong body of believers. That his reaction in turn is affective, is hardly surprising. He would be a strange believer himself if he were not downcast at discovering that, like Abraham, his true home is not where he has thought it to be.

In sum, when the theological conception to which he has won his way is rebuffed by facts, events, his thoughts in one sense may not change, but that means that his life must change. This is why the history of his religious opinions has to be a *history of events*, not just of thoughts. And that is why, finally, the story of Tract 90 is recounted where it is. That Tract has to be the axial point of his story, even though all it tells him at the time is not where he should be but only where he can no longer be at home. The linear development of his opinions must contrast and yet merge with the reversal of his life situation.

V

In conclusion, I want to remark on three significant differences.

First, it would be ridiculous to subtitle Augustine's work, "A History of His Religious Opinions." It is, after all, addressed to God, a confession of praise and thanksgiving for drawing Augustine to Him. His readers are in the position of overhearing what Augustine is saying to God. The work is not addressed to them; they are referred to in the third person. Moreover it is not a history, but a confession. Newman, if I am not mistaken, never addresses God directly in his narrative though he does use "you" for his readers. His aim is to convince his readers, if possible, that his remaining in the Anglican Communion was not only honest but indeed his duty.

Second, it is striking that Augustine emphasizes that his conversion is an entry with others (Alypius, in particular) and toward others (his mother, in particular) in the Heavenly Jerusalem. Newman, in contrast, stresses again and again the solitary character of his journey,[25] to the point of not even mentioning that other friends are received into the Church alongside him. Perhaps this is related to my next and final observation.

For the third difference, I want to pose a question to which I am not sure my response is correct. It is this: Augustine's story is a confession of how the God who is "most hidden and most present" graciously led him through the events of his life to faith, to Catholic Christianity. What seemed at the time his effort to find the truth was, as he discovered in retrospect, all God's doing. Surely Newman must have had the same awareness in telling his story. Yet as we noted at the beginning, his remarks about the wider horizon of his present understanding ("I little knew it at the time" [82]) seem to leave it open whether his present retrospective understanding is of God's hidden hand or simply results from knowing now things which he didn't know then. To put it in another way, his story can be read as his steadfast search for the true Church, crowned by winning his way to certainty. Although he twice comments discreetly and tentatively (79, 173) about God's Providence in his journey, he never draws it to salience.

There are a number of his letters in the contemporary period (1841–1845) in which he mentions his confidence in God's providential care during this difficult time.[26] But one hardly needs such overt allusions: it would have been impossible for a person of Newman's spirit not to have thought and prayed that God would guide his steps. Why then does he never speak in the *Apologia* of his journey in such terms?

It seems to me that the reason for this difference is that Augustine intends his story to be a paradigmatic account of how God is hidden yet present to all, guiding their steps and calling them. He tells joyfully of the conversions of Alypius, Nebridius, Adeodatus, Verecundus.[27]

But Newman, reserved and sensitive to the religious convictions of his former fellow Anglicans, does not want to present his path as paradigmatic. "One man's meat is another man's poison," he twice remarks, (125, 137):

> I am not setting myself up as a pattern of good sense or of anything else; I am but giving a history of my opinions ... (36) ... as soon as I turned my face Romeward, [1843] I gave up, as far as ever was possible, the thought of in any respect and in any shape acting upon others. (169)

Hence, shortly after his entry into the Catholic Church, he responds to a letter from Cardinal Acton:

> If I might ask of your Eminence a favour, it is that you would kindly moderate those anticipations. Would it were in my power to do, what I do not aspire to do! At present certainly I cannot look forward to the future, and, though it would be a good work if I could persuade others to do as I have done, yet it seems as if I had quite enough to do in thinking of myself. (182)

So the difference between the respective points of view which Augustine and Newman adopt—I mean the fact that Augustine tells of his journey as the work of God's providence, while Newman seems to tell of his only from the perspective of the historically later narrator—is not that Newman had declined to share God's providential view of those years. It is rather because he is telling the tale from below, so to speak, in order to bring out its inner and human integrity. That, after all, is his avowed purpose in writing: to show that his actions had been congruent with his state of mind, and never dishonest, however much that may have seemed so to some.

Moreover—and I think this *is* a difference in their respective viewpoints—Newman, as we noted above, saw providence as more closely oriented toward the individual. His path was not a pattern: that was not only rhetorically unoffensive to his Anglican readers, it expressed his own conviction. It was *his* path, he tells it to justify the intellectual honesty of his conversion, but the convergence of the water of probabilities into the wine of certainty may be different for others. It is the *Apologia pro vita sua*, of *his life*.[28]

CHAPTER SEVEN

Proof and Presence

It may be helpful to note some preliminary reference points in order to give a sense of the orientation of these reflections, and so to provide the reader with some of the conscious assumptions and perspectives within which they unfold.

I take the notion of the presence of God to be a constitutive element of both religion and faith, these two terms being used in the senses that Thomas Aquinas expounds. But I want to avoid any understanding that the concept of presence is, on my own part or that of the reader, appended to an autonomous ego cogitans or transcendental subjectivity. Hence I am trying to anchor that concept and its relevant corollaries into historical strata which underlie the emergence of the cogito and the emphasis on consciousness in the modern period. I have elsewhere tried to explore that anchoring in the *Confessions* of St. Augustine,[1] and here I shall be concerned primarily with some of Thomas Aquinas's discussion of these issues. For similar reasons, I want to keep the exploration of the notion of presence within a social context and a tradition, which will serve as dialectical complements to keep that notion from standing in itself and by itself.

I choose Aquinas for many reasons, but important among them is the common view that he is an intellectual believer who gives reasons for his faith, so far as possible, by rational arguments. Yet Aquinas's doctrine is one in which faith-knowledge is the paradigm of knowledge, so that it serves as the touchstone for rational assessment. Nor is this position arbitrary or unfounded, for the God whom he affirms is Truth and Goodness.

In the third book of the *Summa Contra Gentiles*, in the course of considering a *per impossibile* argument, he remarks in passing,

> it is not possible for the knowledge of faith to be false and empty, as is evident from what we have said in the opening Book.[2]

Intrigued by such a statement, one turns back to the referenced locus and finds four arguments, of which the first is typical:

> It is clear that those things [the principles of rational discourse] which are implanted in reason by nature, are most true, so much so that it is impossible to think them to be false. Nor is it permissible for that which is held by faith, so evidently divinely confirmed, to be believed to be false. Since therefore only the false is contrary to the true, as is apparent from their definitions, it is impossible for these principles naturally known by reason to be contrary to the truth of faith.[3]

Note that it is the principles of reason—the laws of noncontradiction, transitivity, parts and wholes, etc.—which cannot be contrary to the truth of faith. Whatever is not so self-evident, but appears to follow according to them, if contrary to faith must be wrong:

> any arguments alleged against the teachings of faith do not follow correctly from these self-evidently known primary principles of nature. Hence they do not have demonstrative force, but are either probabilistic or sophistical, and hence there is a basis for refuting them.[4]

So must say any scientist when confronted with an alleged fact or argument which contravenes the premises and criteria of evidence of rational inquiry into nature.

It is important, I think, to stress here that it is his confidence in reason as well as his confidence in faith that marks Aquinas's position. There is no double truth doctrine, or more pertinently, reason is not a merely human faculty which must falter and yield when it inquires into the Divine Truth. The principles of human reason are based on the intelligibility of being and thus are not alien to the understanding of God. No more than we can God understand—or make—something to be both four and greater than four. This claim carries recursively all the way back to *any* exercise of reason. If God could make something self-evident to us to be not true then no evident judgment can be known to be true. Descartes' admission of this possibility underlies the well-known circle which his argument for God's existence exhibits. Aquinas's contention is not, like that of Descartes, that a benevolent God did in fact endow us with reliable insight, but that He could not not do so.

The affirmation of faith that God is Truth thus meshes perfectly with the exigencies of rational insight. And as the Author of our rational nature He cannot not have "taught" us rightly in endowing us with reason: "it is not possible to say of God that He taught us misleadingly" (ibid.). The *malin genie* appears only when faith is doubted or set aside.

Nevertheless, the affirmations of faith are more encompassing, more fundamental, and more imperative. They are self-grounding, not requiring confirmation or validation by rational insight or argument. Indeed, Aquinas holds that the merit of faith is diminished if a person believes only when human reasons are provided. Even though one may have reasons confidently based on demonstrations of the existence of God, he should be willing to believe on the authority of God alone.[5] Similarly, although the knowledge of the existence and unity of God is a necessary condition to further matters of faith, it is not necessary that these be established by demonstration, but "those who do not hold them by demonstration must at least posit them by faith."[6]

Those truths about God which are in principle susceptible of being rationally known he calls the "preambles" of faith. But it should be noted that these truths are not necessary conditions for a judgment of the reasonableness ("credibility") of the propositions of faith. St. Augustine's famous remark that no one believes anything unless he already understands it to be believable is relevant here.

Let us examine several of Aquinas's statements about the relation of these preambles to faith.

Theology makes use of philosophy "to demonstrate those truths that are preambles of faith and that have a necessary place in the knowledge of faith. Such are the truths about God which can be proved by natural reason: that God exists, that God is one; such truths about God or about His creatures, subject to philosophical proof, faith presupposes."

God's being one insofar as it is demonstrated is not said to be an article of faith, but presupposed to the articles: for the knowledge of faith presupposes natural reason, as grace does nature.

The existence and unity of God "are not articles of faith but preambles to the articles."[7]

Now these texts might be understood—and historically have been understood—to mean that for the act of faith to be warranted, reasonable, one must already have attained on rational grounds the knowledge of God's existence, unity, etc. But in fact as we have seen, Aquinas explicitly says that they may be posited by faith itself.

For a long time, beginning in the seventeenth century and down to our own time, commentators on St. Thomas and Catholic apologetics have held such a rationalist position, namely, that the credibility of revealed truths required a prior demonstration of God's existence, truthfulness, etc.[8]

The confusion with respect to Aquinas's position arose by taking him to mean that the preambles are necessary conditions to the *act* of believing, whereas Thomas takes them to be logically necessary conditions to the *articles* of faith, that is, the specifically revealed truths of Christian doctrine. Hence the preambles, as the intersection of the areas of faith and reason can be held either by belief or by demonstration and must be held (as necessary conditions) in one way or the other.

As we shall see, however, even this schema makes Aquinas seem more of a rationalist than I believe he is. For the area of intersection can, in fact, only be adequately delineated by the knowledge of faith.

So it is that Aquinas distinguishes as one of the component parts of the act of faith, believing in a God, along with believing God and believing in God.[9]

It is not inconsistent with this for him to hold not only that strict demonstration of the existence of God is possible, but that

> natural reason tells man that he is subject to a higher being on the basis of the defects which he perceives in himself and by reason of which he needs help and direction from someone above him: and whatever this being may be, it is that which is called God by all men.[10]

Such an apprehension is not a logically necessary condition for faith but manifests a converging gradient in human experience, one which testifies again to the fundamental compatibility between faith and reason.

Compatibility does not mean agreement: the inclination of natural reason toward such a recognition may remain so general as to ground quite diverse religious beliefs ("called God by all men"), and Aquinas is quite willing to say that those who do not have faith do not succeed in referring to God whatever they may call Him:

> Those who do not have faith cannot be said to believe in a God as we understand it in relation to the act of faith. For they do not believe that God exists under the conditions that faith determines; hence they do not truly believe in a God, since as the Philosopher says, to know simple things defectively is not to attain them at all.[11]

This is one of the corollaries of his understanding of "religion" as distinguished from "faith." He adopts Cicero's definition of religion as consisting in "offering service and ceremonial rites to a superior nature that men call divine." As distinguished from faith, which is a "theological virtue" having God as its object, religion is a moral virtue (indeed the chief moral virtue) which has God as its end, but not as its object:

> the acts whereby God is worshipped do not attain to God Himself, as when we believe God we attain God by the believing.[12]

Several things are worth noting about his conception of religion. First, it is interesting that he takes over the definition of a pagan philosopher, although not surprising precisely because for him religion is a natural virtue, one whose origin and intent are wholly within the human sphere.

Second, religion is a moral virtue: it is concerned with behavior and indeed with social behavior. It is concerned with service and cult, with prayer and sacrifice, with oaths and oblations. Like Durkheim, Aquinas locates religion in actions which relate to the good of the social community, although that good and the right actions with respect to the divine which it entails will differ as the good is differently perceived. Unless it is instituted by God, religion will be diversified in the same way that political regimes are diversified, which does not mean that there are no natural norms underlying it. Hence, God is the "end" but not the "object" of religion.

Third, "religious experience" is not an integral component or goal of religion (in the sense in which William James speaks of the varieties of religious experience). Aquinas does refer, in a text cited above, to the sense of dependence on God's help which he contends is common to all men, but the object of religion is the behavior which is perceived to be appropriate toward God. The essence of religion does not consist of that sense of dependence, but rather of a way of life, whether always accompanied by feelings or not.

To sum up: faith (and the same can be said of religion) is not logically dependent on a prior demonstration of the existence of God. In fact, natural reason was not in Aquinas's view able to determine adequately the nature of God's unity:

> by faith we hold many things about God which the inquiries of the philosophers by natural reason were not able to discover, for example about His providence and omnipotence and that He alone is to be worshipped.[13]

The "common and confused" knowledge of God (communis et confusa cognitio Dei) which he thinks inclines most men to the acknowledgement of a superior being does not make clear who or what sort of being

He is, or whether He is one (Quis autem, vel qualis, vel si unus tantum: SCG III, 38).

It may indeed be possible for unaided human reason to demonstrate the existence of God and something of His unity;

> But if there have been any men who have discovered the truth about divine things by way of demonstration without any admixture of falsity, they have certainly been very few . . . and this knowledge includes much uncertainty, which is shown by the diversity of conclusions about divine things among those who have tried to discover them by demonstration.[14]

When reason is illumined by faith, the probability of finding an adequate demonstration is significantly increased, since we already know what it is we want to prove. Logically speaking, this is not a unique case, as Galileo's Salviati shows: Aristotle, he says, first obtained his conclusions in natural philosophy by observation and then

> he sought means to make them demonstrable. That is what is done for the most part in the demonstrative sciences; this comes about because when the conclusion is true, one may by making use of analytical methods hit upon some proposition which is already demonstrated, or arrive at some axiomatic principle; but if the conclusion is false, one can go on forever without ever finding any known truth—if indeed one does not encounter some impossibility or manifest absurdity. And you may be sure that Pythagoras, long before he discovered the proof for which he sacrificed a hecatomb, was sure that the square on the side opposite the right angle in a right triangle was equal to the squares on the other two sides. The certainty of a conclusion assists not a little in the discovery of its proof.[15]

Galileo would appear to provide support for Michael Polanyi's contention, as against Karl Popper, that the inquirer into nature seeks to prove what he holds to be true, rather than to falsify it. In our context, it would seem to be appropriate to say that Aquinas's conception of the logical place of proofs for the existence of God is fundamentally An-selmian. That is, although the premises of the proof are not held by faith, the conclusion is: the proofs are sought retrospectively. And this is the case not just factually or historically but on the logical grounds re-ferred to: only by knowing what it is we want to prove, on other grounds, do we stand a chance of finding a proper demonstration.

So it is that what has been called the "principle of charity" in recent discussions of convergence of theories in the history of science functions also for Aquinas. Although nothing corresponds exactly to the inade-quate conceptions of the divine which earlier philosophers and religions elaborated, we can see what they were trying to attain, to refer to, and make use of adapted forms of earlier proofs.

Just because of the retrospective character of the proofs, and their resting in the sense indicated on the firmer ground of faith, the elabora-tion of them is not a central concern for Thomas. And this is why, I believe, he lumps all five "ways" into one article of one question of his *Summa*.

Do we have any demonstrations in the case of the existence of God? Negative rejoinders to this question are often based on the observation that alleged demonstrations are not universally accepted. By itself, that non-acceptance is not logically sufficient ground for abandoning an ap-parent proof and might simply send the demonstrator back to his work more cautious and more determined to scrutinize each step of the argu-ment. But when it is observed that virtually no one accepts such a proof who does not already believe in the existence of God, the pertinence of non-acceptance is given more weight. For it tends to suggest that the belief has surreptitiously found its way into the demonstration, so that the conclusion is not simply known by faith in the way that Salviati approves but some of the premises or steps also rely on belief, and hence the proof as a whole does not, as it purports, rest simply on what is knowable by human reason.

I think that this common view is not as cogent as it appears. My reason for so thinking is derived from a reading of several controversies in the history of science in which demonstrations were presented and rejected, but later came to be accepted as demonstrations. What is per-ceived as an argument may come to be seen as a demonstration when it is placed in a different context. That is to say that the notion of a proof is relative to a context, and that context is not merely logical (an axiomatic system, for example) but may be constituted by a specifically different attitude toward the world and toward the way in which we understand and even perceive the sense of things.

A brief discussion of two of these controversies will illustrate my reading.

The starry sky above has been from earliest ages perceived as totaliter aliter, as a region of power and unchangeableness. We can still recapture some of that sense of glory when we find ourselves at night far from the city lights and gaze up at that imperceptibly, majestically moving pageant of the sky. It has always been perceived as related to, if not the home of, divinity. Galileo wanted to establish the earthlike nature of those heavenly bodies and to prove the Copernican theory. But he found that in order to do so, he had to demythologize the heavens. It is, he said, "vanity to imagine that one can introduce a new philosophy by refuting this or that author. It is necessary first to teach the reform of the human mind, and to render it capable of distinguishing truth from falsehood," which no mere observations could do.

That reform must go very deep indeed, for the conviction of the inalterability and perfection of the heavenly bodies is linked with man's deepest fears and emotions:

> Those who so greatly exalt incorruptibility, inalterability, etc., are reduced to talking this way, I believe, by their great desire to go on living, and by the terror they have of death.[16]

The Copernican revolution is often described as a revolution in our way of conceiving the universe and of locating ourselves within it. But I think it would be difficult to overestimate the power, both perceptual and effective, of the phenomenon referred to here. It can be put contrastingly by saying that we today no longer *see*, with our own eyes, anything palpably immutable, a visible sign of the eternal and unchanging God. It was the very way in which man inhabited the universe, the claim of the "higher things," the very evidence of the senses which blocked the way to seeing another significance of the stars.

Cannot the seeing of sunspots show that the sun is a changeable body? "An illusion of the telescope," "a fallacy of the lenses" reply his critics.[17] The difference which Aristotle postulates between the natural motions of heavenly and terrestrial bodies (which Galileo says underlies all the other differences), viz. circular and linear motion, can be shown to be possibly relative to the position of the observer, i.e., standing on a rotating and orbiting earth. But even if we grant that this is mathematically possible to demonstrate, can we succeed in *seeing* a dropped cannonball move in a circular path or the horizon sink beneath the sun at "sunrise"? And the Bible, Aristotle, tradition are all against such a view.[18]

The required reform of the human mind must be pursued by something like persuasion, assisted by arguments which will eventually turn into demonstrations, i.e., be accepted as such. It is not by accident that Galileo's great work on this takes the form of a dialogue. Wittgenstein remarks,

> I can imagine a man who had grown up in quite special circumstances and had been taught that the earth came into being 50 years ago and therefore believed this. We might instruct him: the earth has long . . . etc.—We should be trying to give him our picture of the world. This would happen through a kind of persuasion.[19]

My second instance may conveniently be linked to Galileo, who noted that the positive integers may be placed in one-to-one correspondence with the even integers, although one would intuitively suppose that the latter set must be smaller than the former. He puzzled over this and seems to have decided that it was impossible to compare infinite quantities. "Infinity and indivisibility are in their very nature incomprehensible to us," he wrote. There is something indeterminate about the notion of the number of infinite numbers, and if we try to give it definiteness we get self-contradictions. Those parts of mathematics which dealt with the notion of infinity, such as the infinitesimals of the calculus, lacked a satisfactory theoretical foundation for several centuries and suffered the guerilla attacks of philosophers and cantankerous mathematicians. Not until Cauchy's work on analysis in 1821 which formulated the concept of a limit did the calculus acquire such a foundation.

But even then, one simply replaced the notion of infinitesimals with that of approaching a limit as closely as desired, thus circumventing the talk of an infinitely divisible interval. Gauss, the foremost of the nineteenth-century mathematicians, protested against the use of "infinite magnitude," which he said was never permissible in mathematics.

But in the 1870s, Cantor began to publish a series of articles in which he proved the existence of transfinite numbers, showed how different transfinite numbers could be distinguished from each other with sufficient determinateness to formulate theorems about their relationships with each other and with their parts. His work was, however, rejected by the mathematical and academic community and bitterly attacked by such eminent mathematicians as Kronecker and Poincaré. A large and indeed fundamental part of the basis for rejecting his work was the weight of the centuries-long traditional understanding of infinity as implying the possibility of going on indefinitely. Cantor's critics felt that these puzzles, i.e., contradictions, would undermine the certainty of mathematics. The contradictions of infinite magnitudes (or the paradoxes, as they came to be called) aroused the same sort of scornful rejoinders which the Copernican theory aroused in Galileo's day.[20]

Cantor was keenly aware of the philosophical context which set his understanding apart from that of his peers, and of what he saw as its theological implications. He corresponded with several Cardinals in the Vatican about theological pronouncements on actual infinities and even wrote to Pope Leo XIII on the subject.[21]

Were his proofs proofs? They are certainly so accepted now; they were certainly rejected then. As a mathematician colleague once commented to me in discussing this question, "Well, we understand infinity differently now." For a proof to be accepted as a proof, one is tempted to say, its conclusion must be possible and plausible, intellectually admissible, and the criteria for those qualities are related to one's *Weltbild*. But while the *Weltbild* is not merely a conceptual framework—its roots may be very deep, as we have seen—neither is it a *Lebensform* which encloses its own justification and hence is impervious to rational criticism. Cantor himself commented on his discovery, "I was led on step by step, almost against my will"; he had, in fact, started out to show that the notion of an infinite magnitude was untenable. "Je le vois mais je ne le crois pas," he wrote to his friend, Dedekind, in recounting the steps of the demonstration.[22]

But if this casts some light on a possible reason why proofs for the existence of God are not generally accepted, it has not yet been made clear why such a proof is neither a necessary nor a sufficient condition for faith. That it is not necessary for Aquinas is clear. I want to say that the proof is not sufficient because what faith affirms is the *presence* of a living God, and no proof can establish that. He cannot not be thought of as present to the believer, and it is this intellectual affirmation which grounds our direct address to Him in prayer and our union in love:

> the thing believed is not made perfectly present to the intellect by the knowledge of faith, since faith is of things absent, not of things present . . . Yet God is brought into the presence of love through faith.[23]

> So long as we are in the body, we are said to be absent from the Lord, in comparison with that presence whereby He is present to some by the vision of sight . . . Nevertheless even in this life He is present to those who love Him, by the indwelling of His grace.[24]

But doesn't the affirmation of something's presence logically depend on the affirmation of the thing's independent existence? Only if the presence is contingent with respect to the reality, i.e., if the reality is knowable apart from its presence to someone. Compare proving that the external world exists. Can we say, it's present but does it really exist? For a long time this seemed a real problem, and the present-world was taken to be separate from the real world, internal to consciousness or to the theater of the mind. Today we find it hard to give more than a notional assent to that problematic: the very language in which the present-world was described betrays its rootedness in the perceptions of things in the world, and not apparent things. The reality of the world is existentially and cognitively inseparable from its presence: the world is what is given to me in perception.

Similarly, Aquinas argues in the First Part of the *Summa* that God by His very nature is present to all things (He is everywhere by essence, presence, and power). But like Augustine's discussion in the first book of the *Confessions*, presence here is construed as unilateral omnipresence. It is, so to speak, a metaphysical presence (as causally sustaining) which carries no implication of being recognized by what is sustained (I, 8c). Only when he comes to discuss faith and religion does he delineate the reciprocal of that presence, namely, the way in which God is experientially present to man's awareness in a *unio affectus*. God is present to man by nature, we can say, but man is present to God in the exercise of the natural virtue of religion as well as by faith. The acknowledgement of His presence is implicit in prayer (an act of religion), which has as a necessary condition that "the person who prays should approach (accedere) God to whom he prays."[25] I think "approach" here must be construed in the sense of "turning to" rather than of proximity: far and near are both dimensions of presence. Jesus on the cross felt abandoned by God, but He expressed that in a prayer, i.e., by direct address.

The natural sense of the presence of God Aquinas traces not to one of the "Five Ways," all of which begin from observations about the way the world is, but to the apprehension of man's dependence on a power not his own. That apprehension opens a space of encounter, an intentional space characterized by the numinous quality of its intentional object. It opens or discloses, that is, a dimension of meaning which events and actions can come to participate in. Occurrences, objects, behavior can acquire the intentional quality of the preternatural by virtue of their reference to the divine. We can speak of encountering the divine in such events.

But the sense of the presence of the divine itself is, in this sphere, unstable. The "high gods" may be absent: prayers may not be heard. Or power may not be undivided: heard prayers may not be efficacious because, as Vergil muses, other powers may harbor animosity.

The God announced by Christianity is One who is present by His nature, whose power is undivided, whose goodness is unqualified. But the knowledge of that God is mediated: it comes through hearing.

> One who believes gives assent to things that are proposed to him by another person, and which he himself does not see. Hence, faith has a knowledge that is more like hearing than seeing.[26]

Faith is not a mystical or direct apprehension; it is an act of rational assent to what is heard.

So it is that Aquinas allots the experiential component of faith to the affective domain of the will. *Believing* in the irrevocable presence of the God whose nature specifies and fulfills the empty intention (to borrow Husserl's language) of natural apprehension, the heart of the hearer leaps up in joy, for what is naturally loved as the highest good is with us. Joy is the awareness of the presence of the beloved.[27]

While that awareness is personal, it is not merely subjective in a psychological sense. For it derives not from private intimations but from a public source: the propositions which are handed on to us by a historical tradition. And the affective union of love is kindled and quickened not merely by the hearing but in the communal rituals and celebrations and symbols of Emmanuel.

Hume's Unnatural Religion
(Some Humean Footnotes)

On the title page of his first publication, *A Treatise on Human Nature* (1739), Hume chose a motto from Tacitus: "Rare those happy times when you can think what you will and are permitted to say what you think." The observation accurately reflected the constraints on the discussion of religion in eighteenth-century England and Scotland, and Hume tells in a well-known letter to a friend in 1737 of revising the *Treatise* for publication and excising his discussion of religious topics (among them that of miracles) because of the possible consequences. Ten years later, when he is preparing the *Essays Concerning Human Understanding* (1748) for the press, he is less fearful of being indiscreet— partly because he has learned something from classical authors about the rhetoric of religious discourse, partly because he has surrendered some of his hopes for public preferment. At any rate, he now (1747) writes to another friend about including his discussions of miracles and the design argument, Chapters 10 and 11 of the *Essays* (renamed *Enquiry Concerning Human Understanding* in the 1758 edition): "I see not what bad consequences follow, in the present age, from the character of an infidel; especially if a man's conduct be in other respects irreproachable."[1]

By the reference to "the rhetoric of religious discourse," I mean not only the conventional pieties with which Hume learned to surround his critical discussions—for example, the opening and concluding paragraphs of the essays on miracles, on the immortality of the soul, and of the *Dialogues Concerning Natural Religion*—but even more the rhetorical forms themselves in which he henceforth cast his essays on religion. This claim takes Chapters 10 and 11 of the *Enquiry* as forming a complementary pair; complementary not only in their subject matters but in their literary forms.

Chapter 10 is a treatise, the famous critical analysis of miracles, which after arguing that the probability of the truth of testimony cannot be assigned independently of the probability of the events reported— and that miracles have a virtually zero probability—concludes as noted with a conventional, if tongue-in-cheek, affirmation that the faith necessary to believe in miracles is itself a miracle that subverts all reason. Chapter 11, without any transition, opens with a narrator "I" who proposes to report a conversation with a friend whose theses, although the narrator can "by no means approve" of them, are yet relevant to the larger "enquiry." Chapter 11, which is entitled "Of a Particular Providence and of a Future State,"[2] in fact says little about these topics directly but rather discourses on what is asserted to be one of their necessary conditions, namely, divine existence as demonstrated by the design argument. The views expressed here are hardly different from those embodied later in the *Dialogues Concerning Natural Religion*. The dialogue form, however, is here utilized much less artfully than in the later work; there are only two characters including the narrator, and most of the space is given over to the anonymous friend.

What is worth remarking is that Chapter 10 deals with positive or popular religion and its foundation and takes the form of a treatise apparently in *oratio recta*, while Chapter 11 deals with natural religion and its foundation (namely, the design argument) and takes the form of a reported dialogue. Why should the second rather than the first take a dialogue form? Not, I think, as has been said, because the dialogue form is one "in which disagreements could be clearly displayed,"[3] but rather primarily because the dialogue allows the author to recede from view or to hide himself, as Plato's Socrates noted. In Chapter 11[4] the author hides himself only to the extent of speaking as an anonymous "I" who reports the views of an interlocutor and occasionally makes an objection. Why should Hume want to do that for a discussion of natural religion?

Because it had been acceptable for a long time, and exploited for several centuries before Hume wrote, both to criticize superstition in general and the practices of other religious traditions in particular, and also to characterize religious doctrines as above reason.[5] As long as one was careful not to take examples from the surrounding religious tradition, one was not liable to be denounced, however suspicious some might be. On the other hand, to raise questions about what was common to all religions, namely, the existence of God, and what had been claimed by philosophers as a question decidable by natural reason, namely, the rational arguments for the existence of God, was much more subversive. Reasonable men might disagree about transubstantiation or the relation between faith and works but not about the existence of a providential God, whose handiwork was only made more apparent as the natural sciences advanced. But the critique in Chapter 11 goes beyond suggesting questions about the cogency of the argument from design. Even if the argument were logically compelling, it would not establish the existence of a God whose providence goes further than the orderliness of nature, namely, a God of "particular providence," one who intervenes in history.[6]

So if we read Chapters 10 and 11 as a unit, we find that they make a radical cut between "popular" religion and philosophical religion, between the God of miracles and particular providence and the God of the philosophers. Each of these two forms of theism must stand on its own—they do not reinforce each other—and neither stands on very solid ground.

What Hume did in Chapters 10 and 11 of the *Enquiry*, I want to say, he repeated in the two works that he wrote soon afterward, the *Natural History of Religion* (1757) and the *Dialogues Concerning Natural Religion* (1779).[7] The *Natural History* is a treatise that deals with popular, not philosophical, religion, while the *Dialogues* are a reported conversation on the design argument in which Hume does not speak in his own voice, that is to say, is not the narrator of the conversation as he apparently is in his two previous dialogues. Although I think that parallel relations are clear once they are remarked, the fact that the *Dialogues* were not published until some twenty years later, after Hume's death, has made the parallelism less salient. But unless one takes it into account, one is liable to misinterpret Hume's own views. For example, in the *Natural History* there are half a dozen favorable references in passing to the design argument (the argument is never discussed directly) and few critical remarks about it.[8] The reader might think (and a number of modern readers have so thought) that Hume accepts the design argument or at least does not reject it. But if the *Dialogues* are taken as a diptych to the *Natural History*, then it is clear that Hume is simply not opening more than one front at a time. Philosophical demonstrations simply have nothing to do with the origin or the justification of ordinary religiousness. Positive religion is one thing and natural religion is another, and the one needs different assessment (both rhetorically and logically) than the other.

So let us look first at the *Natural History of Religion* and then at the *Dialogues*.

The Sources of Popular Piety

The opening sentence of the *Natural History* introduces a distinction between the reasons for and the causes of religion, between the questions "concerning its foundation in reason, and that concerning its origin in human nature."[9] The first question, it is said, "admits of the most obvious, at least the clearest solution," namely, the evident design character of the whole frame of nature, about which "no rational enquirer can, after serious reflection, suspend his belief a moment." But the order of nature is not the source of religiousness, Hume claims against the Deists, nor on the other hand does it spring from "an original instinct or primary impression of nature" (21). Religion is not natural to man—as is shown, he says, by the facts that it is not universally found among all nations and ages and that it does not have a fixed and determinate object. So one must give an account of the genesis of religion that neither presupposes that early man had inferred the existence of God nor that man is by nature a religious being, that is to say, by nature inclined toward the worship of a deity. Indeed, such an account should not even presuppose that there is a God.[10]

Hume proceeds to trace its origin rather to a weakness in human nature, namely, an inordinately fearful concern about what will befall us tomorrow, hence with the unknown causes of those future events; and the conjunction of this concern with a "universal tendency among mankind to conceive all beings like themselves" results in the conceiving of these causes as having sentiment and intelligence (29). Conceiving of the unknown causes of our good and bad fortune anthropomorphically, as conscious, intentional agents, we ascribe to them the same passions and thoughts as human persons, and so are led to try to influence their attitudes toward us. So it is not out of the experience of a "universal presence" or through observation and reflection that religion arises, but from our emotions, from "an anxious fear of future events" (65).[11] And its object is not some observed or known cause of events, but an imaginary object, an invisible cause of the events about which we fear and hope.

Given this account of the origin of religion, and so the rejection of the Deistic attempt to trace its origin to the perception of the order of nature, Hume proceeds to argue that it is both logical to expect, and confirmed by all our historical data, that polytheism was the first form of religion. It is not the unity and order of nature that lies at the foundation of religion but rather the disorder or unpredictability of the events of human life, the things that happen to us individually and collectively and constitute our misery or good fortune. What the perplexing variation of connection between action and reward suggests is that there are multiple conflicting causes, not one consistent agent. So, concludes Hume, we are "necessarily led into polytheism" (27).

No more is the genesis of "theism" (monotheism[12]) out of this original polytheism a matter of men's observation and reflection. Rather, the exaggerated worship and praise to which religion inclines human beings leads to the magnifying of one divinity as higher and more glorious than all the others. From fear of his powerful displeasure and from fear of admitting to ourselves that he might not have control over future events, any suggestion of limitations of power and knowledge becomes unthinkable in praising him. And, as this process reinforces itself over time, it ends by elevating one supreme divinity over mere messengers and mediators, and thus finally arrives at the maximal theism of an infinitely perfect being, creator of the world.

Thus far, even a contemporary might have found these views, if rather untraditional, at least not subversive of the established religion.[13] Indeed, the first chapter of the *History* ("That Polytheism was the primary Religion of Man") explicitly suggests the development of religion from lower to higher, from polytheism to monotheism, by language such as the following:

> [I]f we consider the improvement of human society, from rude beginnings to a state of greater perfection, polytheism or idolatry was, and necessarily must have been, the first and most ancient religion of mankind. (23)

> [A]ccording to the natural progress of human thought, the ignorant multitude must first entertain some groveling and familiar notion of superior powers, before they stretch their conception to that perfect Being.... (24)

> The mind rises gradually, from inferior to superior ... [in a] natural progress of thought.... (24)

But these presuppositions, on the basis of which we have been following the evolution of polytheism into theism, are suddenly not merely questioned but reversed by Chapter 8, which is the middle chapter of the book. The title of the chapter is "Flux and Reflux of Polytheism and Theism"; and Hume tells us there that "men have a natural tendency to rise from idolatry to theism, and to sink again from theism into idolatry" (46–47), and that "so great is the propensity, in this alternate revolution of human sentiments, to return back to idolatry, that the utmost precaution is not able effectually to prevent it" (48).[14] Hume seems to have indicated the singularity of this chapter by placing it in the center of the fifteen chapters.[15]

Two other claims, made in Chapters 4 and 12, also subvert the opening picture of an evolution from lower to higher forms of religion.[16] Chapter 4 (quite in contrast to its title, "Deities not considered as creators or formers of the world") asserts that the so-called gods of polytheism are rather more like the elves and fairies of our ancestors, that is, not truly deities at all. Indeed, Hume says, such pagans are closer to atheists than they are to genuine theists. It is, he says, "a fallacy, merely from the casual resemblance of names, without any conformity of meaning, to rank such opposite opinions under the same denomination" (33). Polytheism and theism are thus not two species of the same genus, related as lower and higher, but disparate. (This is obviously related to Hume's thesis that religion is not a disposition natural to man, because it has no precise determinate object.[17]) In addition, Chapter 4 introduces in connection with its depreciation of polytheism and the power of its divinities an alternative account of the origin of the universe, namely, by generation, an account that is developed at length in the *Dialogues Concerning Natural Religion* as the major alternative to the argument from design.[18]

Chapter 12 is the concluding chapter of four chapters that deal with the comparison between idolatry and theism. If it is read with care, it reveals clearly that the author's view is that modern religion is no less absurd than ancient religion. Still, the chapter concludes explicitly that the human consequences of idolatry are less corrupting, so that of the two, idolatry laid the lighter yoke upon life and mind. Far from popular theism being an advance upon and superior to mythological religion, idolatry scores higher on Hume's card.

So if the opening chapter suggests that there are two species of theism, that there is a progress from the one to the other, and that the later stage is higher, we can say that those opening impressions are subverted in sequence, in Chapters 4, 8, and 12. The final chapter draws the conclusion that if there is no significant distinction between ancient and modern religion (one is not higher nor lower, nor more or less absurd), then the prudent thing to do is to suspend judgment[19] on "the whole . . . subject." We can maintain the suspension only by "opposing one species of superstition to another [and] set them a quarreling; while we ourselves, during their fury and contention, happily make our escape into the calm, though obscure, regions of philosophy" (76). This counsel implies that we have nothing before us in this whole subject except comparable superstitions, and that "we" recognize that. To recognize that, of course, requires that the case against any superiority or uniqueness of Christianity has been understood. It requires that we become one of the few "bystanders" (57) to whom the work is primarily addressed.

The Justification for Natural Religion

The *Natural History of Religion* is not a straightforward, unfeigned enquiry into the origins of religion, although a recent editor of the work describes it as "in the form of straight exposition" (11) in which we have no reason to doubt "Hume's philosophical sincerity and honesty" (16). In fairness, it is right to note that he explicitly disclaims any concern with "questions of biographical interest" such as "whether Hume retained genuine respect for 'the primary principles of genuine Theism and Religion' or whether he was merely willing, at times, to work within the conventions of his age." Rather, he says, "what we are left with [after setting aside biographical questions] is the argument itself" (9).

I do not want to deprecate the role of analysis in assessing an argument but rather to raise the question of whether we can always know what an author's argument is without attending to the issue of whether different audiences are being implicitly addressed. It is always possible to dissect an argument out of a text, and that may be useful and very important to do, but it is another question to ask how the author means it to be taken. No difference is more fundamental for the author of the *Natural History of Religion* than that between the vulgar and the few, and it is at least fair to reflect on whether an author intends to address both audiences in the same way, to the same purpose.[20]

Perhaps one of the reasons why this issue has often not been given sufficient attention is that an influential model of language does not make it salient. A contemporary British philosopher writes, "The task of the philosopher [of language] is to obtain some stable conception of this triangle of speaker, language, and world."[21] What is left out in this picture is a fourth element, namely, the addressee(s). In construing the meaning of an expression, it may be safe to ignore that element if there is only one (specific or generic) addressee, if in effect the words are meant to have the same meaning for all readers or hearers.

These brief remarks are a prologue to the examination of the *Dialogues Concerning Natural Religion*, which both contemporary readers[22] and Hume himself[23] rank among his most carefully written works. It is the more remarkable that it has received the most diverse interpretations and that there is no agreement about what Hume's position on the issues discussed was.

Let me briefly summarize the *Dialogues*. They consist of a conversation recounted by a schoolboy, Pamphilus, to a friend, in which three interlocutors discuss questions of God's nature and existence. The character of the interlocutors is characterized by Pamphilus as "the accurate philosophical turn of Cleanthes . . . the careless scepticism of Philo [and] . . . the rigid inflexible orthodoxy of Demea" (128). (Of course one has to take those descriptions as coming from a youth, and one who is in fact a student and protégé of Cleanthes.) Cleanthes is an "empirical theist" who defends the argument from design as the only foundation for a reasonable religiousness. Philo criticizes it, offers alternative hypotheses for the apparent order of the world, and shows that, in any case, no moral or religious attributes of God can be inferred from the design argument. Demea, who thinks Philo is on his side, offers an a priori argument for God's existence (from contingency and necessity), and after a lethal critique by Cleanthes, admits that his religiousness is really founded on the experience of evil and suffering in the world. At the end of Part 11, he leaves, and in the last part, 12, Philo appears to change his attitude toward the design argument—he now seems to accept it—and hence to reach some kind of consensus with Cleanthes. The work ends with Pamphilus commenting to his friend that he (Pamphilus) thought the position of Cleanthes was nearest to the truth.

The question "Who [among the interlocutors of the dialogue] speaks for Hume?" has preoccupied at least a third of the large number of essays on the *Dialogues* in the last fifteen or twenty years.[24] Of the four characters—Pamphilus, the schoolboy narrator of the discussion; Demea, the pious and orthodox; Cleanthes, the empirical philosopher; and Philo, the skeptical challenger—only Demea has never been identified as Hume's spokesman by anyone.[25]

It is tempting to propose that one of the reasons for the disagreements about what Hume intended is that some have read the *Dialogues* as Demea might, literally and unsuspiciously; some like Cleanthes, focusing concentratedly on the analysis of the design argument; and some like Philo, conscious always of the differences between the interlocutors.[26] Perhaps one could suggest that the best way to read the work would be successively as Demea-, Cleanthes-, and Philo-like, passing to the subsequent hermeneutic only when the motive is appropriate.

However that may be, to refer to different levels of understanding is not merely or primarily to refer to the ironical remarks of Hume in his other writings on religion and of Philo here—an irony commonly noted by some and denied by others—but rather to the difference of levels instituted by the form of the work; for example, in a dialogue, to whom is what is said addressed? Some remarks have their irony, their double meaning, built in, on their face, so to speak: it does not depend on character or context.[27] If we take into account the form of a work—for example, the dramatic structure of a dialogue—then different meanings of what is said may derive not only from what is said but to whom and when and in what circumstances it is said. It certainly cannot be assumed in a dialogue that what a speaker says can be taken as what the author thinks. But this is often overlooked. Consider the following hermeneutical principle: "[O]ne must assume that, no matter who the speaker, those arguments which seem most cogent, are probably to be ascribed to Hume."[28]

So before the question "Who speaks for Hume?" we have to place a prior issue. What Philo says to Demea and what he says to Cleanthes and what he says to Pamphilus may have to be evaluated differently. If Philo is always taken as speaking candidly and uniformly, then we arrive at the contradictions or inconsistencies that so many commentators have found in the *Dialogues*. Moreover, in a dialogue with more than two interlocutors, one may also have to consider how the different speeches might be taken by the listener(s). For example, it is perfectly clear that the speeches of Philo through Part 11 are not only a running criticism of Cleanthes and the design argument but that they are also intended to sound orthodox to Demea. Philo makes an explicit point several times of allying himself with Demea, not only in the critical responses to Cleanthes but in the vivid descriptions of the evil that men suffer in this world. (The only brief exception is at the end of Part 9 when Philo allows himself to endorse the criticisms that Cleanthes has made of Demea's metaphysical argument. But this is followed immediately by their duet of lamentation on the evils in the world, introduced by Demea's admission that his belief is not based on the refuted arguments but on the human situation.)

The fact that the dialogue of Cicero *On the Nature of the Gods* served as Hume's model in more ways than one—not only in form but in content—means that it may be worthwhile to look at some ways in which he departs from his model. One way in which he changes the dramatic structure is by having one of the interlocutors, Demea, leave before the end of the dialogue. The most discussed question among recent commentators has been why there appears to be a change, indeed to some a reversal,[29] in the position of Philo at the end of the dialogue (Part 12). He now seems to accept the design argument which has heretofore been the object of his unrelenting critique. It would appear likely that these two changes are connected. How?

In the first eleven parts, as noted earlier, Philo seeks to ally himself with Demea by implying that his criticisms of Cleanthes' design argument are meant to support a pious orthodoxy. (Compare the way in which Socrates often seems to ally himself with his interlocutors, e.g., Euthyphro.) This is why Cleanthes is brought forward as critic of Demea's metaphysical argument rather than leaving that role to Philo.[30] But after Philo and Demea join in magnifying the evil in the world in the first half of Part 10, Philo goes on to suggest the argument from evil and the difficulty that this causes for an empirical theist[31] like Cleanthes. Cleanthes responds (11) by proposing the "new hypothesis" of a finite God to account for evil, and Philo shows that this would still leave us with the same difficulty of inferring the existence of a benevolent and providential God—even finite—from the reality of the evil around us. As he warms to his argument he even draws the conclusion that the more powerful God is taken to be, the more must we think him responsible for the evil. At this point (the end of Part 11) Demea, who has been silent since the first section of 10, at last comes to see that Philo has not been his ally all along, and he shortly finds "some pretence" to depart.

And now a change does take place, but it is not a material change in Philo's position. He has never denied the appearance of order in the world, only that a designer was the best or even a very probable explanation of it. His own preference, if he had to defend a position, would be to argue for an internal principle of order like that of organisms (174), which, he agrees with Aristotle as against Thomas Aquinas, does not presuppose mind or design (179, 146). But now that Demea is gone, he can behave toward Cleanthes just the way he has behaved toward Demea: by stating his position in such a way as to maximize the area of agreement, to suggest his alliance with Cleanthes.

He readily concedes that not only is it logically possible to pose the hypothesis of a designer (he has all along conceded that much, arguing only that the confirmation for it was very weak and that such a designer is not the God of popular religion), but that the semblance of finality engages a strong propensity in us. "A purpose, an intention, or design strikes everywhere the most careless, the most stupid thinker" (214).[32] If there is a cause of order, analogous to that of organisms or of thought, isn't it merely balking at words to refuse to call it "mind" or "intelligence" or even "God"? But—and now he steps back from the debate—isn't the whole question a matter of words anyway, a verbal dispute? The theist will agree that the analogy with human design is very remote and hypothetical, the atheist will agree that there is some "remote inconceivable" analogy between whatever explains the order of nature and whatever explains "the rotting of a turnip, the generation of an animal, and the structure of human thought" (218).

> Where then, cry I [Philo] to both these antagonists, is the subject of your dispute? The theist allows, that the original intelligence is very different from human reason: The atheist allows, that the original principle of order bears some remote analogy to it. Will you quarrel, Gentlemen, about [that] . . . which admits not of any precise meaning, nor consequently of any determination?

When I read this passage, I cannot understand those commentators who say that Hume is defending a "minimal theism" at the end of the *Dialogues*. The conclusion is that no rigorous resolution is possible in estimating *how* similar the world is to a machine, or *how* similar its hypothetical designer would be to human designers. What leads to the difference between the two antagonists is not the empirical evidence or the logic of the argument but the inclinations that carry each one beyond the evidence.

What I want to argue, then, is that the only change in Part 12 is rhetorical, that Philo is behaving toward Cleanthes just the way he had behaved toward Demea in the first speeches of Part 1. Just as he had allied himself with Demea to attack Cleanthes' rational religiousness, so now he allies himself with Cleanthes to attack Demea's vulgar religiousness. His "reversal" is less substantive than it has appeared to some commentators, because it is not the admission of any data or inference that he had not admitted before but only the way in which he describes the argument. Not only does this seem evident in the language just cited (and even more in the summary conclusion at the end of the dialogue), but there are other signs of the shift. One is the change in vocabulary that appears in 12. Philo now denounces, in a duet with Cleanthes, the "bigots" and the "vulgar superstitions" that Cleanthes calls "false religion" (224). In fact Philo uses the pejorative term "superstition" ten times in Part 12, but he has not used it even once before.[33] "True religion" appears for the first time as opposed to "bigoted credulity" or "popular religion" or "vulgar superstitions." Clearly, Philo now feels able to use a vocabulary that he can share with Cleanthes but could not share with Demea, just as previously the two of them have spoken of the "theistic hypothesis" or the "hypothesis of design," while Demea spoke only of "perfect evidence" (145) and "infallible demonstration" (188).[34]

Moreover, Philo reiterates his earlier insistence that for a philosophical theist like Cleanthes, there is no way of inferring a providential and just and good God on the basis of the human situation. Even if there is order in nature, there is none in human life and history that bears witness to a just God, as Job long ago complained. Cleanthes makes no reply except to say that religion still offers the most agreeable picture that "human imagination" can suggest (224).

True, in his last words in the *Dialogues*, Philo returns to recommending philosophical skepticism as the most essential step toward being a "sound, believing Christian."[35] He explicitly notes that he is addressing this remark to Pamphilus—which tells us something about his perception of the latter. But this position, which he has maintained from his opening remarks in Part 1, is perfectly consistent with the claim that philosophical theism does not arrive at the Christian God.

So what is Philo's position in the end? Well, that neither theism nor atheism is proved or refuted by the admission of there being some principle that accounts for the order of nature; one can live with either in peace[36] so long as it is conceded that the inclination to assent to the proposition that God exists is motivated not by the evidence but by temperament and early training. "If this proposition be not capable of extension, variation, or more particular explication: If it afford no inference that affects human life, or can be the source of any action or forbearance. . . . [W]hat can the most inquisitive, contemplative, *and religious* man do more than give a plain, philosophical assent to the proposition" (227; emphasis mine).

Does Philo speak for Hume? I agree with Norman Kemp Smith and E. C. Mossner that he does,[37] *provided* that we weigh his remarks not by looking for a merely logical consistency but by considering when and to whom he says what he does. Apart from the reading suggested here, there is a curious bit of evidence in another departure of Hume from his Ciceronian and classical dialogue models.

After the passage quoted earlier in which Philo distinguishes himself from *both* the atheist and the theist ("Where then, cry I to both these antagonists . . ."), Hume added a note to the text that endorses the judgment that both dogmatist and skeptic go beyond the evidence available to them, and insists that the difference between them is merely verbal.[38] The note says, in effect: "What Philo is claiming here is correct." All the same it is a curious interjection.

Hume's own view can then be summarized on the basis of this reading as follows. Theism is a possible hypothesis to explain the apparent order of nature, just as is that of atheism—coupled, say, with the hypothesis of an internal principle of order—but there is no possibility of *proving* either hypothesis. That is why, in his letters and published essays, he declined to believe that there really were atheists (who *know* there is no God), except self-styled ones.[39] This position can be described as a strong, that is, impregnable agnosticism, because given the absolutely singular nature of the case—creating and/or ordering a world—we have no possible basis for compelling demonstration. All demonstration involving cause and effect rests for its cogency on experience, reason in this mode being "nothing but a species of experience" (150) and we do not have sufficient experience of other worlds to draw reliable conclusions.

Moreover, as we have seen, even if we allowed the possibility of the theistic hypothesis being true, no consequences would follow for popular religion, which must assume a particular providence and a just and good God to justify its practice (prayer, sacrifice, etc.). The data for such an inference are simply not consistent. If we *assumed* the existence of such a God, it is *possible* that such an assumption could be made consistent—especially if we abandoned infinity and omnipotence—with our conflicting experience of suffering and injustice (205). But then we are in the region of sheer conjecture, unsupported by prior evidence.

Religion is unnatural then in two ways. First, it is not a natural inclination, as is shown by the fact that it is not universal and has no specific object. Second, it is unnatural in the sense that it has no foundation in reason, contrary to the Deists of the Enlightenment. There is a philosophical kind of religiousness, namely, the mere assent to the proposition that God exists, but it is not motivated by any compelling evidence, it entails no consequences for human life, and it teaches no way of life other than that of ordinary, unreligious morality. Moreover, popular or vulgar religion in fact has historically had nothing but bad consequences for human beings.[40] So neither in its causes nor in its reasons nor in its consequences are there rational grounds for religiousness.

So with Hume, the confidence in proving the existence of the God of Christianity, which seemed to be introduced by Descartes and for which the progress of science had come to be the primary foundation, came to an end. Kant agreed and instead sought to reinterpret rational morality as requiring the presupposition of God's existence. The philosophy of religion took a new turn, or rather recast an old one. The philosophy of religion directed itself to the genealogy of religiousness, to trying to understand why human beings have this propensity toward piety and worship. Cicero had long ago, in the opening sentence of the *De Natura Deorum*, suggested that if we cannot learn about the existence and nature of the divine from such an enquiry, we shall at least learn something about man.[41] Through Feuerbach and Marx and Nietzsche and the rise of anthropology and psychoanalysis the quest to understand religion as a curious human creation grew.

Religion and Faith

I want to end by remarking briefly on some differences between the conception of religion and faith that Hume takes as his target and the conception of religiousness and faith in another tradition, that of Thomas Aquinas.

Why did Hume seek to understand the nature of religiousness by writing a history? A century before he wrote, the emergence of the "state of nature" theories of Hobbes and Locke had opened up the question of whether things that had previously been assumed to be natural to man—for example, being a political animal—were not rather the result of developments in history (or prehistory as we would say). That question expanded as more human properties—for example, language and moral obligations[42]—came to seem susceptible of historical rather than natural explanation. Justice, Hume argued, is "artificial," which does not mean that it is arbitrary—it is extremely useful if not necessary to human society—but that it is not a natural, innate obligation. History came more and more to seem capable of giving an account of what had been called human nature. Hume was consistent in seeing that if this were the case with respect to religion, then the development from polytheism to theism could just as well reverse itself.

Thomas Aquinas, following the classical tradition, denied that there is any dichotomy between the things that human beings bring into existence and those that are natural. What is natural to us is not merely our genetic endowment, but the human goods to which we are innately inclined, even though we may have to experiment and invent in order to discover the proper way to realize those goods. So he can agree with Hume that religion is a phenomenon human in origin, and not founded on any philosophical arguments for the existence of divinity. But he can also locate religion in a yet-unshaped innate inclination of human beings to realize their need for help in achieving their good[43] without their being clear about what that good truly is or how to seek the help. Religion is as natural as that aspiration and that realization are, and it unfolds as the attempt, profoundly shaped by the society we grow up in, to say and do what is needful in order to stand in the right relation to that superior nature "which men call divine."[44]

Undeveloped man may indeed seek his good in the gifts of fortune, and implore the aid of imaginary powers, just as justice may first come into view as helping one's friends and harming one's enemies. But thoughtful reason, over time, exercises some measure of pruning and clarifying the good we seek. Homer's Achilles learns that death is not the greatest of all evils or life the greatest of all goods, and Homer's Odysseus learns that death at home is preferable to immortal pleasures in exile. So religion can be a natural virtue without having to emerge automatically, provided we delineate it from the normative state toward which it inclines. Then we shall say that far from being characterized by a concern with the good and bad fortune of future events, true religiousness teaches us not to worry about the morrow.

As for the Enlightenment notion of a higher form of "true religion" or "true theism," Hume surely thought that superior to ritualistic religion of any kind. "To know God," says Philo to Cleanthes (quoting Seneca), "is to worship Him: it is to think rightly and reverently of Him." That view may commend itself to one for whom nothing is present to the mind but its impressions, but if man is an embodied spirit, his reverence must be more than mental, and religiousness must incarnate the devotion of the soul in corporeal expression. Only so long can it exist in the soul itself.[45] Religiousness for Aquinas is not thinking rightly about God; it is placing the good that God wills for us first in our lives, and part of that good we seek is doing things that acknowledge his holiness, his being above us, as the child honors her father and mother by kissing them goodnight on the way to bed. The action does not so much express the inward disposition as bring it to life, sustain it in existence. Everything is made more perfect by subjection to its superior, Aquinas wrote:[46] body to soul, child to parent, disciple to teacher, man to God. If man is the greatest thing in the universe, then religiousness, which entails the acknowledgment of superiority, cannot be a virtue: that seems to have been the view of Hume and many of his successors. For then indeed *pietas* would have no other object than our parents and the community that has endowed us with what humanity we have.

Cleanthes says that "Locke seems to have been the first Christian, who ventured openly to assert, that faith was nothing but a species of reason, that religion was only a branch of philosophy" (DNR 138). Faith in this view is simply the belief that God exists. Many find it natural so to think today. If someone says, "Do you believe in God?" we commonly take that to mean "Do you think that God exists?" Faith is often taken—as Hume's term "the religious hypothesis" suggests—as tantamount to the belief that God exists.

But for Aquinas, faith is not fundamentally belief *that* some proposition p is true. Faith is, in his conception, a "theological virtue." It has God as its object, it reaches God: it is believing God. *Credere est credere aliud.* Faith, we could say, is believing G that p. It is not primarily a "propositional attitude"; it is not believing that p, or believing other human beings; it is believing God when he speaks to us in the words of men, as Saint Augustine discovered in the Garden.

Making sense of that understanding of faith requires understanding it in the context of time and being and creation, to which Augustine devoted the last three books of the *Confessions*.[47] But that is too far afield for now.

CHAPTER NINE

Religion and Natural Law

I

My aim here is to reflect on the religious origin of natural law and on the later history of that relationship. To begin, let us draw attention to the strangeness of the term "natural law." It may not seem strange to you, so the first thing to do is to recall how paradoxical it originally was. Familiarity breeds understanding, or the illusion of understanding, and we are accustomed to speaking of "laws of nature" in the physical sciences, as well as to speaking of theories of natural law in the field of jurisprudence. A recent book whose author rejects any ontological foundation for natural law nevertheless affirms that "natural law's subject is the moral analysis of positive law."[1] In this—not uncommon—sense of the term, it simply refers to any theory of the moral ground of legislation.

For the Greeks, however, the terms "nature" and "law" (*physis* and *nomos*) designated two quite distinct realms: the realm of things determined by their own proper essences, not by human initiative, and the realm of things called into being by man, by the arts and ordinances and customs of human beings (agriculture and poetry, politics and praxis). The distinction is not wholly unlike that familiar to us as the distinction of nature and culture, namely, that which is already there when homo sapiens comes on the scene, and that which emerges through the extraordinary ability of man to produce a world of human things, the world of culture. Law or human convention could not change the realm of nature, but it could superimpose on that realm the patterns of human ordering—through customs, enactments, technology, and various kinds of shaping of thought and behavior.

To describe the difference between nature and law in this last way—as superimposed—is to suggest a way of thinking about the relation of the two realms which arose explicitly with the Sophists or wise men of fifth-century Greece. They viewed the realm of law or convention as an artificial imposition on human life of ways of acting which were at variance with the natural tendencies of human beings. Human nature was the same everywhere, but the accumulating knowledge of the diversity of forms of social organization, of religion, and of morality led to the conclusion that the conventional ways were artificial (in the depreciatory sense of that word). In a manner which recurs in the modern period, they came to think that our ways, our laws, and our customs are no more right than those of other peoples—that all the different patterns of social organization are equally conventional and equally superimposed upon human nature.[2]

In the dialogues of Plato, we meet many such interlocutors who declare, for example, like Thrasymachus in the *Republic*, that by nature the strong do and should dominate the weak, and that conventional restrictions on that dominance are artificial and have no obligatory validity. In this perspective, law and conventional patterns of belief and action are sheer additions to nature, cloaking the true nature of human beings, and that is why cultures are so many and so diverse. The good life which we seek together, the laws and customs by which we specify what is right and wrong, are mere conventions hallowed only by their ancient character and reinforced by tales of the gods and the afterlife.

Plato's Socrates undertakes to show that what follows from the diversity of social patterns is not that there is no normative standard of justice by which to guide ourselves in legislating and acting but rather that that standard is not sufficiently known to us because it requires the cultivation of rational inquiry; it requires philosophy. Through disciplined inquiry in dialogue, we can come to see that there is a nonconventional and universal good for human beings, that its embodiment in the community and in the individual is justice, and that justice consists in the ordering of our lives not by desire or passion but by reason. The virtues, the truly admirable qualities of a good individual, are the impress of reason on our desire for pleasure and our passion for self-assertion so that our actions acknowledge what is due to others as well as to ourselves. Similarly, the positive laws of a community that is just according to nature will seek what is due to (i.e., what is good for) each of its parts and members.

All of this is only description, of course, not argument. Lest it seem too easy, let me mention one argument against Thrasymachus, as Socrates unfolds it. Do the strong in dominating the weak seek what is good for themselves? (Hard to say no.) Do they seek what is really good for them or what is only apparently good? (Hard to say apparently.) Can they be mistaken about what is really good for them? (Again, hard to deny they may be deceived.) Then there is a good to be discovered which should guide their actions, a good not immediately identical with what they think to be good, and that leads us out into the trackless inquiry.

But the reason for merely summarizing the positions is that the point to be made is simply that Plato's Socrates does not, no more than the Sophists, think of the natural norm as a law. Laws may and should be made by taking one's bearings from the form or essence of justice, but that form exists eternally the same. It is not the product of enactment, by the gods or by any legislator, but exists timelessly as do the truths of mathematics, whether known or embodied now or ever.

Aristotle, although he thinks of the essences not as merely appearing in the phenomena but as actually informing the substances that exist, as existentially multiplied and inherent in them, retains the conviction that there are things that are declared right by law and there are things that are right by nature. If there is nothing that is by nature right then all right is legal or conventional. But we spontaneously and correctly acknowledge the conventional differences among societies—systems of coinage, traffic laws, etc.—while refusing to acknowledge that genocide is merely a matter of such conventional difference in customs. For Aristotle as for Plato, enactments and customs and constitutions can be assessed by reference to what is by nature (objectively, as we would say) right or wrong, good or bad for human beings. For Aristotle as for Plato, the Sophists were wrong to think that nature stands under culture (so to speak): nature stands above or beyond culture as the norm of its laws and customs. For Aristotle as for Plato, *nomos* may and usually will to some extent overlap with *physis*: that is why there will be some things more or less common to the laws and customs of all societies. But because nature in its fullness is hidden, and because its exigencies will differ in different circumstances, laws will also differ.

And now we are in a position to underline the oddity of "natural." Despite all the analysis and argument aimed at discerning a nonconventional foundation for politics and morality, a foundation in nature, the term "natural law" does not come into regular use until the first century A.D., in the writing of the Jewish philosopher Philo of Alexandria. There are, in all the corpus of Greek writers over the five centuries, only a handful of occurrences of the term "natural law" or "law of nature," and in none of them is the term used to mean a law which is a nonconventional standard for morals and for political enactments. Helmut Koester has shown persuasively, I think, that the common attribution of the concept to the Stoics is mistaken.[3]

Among Latin writers, it is, of course, Cicero who has been considered the primary source of a natural law teaching, prior to the introduction of the Biblical revelation. However, Cicero does not maintain that there is a law of nature or in nature, although his language has been read as embodying such a position.[4] There are several reasons for this standard reading. First, Cicero does speak of a *vera lex* (*Aeterna lex*, etc.) as the measure of civil law, and of a *jus naturae*, but he rarely speaks of a *lex naturale* (or a *lex naturae*.) So far as I know, the latter occurs only once in the *de Natura Deorum* (1.36) (where Koester has shown it is a [mis?] translation of the Greek *logos physeos*, not *nomos physeos*), once in the *de Legibus* (1.21.56) (where Quintus speaks of *naturam sequi et eius quasi lege vivere*), and several times in the *de Officis*. As for the term *jus naturae*, that is hardly conclusive since it normally means what is by nature right, as in Aristotle's *to dikaion physikon* (*N. Ethics*, 1134b). (Compare, e.g., *de Leg*. 1.10.28.)

What about *vera lex*? This term appears both in the *de Republica* (3.22.33) and the *de Legibus* (2.4.10) in conjunction with the grounding of such a true law in nature, a law which precedes all written law. What exactly is this unwritten law? Here is the definition offered in *de Legibus*:

Law is the highest reason, implanted in nature, which commands what ought to be done and forbids the opposite. This reason, when firmly fixed and fully developed in the human mind, is law.[5]

This is the sort of language which later Christian thinkers can and will take over to characterize what they call natural law. But Cicero continues:

> Therefore, since there is nothing better than reason, and since it exists both in man and god, the first common possession of man and god is reason. But those who have reason in common must also have right reason in common. And since right reason is law, we must believe that men have law also in common with the gods. . . . Hence we must now conceive of this whole universe as one commonwealth of which both gods and men are members. (1.7.23)

So this unwritten law is reason, which is a possession common to men and gods and makes them members together of one commonwealth. But not just reason: it is reason characterized by its rectitude (*recta ratio*), by its wisdom, by its insight. Insight into what?

> Therefore law is the distinction between things just and unjust, made in agreement with that primal and most ancient of all things, nature; and in conformity to nature's standard are framed those human laws which inflict punishment upon the wicked but defend and protect the good. (2.5.13)

Note that it is human laws (discussed in book two) which punish and protect. The true or eternal law has no such sanctions, according to book one.

> But if it is a penalty, the fear of punishment, and not the wickedness itself, that is to keep men from a life of wrongdoing and crime, then no one can be called unjust, and wicked men ought rather to be regarded as imprudent; (1.14.40)

Right (*ius*) is based, not on men's opinions, but on nature (1.10.28). Cicero's position—as I read it—is that reason, as it exists in the wise, apprehends nature, that nature is a norm, and that in rightly apprehending (*recta ratio*) that norm, reason commands right conduct, i.e., conduct according to that norm. As thus commanding, reason *is* law, indeed *vera lex*. If this is a correct reading, then to speak of an unwritten, eternal, true law is not to speak of a law *in* nature, but rather of a law which is based on nature as a norm. It is reason, not law, which is *insita in natura*.

But this position is not fundamentally different from that of Cicero's Greek predecessors. Socrates, in the *Republic* of Plato, speaks constantly of human nature and of the nature of the virtues as a standard which the philosopher-king, as legislator, must come to know (e.g., *Rep.* 501[b]). That human law should be based on nature insofar as possible is a common teaching of classical philosophy.[6]

It is easy to see how Cicero's language provides an occasion for reading back into his dialogues the subsequent ideas of natural law. In fact, his language in book two of the *de Legibus* made this all but inevitable. For there he speaks of "that law which the gods have given to the human race" (2.4.8) and asserts that "the true and primal law, applied to command and prohibition, is the right reason of supreme Jupiter" (2.4.10). Moreover, he there specifies that "god himself will deal out punishment" to wrongdoers, something which, as we have seen, he explicitly denies in book one. Why the difference?

Cicero himself carefully notes the ground of the difference at the end of book one.

> ...when [the divine and eternal mind of man] realizes that it is born to take part in the life of a state, it will estimate that it must employ not merely the usual method of subtle dialectic [*disputatio*], but also the more copious method of exposition [*perpetua oratio*], considering, for example, how to rule nations, establish laws, punish the wicked, protect the good ... [and] publish to fellow-citizens precepts conducive to their well-being ... (1.24.62)

For political purposes, it is not enough to show that reason can discern what is by nature right and wrong. Not all will be able to achieve the *recta ratio* which is capable of such discernment, and thereby to see the harm they do to themselves in acting wrongly. These will need to have a law given to them, given by the gods, and sanctioned by divine punishments and rewards. This law is unfolded at length in the subsequent chapters of the *de Legibus*, but its functional character is clearly indicated in the above quote (compare 2.3.7).

> Who will deny that such beliefs are useful when he remembers . . . how many persons are deterred from crime by the fear of divine punishment, and how sacred an association of citizens becomes when the immortal gods are made members of it, either as judges or as witnesses? (2.7.16)

It is not irrelevant to note that the Stoic theology which underlies the discussion of books two *et seq.* was subjected to lethal and unanswered criticism in the *de Natura Deorum*, written in the same period.

Philo of Alexandria, who stands in the confluence of the Judaic and Greek philosophical traditions, is the first writer to employ the term systematically and commonly in his texts. The reason does not seem far to seek: it rests in the conception of creation and the Creator-God who has brought all things into being. Natural law is an ontological concept, a corollary of the notion of a Sovereign who rules the whole which He has created and providentially guides, whose will is law. Just as the political legislator orders the lives of the citizens by the laws which direct or proscribe behavior, so the Divine Legislator, in Philo's view, orders the behavior of His creatures which He has brought into being.

> [Moses' account of creation] consists of an account of the creation of the world, implying that the world is in harmony with the Law, and the Law with the world, and that the man who observes the Law is constituted thereby a loyal citizen of the world, regulating his doings by the purpose and will of nature, in accordance with which the entire world itself also is administered.

> Now since every well-ordered state has a constitution, the citizen of the world enjoyed of necessity the same constitution as did the

whole world: and this constitution is nature's right relation, more properly called an ordinance or dispensation, seeing it is a divine law. . . .

. . . God also exercises forethought on the world's behalf. For that the maker should care for the thing made is required by the laws and ordinances of nature, and it is in accordance with these that parents take thought beforehand for children.[7]

As this political analogy suggests, the law of the Creator need not be thought of as inherent in the nature of each individual thing: it may be simply the ordinance which the Creator prescribes to their action. And that indeed appears to be the way in which Philo thought of the law of nature. It is, so to speak, an objective genitive rather than a subjective genitive: it is for the law *for* creatures, the law given to them by God.

And again, the reason why Philo thinks of it in this way does not seem far to seek. There is, as is well known, no term in the Hebrew Bible for the Greek notion of "nature" (*physis*). Leo Strauss among others has noted that, for the Hebrews, revelation had primarily the character of law, Torah, while for Christianity it had primarily the character of truth, of Logos. So for Philo, thinking in the Hebrew tradition, "the law of nature is not an immanent law, but it is the law of the transcendent creator who rules His creation."[8] The law of nature is for him the Torah, understood in an encompassing sense as God's ordinances for the created world. The Maker of the world is also its lawgiver, and so the Greek distinction—and sometimes opposition—between law and nature is thus replaced by the distinction between God's natural law and the many codes of human societies.

So with Philo, for the first time, the concept of natural law emerges and takes up its place in the Western tradition. And its ontological basis is clear: it is because nature is created by God that it lies under law. Natural law has its source, logically and historically, in Divine Law, and in the Biblical tradition, not in classical philosophy. (That's the first point that I want to make.)

II

St. Augustine, for all his prolific literary production, says very little about natural law or, as he generally calls it, the eternal law. That is perhaps odd, given the prominence of law in Roman civilization and given his constant concern with questions of morality. Only in the early dialogue *de Libero Arbitrio* is there anything like a thematic consideration. In that dialogue, directed against the Manichean teaching on evil, he discusses the intrinsic limitations of human positive law in rectifying man's actions. The scope of law is restricted to a small part of human life, and it can only direct the externality of action, i.e., it cannot compel the right motives. There must be, says Augustine—if God is concerned with the rightness of actions—some "more powerful and secret law" which is known to all human beings and by which their actions are measured.

Here, as commonly with Augustine, there is a Biblical text as well as a philosophical source which underlies his argument. In his Epistle to the Romans (2:14), St. Paul had written that those peoples who do not have the Torah "practise by nature (*physei*) the things of the Law." Since nature is God's creation, it is for Augustine more than a metaphor to speak of a law of nature by which creatures are directed. All we have to do is suppose that the law of nature is promulgated, and experience as well as St. Paul give us ground for so supposing. The eternal law may thus be defined as the divine reason or will of God, prescribing the conservation of the natural order and forbidding any breach of it.[9]

The consolidation and culmination of this teaching about natural law comes in the synthesis of Aristotelianism and Christianity which is the work of Thomas Aquinas. The aspect which I want to address may be approached in the following way: the Gospels use the term *harmatia* for what we call "sin." But for the Greeks, the term connotes missing the mark, going astray—without any reference beyond the natural order. What is the difference between this use which one finds in Aristotle, for example, and the Christian use of it (*peccatum*)? How does Aquinas bring these into harmony?

There is a single question of the *Summa Theologiae* which displays in brief compass the reconstruction of Augustine's doctrine into an Aristotelian framework and the merging of this with the creation context.[10]

Aquinas begins with a general definition: "sin," he says, properly names an inordinate act, a disordered act, and, as such, it is opposed to virtue or to that to which virtue disposes. Disordered with respect to what? Well, just as virtue is a good disposition to act in accord with the nature of the subject having it, so vice is a bad disposition to act in a way not conforming to that nature. Man's nature is specifically rational, so an act not conforming to his nature is an act lacking reasonable order. It is *contra naturam hominis in quantum est contra ordinem rationis*.[11]

Similarly, Aristotle in his *Nichomachean Ethics* describes the human good as consisting in activity which manifests reason, since reason is the species-specific property of human beings. Aristotle does not use the language of "order" in the *Ethics*, but it does not appear alien to his thought. Not only is an individual nature the internal principle of a sequenced development of the individual possessing the nature, but the universe of such natures is itself ordered by their orientation toward a prime mover. "The world is not such that one thing has nothing to do with another, but they are connected," he writes in the *Metaphysics*, and the good of the whole consists in its internal order, which in turn depends on that orientation toward the highest being.[12]

What needs to be underlined here, to see the specifically Thomistic inflection of the teaching, is that Aquinas can describe *harmatia* in terms so apparently congruent with Aristotle's thought (an action contrary to reason) and at the same time (in the same question of the *Summa*) conclude the discussion by asserting that sin is fittingly defined just as Augustine had defined it, namely, "a word, deed or desire contrary to the Eternal Law." The junction between these two perspectives is, once again, the doctrine of creation. Sin is indeed an act contrary to the order which man's reasonable nature discerns as good, but that rational nature is God's work, its innate inclinations are embodiments of God's Eternal Law. Hence Aquinas can write, "to depart from the rule of reason suffices to make an act evil," and at the same time can write, "this turning aside from the rule of reason results from man's turning away from God, to whom man ought to be united by his right use of reason."[13] The theologian will, he says, consider sin chiefly as an offense against God, and the moral philosopher, as something contrary to reason. For both, the norm of rational human nature points to what the good is for man, what constitutes human fulfillment. God, Aquinas writes, is offended by us only because we act against our own proper good, the good that reason sets before us.[14] The synthesis which Aquinas celebrated between a foundation in nature for right and wrong, and the promulgation of a divine Eternal Law for creatures proved to be difficult to maintain in its integrality. The major questions which pressed against it were two, and the first concerned the notion of law itself. For something to be apprehended as a law, does it not need to be apprehended as a command, as an imperative? And is that the way in which what is by nature good is apprehended? Plato and Aristotle seem to have understood the morally good as what presents itself to a reason undistorted by appetite or ambition as naturally desirable. To act contrary to that good is wrong, unreasonable, unwise—but is violating such a standard or rule of right reason *ipso facto* disobeying a command? Is the good, apprehended as to-be-done, or evil, apprehended as to-be-avoided, thereby known as law? Even if we add that the good congruent with man's rational nature is understood as congruent with a *created* nature, so that it is understood as designed by God to be man's good, do we arrive at the notion of law? Is it not necessary to add that God has commanded, by an act of His will, that that good is to be done? It is one thing to know the rules of a game, and even to know that it is good to follow them if the end of the game (recreation, honest victory, satisfaction) is to be achieved—it seems to be something additional to be told or to know that one will be punished by an observer for not following the rules.

Aquinas had maintained that command was an act of the intellect[15] because one can command by nature only if one has knowledge of what is good. The authority of political office may be instituted, and the holder of office may therefore have the authority to command, but though it is desirable that the officeholder know what is good, his instituted authority does not rest on that. Not so with one who has authority by nature. However, Duns Scotus already challenged that claim by asserting that law was an act of the will. It is not enough, he argued, to know the rule or standard of good action; an act of volition, of command, was necessary for a rule to have the force of law and hence to oblige under pain of sanction.

The second question which pressed against the Thomistic synthesis had already appeared in the famous set of theses condemned by Archbishop Tempier of Paris in 1277. One of the propositions condemned was that God could not have created the world differently, other than it is. To maintain this, it seemed, was to deny the omnipotence of God, to suggest that He was constrained by necessities to which He had to bow, to assert that He could do no other. If we combine this with the first question, we can see how one could be led to believe that God's will was supreme, and that the laws which He in fact enacted for His creation might have been quite different. And the crucial consequence of this view is that we cannot know by our unaided natural reason what is necessarily right or wrong for man, because to claim to know that would be to claim to know how God *must* have ordained human conduct. This is the so-called "voluntarist" conception of God's relation to the world, and its consequences for natural science as well as for morality were radical.[16] The conception which is its dialectical opposite we may call the "rationalist" or "essentialist" view—and we may identify that with the view of classical philosophy, the position, namely, that what is of necessity good for man by nature is discernible by unaided human reason. (Let us note that this was not the integral conception of Thomas Aquinas.) And we may, for the purposes of exposition, identify the voluntarist view with that of Philo.

Now the problem with the rationalist view, in the context of the Christian tradition within which this dialectic was unfolded, is that, as we have noted, it is not easy to see how such discernment could have of itself a juridical or legislative aspect. In grappling with this problem, one solution which aimed at maintaining the truth of both of the dialectically opposed views was to distinguish two different senses of law. Gregory of Rimini wrote that one could distinguish an indicative law, *lex indicans*, which evinced the intent of the legislator, and a prescriptive law, *lex praescriptiva*, which bore on its face, so to speak, the imperative or command character of the law. Even if the legislator-God did not exist, Gregory wrote, the natural law would still be knowable by unaided human reason, but only as a *lex indicans*, as a rule or standard by which human actions were to be measured and judged.[17] To know the natural law as a *lex praescriptiva*, as commanding man to act rightly under sanction of punishment, we must know of God's voluntary enactment of the law.

The great Jesuit theologian, Francisco Suarez, in his *De Legibus ac Deo Legislatore*, considered sensibly enough that this distinction was a purely verbal one. A mere *lex indicans*, he asserted, was simply not a law in any genuine sense (*lex vera*). But on the other hand, he said natural law was not a genuine *lex praescriptiva* merely by being an enactment of God's will. God commanded to be done what was right by human nature, so the natural law as His legislation was not merely law because He willed it so, but He willed it so because it was right by nature for human beings.[18] He thus rejected both the pure voluntarist and the pure rationalist views and understood himself to be reasserting the integral position of Thomas Aquinas.

It was in response to the voluntarist conception of natural law that Hugo Grotius, following Suarez and Gregory of Rimini, came to declare that natural law would retain its validity as a measure of human acts even if God did not exist, and it was under this rationalist program that the influential modern versions of natural law and especially that of John Locke were defended.

And that's the second point I want to make: the way in which the notion of natural law was developed within the theological context of scholasticism led to a stressing of its embedding in nature, its independent intelligibility, its accessibility to natural reason. And despite the voluntarist controversy, it came about that natural law seemed to share something of the same sense of scientific objectivity and religious neutrality that the sciences of inanimate nature were so successfully representing.

III

John Locke, at the beginning of his *Second Treatise of Government*, declares that there is a law of nature "which obliges every one: and reason, which is that law, teaches all mankind."[19] It was just the question of juridical obligation which, as we have seen, had preoccupied the late scholastic discussion: if natural law is something accessible to reason independently of any knowledge of God, how is it known as *law*, i.e., as an authoritative command which obliges in conscience and is sanctioned?

Locke finesses this question by following Hobbes in asserting that there is no obligatory and unconditional good-to-be-pursued which is knowable to us—except the instinct or law of self-preservation. That law is obligatory or rather it is inherently efficacious; it is efficacious whether or not we know it as a law. Beyond that fundamental and undeniable good, men legitimately differ on what they conceive to be the human good. Such conceptions differ because human beings find different things pleasant and fulfilling. Thus Locke lays the foundation for contemporary democracy by denying that any person knows more than another about what the human good is: we are all equal in the politically relevant aspect because no one can claim any greater knowledge about the human good than anyone else and hence cannot claim any *right* to legislate for us.

Hence the conception of law and of natural law changes: it no longer directs us toward any telos or fulfillment of human nature or of the human community, because none is reliably knowable. Positive law must rather aim at allowing many conceptions of the good life to be pursued. If all conceptions of the pursuit of happiness are relative to the individual, so far as any objective determination goes, only a society which acknowledges and is founded on that fact is a good society. The good society will be one which allows the liberty of each citizen to choose his or her own way of life, compatible with others doing the same.

Locke consistently draws the consequence of that position: the laws of such a society, apart from having to respect the natural law of self-preservation and the rights consequent upon it, will simply be decided by the majority. And the majority's power to enact legislation is not, as Aristotle had argued, based on their claim to better insight into what is good than any expert, whether theologian or philosopher, but simply on their numerical strength:

> . . . that which acts [for] any community, being [based on] only the consent of the individuals of it, and it being necessary to that which is one body to move one way; it is necessary the body should move that way whither the greater force carries it, which is the consent of the majority. . . .[20]

The majority functions like the mass of a body in Newton's mechanics: it is just a fact that a body will be carried where its center of gravity inclines it.

That is, when you think about it, an incredibly radical position. The emerging democratic forms of government were protected from its consequences by the still-pervasive religious consensus and the tradition of moral law. But the consequences nevertheless worked themselves out as the strength of the religious consensus declined and the tradition of public morality waned.

John Stuart Mill, writing a century and a half later, unintentionally carried the consequences forward while trying to preserve a space for freedom of thought and action against what de Tocqueville had called the danger of the tyranny of the majority. In his essay *On Liberty*, he argued that it was in the self-interest of society to allow unlimited freedom of discussion and of action that was self-regarding, i.e., which did not harm others, however much those others might find it wrong or immoral. The majority, for reasons of utilitarian self-interest, ought not to impose its own opinions of what is right to say or to do on the members of society, or to proscribe the expression of opposing views. It is in society's self-interest to allow such liberty because only by hearing opposing views expressed could the majority have the opportunity to exchange its possibly erroneous opinions for true opinions or at least to have its correct opinions confirmed and clarified.

There is an irony in the fact that Mill's argument was motivated by his sense of intellectual and moral superiority to the opinions of the majority. Indeed he writes—in words which no public figure would use today—that

> No government by a democracy or [even] a numerous aristocracy, either in its political acts or in the opinions . . . which it fosters, ever did or could rise above mediocrity [—] except in so far as the sovereign [Majority] have let themselves be guided . . . by the counsels and influence of a more highly gifted . . . one or few.[21]

The irony lies in the fact that his argument entails that all opinions must be treated as equal.

His dilemma comes about in the following way. In order to make the case for freedom of thought and discussion, he finds himself obliged to argue that we can never be sure that the opinion we now hold is true, and if it is in fact false we will never know that unless we allow it to be challenged. We will thus have denied ourselves the opportunity of exchanging our possibly false opinion for a true or truer one. That sounds persuasive, especially to our democratic ears, until one asks how we will know that the new opinion we arrive at is true, if we can never know for sure that the opinion we hold at any time is true? How will we know that the exchange doesn't go in the wrong direction, and we end up having exchanged a true opinion for a false one?

Why is that a dilemma? Why can't Mill simply say that we know some opinions to be true? Because then one would have a warrant, at least, for proscribing the public promotion of the erroneous opinion or for limiting its access to the organs of its propagation among the people. So although he believes in the superiority of the few and the mediocre minds of the many, Mill is forced back, in practice, to Locke's position that all opinions about what is good for us must be treated as if they were equal. Indeed, it is not only opinions about what is good but opinions about scientific, religious, and philosophical matters which must be treated equally in Mill's view. (The only exception he allows is for mathematics.) Our hope—or our faith—is that, somehow, the opinions we hold and on the basis of which we legislate and act are for the most part true, even though we have no way of being sure.

And that is the end of the third act. Natural law, separated from its connection with the religious idea of creation, separated from its earlier ontological foundation, not only lost the character of a knowable moral *law*, it also lost its previously invested confidence in the knowability of human nature, i.e., of its fulfillment or happiness. By no means does the analysis I have traced imply *post hoc, ergo propter hoc*. By no means does it imply that what is by nature the good life for human beings must be deemed unknowable outside the context of religious belief. Classical philosophy is sufficient counterexample for that. And of course, the axial figures whom I have touched upon are hardly the whole story: many other developments contributed to the denouement.

IV

I want to do two things in the time left. One is to suggest some aspects of the present scene which may perhaps make what I have said seem more recognizable as a self-portrait of U.S. contemporary Americans. The second is to reflect on the present relation of religion and natural law.

First, then, some remarks about the situation in which we find ourselves. Strange as it seems compared to what every schoolboy and schoolgirl knows, even the understanding of the natural sciences has come to stand in Mill's position. The most influential contemporary portrait of the development of natural science, that of Thomas Kuhn in *The Structure of Scientific Revolutions*, has described persuasively how scientific theories succeed one another without having to say that the succeeding theory is truer than the one it succeeds. As for the notion of truth generally, it is presently construed by many philosophers as equivalent to the notion of "warranted assertibility." That is, one is justified in asserting as true what is agreed to be appropriately warranted by the competent participants in whatever form of inquiry we are dealing with. As for politics and morality, we are all familiar with the phrases, "Personally I think that . . . [such and such] . . . is wrong, but I don't have any right to impose my views on others" and "Don't impose your values on me."

I run the risk here, in descending to the vernacular, of sounding like an old curmudgeon. But my aim is to understand where we are as a people, as a political community. My claim is not that anything goes, that there is no agreed-upon set of values. Our world is not in chaos, people doing anything they please, thinking anything they like. There is some good work going on in the writings of moral and political philosophers. But it does appear to me that as a people, as a body of citizens in public discourse, we have lost confidence in our ability to settle differences by rational argument. We do not think and act in a tradition of rational political and moral inquiry but in many disparate ones. We no longer have "self-evident truths" to begin discussion from. As a result, we find ourselves in the position which Locke postulated long ago: the majority decides.

Why do we have as much agreement as we do? Well, partly of course because most of us belong to the majority, and we share the opinions on the basis of which we act and legislate. My concern is that we seem to have lost confidence in our ability to show that those opinions are true, to exhibit their rightness, even to ourselves: our substitute is commitment. And partly we have agreement because the factors which I indicated earlier retarded the consequences of Locke's position are all still operative for us. We are, for example, still an extraordinarily religious people among the Western democracies. We have, despite the Constitution, a de facto religious test for office. By drawing our legislators from a quite small segment of the population, we manage to get a number of what Jefferson called "natural aristocrats" in high office. But it cannot be a politically healthy situation when so many questions deeply affecting the human quality of our lives are decided simply by majority vote. For majority opinion, like all opinions, drifts when it is not anchored by a tradition or by insight.

The second and last thing to do is to reflect on the present situation of religion and natural law in our public life. If the situation which I have just sketched is at all accurate, it is to be expected that the eternal law of God, even when it is presented in the form of arguments deriving from the tradition of natural law, can only be perceived as the assertion of one's private or group religious conscience. For the tradition of natural law was a product of the religious teaching about creation and the Creator. And the notion of nature, of an unchanging objective norm for the guidance of our lives, was in fact carried to us over the centuries in the Church's self-understanding, in its teaching and reflection on its faith. Its self-understanding, elaborated over those centuries, involved a defense of the notion of nature as knowable to all in some measure, so that its moral teaching was consistently, from the earliest times, distinguished from a divine command doctrine, i.e., the mere assertion of God's will. For God created through His Word.

I do not want to sound homiletic. I state the fact that the Church bears witness to the eternal—not only to the eternal God, but necessarily also to the eternal law, to the relation of human beings, whether they know it or not, to an unchanging truth about themselves. The crucial question for man is whether he is related to something unchanging and eternal.

CHAPTER TEN

American Reflections on a Century
of Catholic Social Teaching

The centennial of the School of Philosophy comes at a time helpful for looking back over a century of Catholic social philosophy, for the modern emergence of Catholic social teaching may reasonably be said to have begun with the encyclicals of Leo XIII, *Rerum Novarum* in particular (1891). Not only did that encyclical enunciate many of the principles of such teaching and formulate their application to the contemporary political economies of the West, but it became a reference point for the later papal teaching of such encyclicals as *Quadregesimo Anno*, *Populorum Progressio*, and *Centesimus Annus*.

   I want to remind you of two topics in particular that were emphasized by Leo XIII and to trace some of their subsequent evolution. They are, first, the responsibility of the state to ensure justice in the economic relations of workers and employers and, second, the responsibility of the state with respect to religion. I want to reflect on the conceptions of the nature of political society and of the state as they present themselves in that evolution. As will become clear, the two topics have some interconnected philosophical issues in common. And so I shall track three Catholic thinkers—indeed Thomists—in America (two of them transplanted) who have written on those issues.

I

Leo saw the responsibility of political authority for the promotion of justice in the area of economics as steering between the two opposing doctrines of ownership by the state, on one hand, and the proscription of any state "meddling," on the other: socialism vs. laissez-faire. Against the first he defended the right of private property and the usefulness of a market system, and against the latter he affirmed the right and responsibility of the state to insure that the requirements of justice were not lost sight of in the inequalities produced by the laissez-faire capitalist economies.

More specifically, in seeking to outline the need for insuring greater equality between the contracting parties of entrepreneurs and workers, he asserted, for example, the right of the workers to organize themselves into unions in order to aggregate some bargaining power in negotiating employment with the owners and managers of capital. That teaching, reinforced and articulated by Pius XI, had a strong and lasting influence in this country during the period of the 1920s and 1930s when industry-wide unions were fighting to organize themselves. The social program of the "New Deal" of Franklin Delano Roosevelt was powerfully assisted in its pursuit of justice for labor by the teaching and support of the American church, and of course one of the strongest voices developing the papal teaching was the well-known moralist Msgr. John A. Ryan of the Catholic University of America.

Leo XIII not only asserted the need for justice in the treatment of the working classes, he made that the responsibility of the civil authority. To illustrate the classical context of his teaching, let me quote from *Rerum Novarum*:

> We have insisted ... that, since the end of society is to make men better, the chief good that society can possess is virtue. Nevertheless, it is the business of a well-constituted body politic to see to the provision of those material and external helps, "the use of which is necessary to virtuous action." ... Justice, therefore, demands that the interests of the working classes should be carefully watched over....

[I]t lies in the power of a ruler to benefit every class in the State, and amongst the rest to promote to the utmost the interests of the poor, and this in virtue of his office, . . . since it is in the province of the commonwealth to serve the common good. And the more that is done for the benefit of the working classes by the general laws of the country, the less need will there be to seek for special means to relieve them.[1]

At the same time, that classical context in the encyclical is sometimes coupled with unclassical language and ideas, for example, that

man precedes civil society (respublica) and, prior to the formation of any civil society (civitas), must have by nature the right to sustain his life and care for his body.[2]

However that may be, it would take us too far afield to pursue the issue of "rights" language and its appropriate role in understanding the nature of political society and of citizens.

Rather I want to remark on a similarity between the teaching of *Rerum Novarum* and *Populorum Progressio*. The same principles lie behind the discussion there, although the field of application is different: it is not the relation of worker and owner but the field of trade relations between the rich and poor countries. Like Leo, Paul VI observes that the free trade of a market economy has evident advantages when the parties involved are not economically too unequal, but when they are, like Leo, he calls into question the justice of the "fundamental principle of liberalism," i.e., the justice of free trade.

Indeed Barbara Ward remarked on the resemblance of the people of the post-colonial countries in the third world and the situation of industrial workers in the capitalist economies of the nineteenth and early twentieth centuries. Like the industrial workers, these third world countries, she says,

have been drawn into an economic system they did not initiate and do not control. Like them, they earn a disproportionately small share of the wealth they are helping to create. Like them, they still lack the power to act together to redress the balance.[3]

Paul VI explicitly cites the same principle as Leo:

The teaching of Leo XIII in *Rerum Novarum* is still valid: if the positions of the contracting parties are too unequal, the consent of the parties does not suffice to guarantee the justice of their contract, and the rule of free agreement remains subservient to the demands of the natural law.[4]

But now who is *responsible* for the pursuit of justice in the common good of nations, of mankind, in the way that the government is responsible for the pursuit of justice in the common good of a particular political society? Well, one answer to that question is to say that some "world authority" or world government is going to be necessary to address those substantive questions of justice as well as the more practical ones of order and security.[5] That is an idea that we do not find strange, whether we support or oppose it. Provinces or states have a central government; nations presumably could have a world government.

And yet, as Jacques Maritain insisted, there is a problem about the very concept of world government. The problem is not that it is utopian in the sense of unrealizable, impossible, but rather that two quite different notions are confused in our common talk.

If "world government" means a system of administration—legislature, executive agency, judicial bodies, etc.—having authoritative jurisdiction over all nations, then one is thinking of what Maritain calls a "merely governmental theory of world organization."[6] But, he affirmed,

the basic political reality is not the State [i.e., the set of offices and their holders] but the body politic . . . and the moral community which grows out of it. . . . The State is [only] the particular agency which specializes in matters dealing with the common good of the body politic . . . its functions are merely instrumental [with respect to that moral community];[7]

The issue is not simply world government, it is world political society, and even if the world government officeholders were chosen by popular election and representation, that would only fulfill a necessary and not a sufficient condition for a truly political world government. Democratic election of a "merely governmental" world authority, Maritain insisted, would only be a technical or juridical procedure and "would be entirely insufficient to change in any way the fact that I am pointing out." It would only create a State without a body politic or a political society of its own, "a world brain without a world body." It would result in a "democratic multi-national Empire, which would be not better than the others."[8]

It's not that we couldn't create such a "merely governmental" world authority; it is rather that such an authority would not *ipso facto* have the common good of the human community as its goal. For that there must be sharing in a sense of the common good of one human people in a worldwide political community, a common good on the basis of which deliberations about the justice and injustice of actions and situations would be possible, and through which a sense of civic friendship could animate our relations with other peoples. Without a sense of forming one community, economic interdependence tends to produce not togetherness but conflict.

For a sense of what is involved in the notion of a common good, think of the community formed by a family. Here the good is a life together, a life of doing things with and for each other and for the group's good. There is a shared human and moral good, achieved through and realized in their actions: sharing, learning to be and being fair, thoughtful of others, honest, loving. . . . There is a life together to which each contributes (not merely by doing their assigned "chores"), which has its celebrations and its rituals, and from which each one draws an essential part of his or her identity, and finally where each learns that the good of the whole—which is also the good of each of the parts—comes before the private good of the individual parts.[9]

It is not a question of the homogenization of cultures: Maritain championed what he called a "pluralist unity, taking place only through the *lasting* diversity of the particular bodies politic, and *fostering* that diversity."[10] It is rather that "*one* body politic is *one* organized people." To ask presently, for example, that people in the developed countries accept a serious lowering of their standard of life in order to provide people on the other side of the world with an equivalent raising of their standard of living would be to ask for heroic virtue. But in a world political society, one people with a common good, justice would claim a certain relative commensuration of the living conditions of all persons, of those who would be fellow citizens of those of us in the developed countries.[11]

So the critical issue here is not the institution of a "merely governmental" world government that would try, like the United Nations, to adjudicate claims between distinct constituencies. It is rather the need for a world political society, united in sharing the sense of a common human good and of the responsibility we have to each other.

II

The second issue to be examined is that of the relations between the state and the Church, or, in later terms, the question of religious liberty.

Consistent with his view of the responsibility of the state for the promotion of the human good of its citizens, Leo XIII asserts that

> ... men living together in society are under the power of God no less than individuals are, and society, no less than individuals, owes gratitude to God who gave it being and maintains it.... Since, then, no one is allowed to be remiss in the service due to God, and since the chief duty of all men is to cling to religion in both its teaching and practice—not such a religion as they may have a preference for, but the religion which God enjoins ... it is a public crime to act as though there were no God. So, too, it is a sin for the State not to have care for religion, as though it were something beyond its scope ... for we are bound absolutely to worship God in the way He has chosen.... [O]ne of the chief duties [of those who rule] must be to favor religion, to protect it, to shield it under the credit and sanction of the laws, and neither to organize nor enact any measure that may compromise its safety.[12]

And if the Catholic Church is the true church, then it is in principle the responsibility of the state to promote the well-being of that church.

(At the same time—in the same encyclical—he affirmed that no one could or should be forced to embrace the Catholic faith against his will.)

Alexis de Tocqueville had remarked on how the independence of church and state in the United States had been a healthy state of affairs for religion there. Leo, in a message to the American hierarchy in 1895, commented favorably on the freedom of the American church to live freely and act without hindrance. However, he wrote,

> it would be very erroneous to draw the conclusion that in America is to be sought the type of the most desirable status of the Church, or that it would be universally lawful or expedient for State and Church to be, as in America, dissevered and divorced.[13]

So although it is not the optimal solution to the relation of the two powers, it may be the best solution available under the circumstances to make the "establishment" of any church unconstitutional in such a religiously pluralistic political society.

This teaching remained the standard for most of the twentieth century. Perhaps the most widely disseminated and influential statement on this teaching was in Msgr. John A. Ryan's book *The State and the Church* (1922, reissued in 1940 as *Catholic Principles of Politics*). Ryan stated the principle as "the State should officially recognize the Catholic religion as the religion of the commonwealth"; but he discussed the dangers of abuse in such an establishment and insisted that no particular historical arrangement could serve as the norm for such a relationship.

In Ryan's account, the reason for the principle is that the state is responsible for promoting the common good of its members, and if religiousness is part of that human good, then the true form of religiousness should be sought by the state for its members.

The reasons for accepting a situation of religious pluralism where no religion is privileged over others—the First Amendment situation—are, first, the classical principle that more harm than good would likely follow from the attempt to give political primacy to the true religion and, second, that if religious freedom is a fundamental constitutional provision, then the obligation to respect that freedom is binding in conscience.

Nonetheless, Ryan honestly confronts the question of whether, if a state became predominantly Catholic and any such constitutional provision could be amended, the Catholic Church ought not to be given singular status. His response is candid: yes. But, he adds,

> the event of its practical realization in this country is so remote in time and in probability that no practical man will let it disturb his equanimity or affect his attitude toward those who differ from him in religious faith.

Some people, he acknowledges, will continue to attack the Church on these grounds, but,

> we cannot yield up the principles of eternal and unchangeable truth in order to avoid the enmity of such unreasonable persons. Moreover, it would be a futile policy; for they would not think us sincere.[14]

And he adds that he is

> confident that the majority of our fellow citizens will be sufficiently honorable to respect our devotion to truth and sufficiently realistic to see that the danger of religious intolerance toward non-Catholics in the United States is so improbable and so far in the future that it should not occupy their time or attention.[15]

But of course that is a legal and moral position awkward to hold vis-à-vis one's fellow citizens, and of course it *was* attacked as un-American. There is, however, a way to avoid it without accepting all religions as equally true and thus surrendering the Catholic Church's claim of uniqueness. That way is to reconceptualize the nature of the state and to restrict its responsibility to protecting the rights of its citizens and securing public order. And that is the position that Fr. John Courtney Murray found his way to.[16]

On Murray's account, the transition from the one conception of the state to the other had already taken its decisive steps by the time of Pius XII.

He [Pius XII] abandons Leo XIII's ethical concept of the society-state.... Instead he adopts the juridical concept of the state (*Rechts-staat*), whose genesis owed more to Christian inspiration. The state is ... an agent of society for certain limited purposes.[17]

And he quotes Pius to validate that claim. Pius said:

To protect the inviolable rights that are proper to man, and to have a care that everyone may more readily discharge his duties—this is the chief function of the public power.[18]

Murray comments:

Pius XII shows his awareness of the distinction between society and state, between the *total common good of society* and the *elements* of the common good that are committed to the power of the *state*. In his own idiom, the distinction is between the wider order of "social life" and the narrower "juridical order of society."[19]

If the total care of the common good were committed to the rulers of states, what would follow, Murray says, is "the disappearance of the distinction between society and state."[20]

On the issue of religious freedom, then, Murray argued that the state's responsibility was simply to protect the right to that freedom. Could the exercise of religious freedom be restricted, and, if so, on what grounds? He maintained that it could not be restricted by the state on either theological or moral grounds but only on grounds consistent with the state's competence and responsibility—namely, public order. He was willing to include a moral dimension in "public order" provided that the standards invoked were "commonly accepted standards of public morality."[21] And he also included justice in the state's charge, justice understood as what is due to the people, namely, protecting their rights.

So religion is indeed "a social good, a fundamental element of the common temporal good of *society*" but "*governmental* favor of religion formally means favor of the freedom of religion." Government "must somehow stand in the service of religion" but "this duty of service is discharged by service rendered to the freedom of religion in society."[22] It should be noted that Murray insisted that the grounds for the claim to religious freedom from state interference were different for the Catholic Church and for other religious associations: for the Church, it is its divine mandate; for other religious associations, it is the dignity of the human person.[23]

When I pressed him, at a meeting at Notre Dame in 1965 (he died the following year), on whether the state could not legitimately promote the free exercise of religious acts by its citizens, he responded by saying that in his view all the fundamental human rights are immunities and he didn't understand how you could promote an immunity. The underlying issue here, to which he candidly referred, was a clause inserted into the final draft of the Declaration on Religious Freedom (of which he was the primary architect) by bishops at the Council, which stated that

> Government, therefore, ought indeed to take account of the religious life of the people and show it favor, since the function of government is to make provision for the common welfare.[24]

He went on to say that he interpreted that to mean not that government could favor religion as such but that since having religious citizens may benefit society in terms of justice and order, it is appropriate for government to favor it in that respect.

This line of argument certainly secures the right to religious freedom by making the state incompetent to legislate about religious acts. Note that to avoid the awkwardness of the John A. Ryan position, Murray must accept (as he did) that this conception of the state having no competence to seek the fuller human good is not simply a de facto situation, but that this conception is an advance and clarification in our understanding of the nature of the state.

But it seems to entail a number of consequences about which one might have hesitations. I think Murray himself was not completely comfortable with some apparent implications of the argument. For example, he quoted approvingly what he called the basic rule of jurisprudence:

Let there be as much freedom, personal and social, as is possible; let there be only as much restraint and constraint, personal and social, as may be necessary for personal order.[25]

That sounds very much like the classical modern conception of the liberal state that stems from John Locke and John Stuart Mill. (And it requires the kind of pragmatic reading that Murray gave of the Declaration's statement that the state ought to favor the religious life of the people since it is concerned with the common good.) But if the state has no responsibility—and no competence—to seek justice (other than by respecting immunities), then it would seem also to be required to stay out of the economy. The argument would seem to encourage if not to require a laissez-faire attitude towards the market.[26]

Murray does allow the juridical object of the state's mission—public order—to include justice, but as we have seen, he seems to limit justice to the securing of immunities (rights). And if he includes "public morality" in the state's responsibility, it is only in the sense of "moral standards commonly accepted."

Moreover, if the state has no mandate to promote justice (beyond assuring immunities) and moral values (beyond commonly accepted standards) as a component of the common good, it is hard to see how the Church's social teaching about justice can be appropriately directed to governments. Such teaching could still be directed to *society* because, as we have seen, on Murray's account there is a "total common good" of society as distinguished from those "*elements* of the common good" that are committed to the power of the state.

I mention these possible consequences not to "refute" Murray's argument but simply to articulate what appears to be involved in accepting—not without reasons—the modern liberal conception of the state. He retains the notion of a "thick" common good but allocates responsibility for it to political society.[27] But is society capable of assuming that responsibility?

III

Alasdair MacIntyre has developed in several books an analysis and critique of the present situation of public discourse, discourse about what to do, in which we members of liberal democracies may be able to recognize ourselves.

Our situation is one in which the public realm has been reconstructed by the culture of liberalism, a liberalism that was born in the attempt to replace the tyranny of tradition by principles that every rational person ought to accept. The liberal claim was to provide a political, legal, and economic framework within which persons with widely different, even incompatible, conceptions of the good life could live together peacefully. Liberalism claimed to rest its frameworks not on any specific conception of the good life but only on principles that anyone could see to be reasonable. As MacIntyre puts it,

> Every individual is to be equally free to propose and to live by whatever conception of the good life he or she pleases . . . *unless* that conception of the good involves reshaping the life of the rest of the community in accordance with it.[28]

So there is a limit to conceptions of the good that are tolerated.

And that means that there are rules for entering into the debate of the public arena.

> What is permitted in that arena is the expression of preferences, either the preferences of individuals or of groups. . . . It may well be that in some cases it is some nonliberal theory or conception of the human good which leads individuals to express the preferences that they do. But only in the guise of such expressions of preference are such theories and conceptions allowed to receive expression.[29]

It is the aggregation of such preferences which exercises influence or authority in public discussion. And of course, given the fact that the liberal state eschews any conception of the human good, there is no rational principle for the ordering of these preferences. So the resolution of differences among preferences, or the resolution of conflicts, comes through political procedures of arbitration and bargaining.

Practical reasoning in this situation proceeds not from a premise about what is good or right but from the premise "I/we want it to be the case that such and such." Such a premise no longer merely expresses a *motive* for action—it becomes itself a *reason* for action. Hence polls and surveys come to exercise an important function.

It therefore may (or may not) be interesting that you think that "such and such" is morally wrong, inhuman, or that judgment may enter into the public arena only as the expression of a preference (e.g., sexual preferences) or a right (e.g., to privacy) or an interest (e.g., of a group). The consequence of the predominance of this form of practical reasoning is that there is a change in the character of public discourse. One must now

> understand arenas of public choice, not as places of debate, either in terms of one dominant conception of the human good or between rival and conflicting conceptions of that good, but as places of bargaining between individuals [and groups of individuals], each with their own preferences.[30]

And so resolution comes about through counting votes and doing market surveys. Debate is barren, since the discussion does not and cannot appeal to a shared set of moral premises:

> rival appeals to accounts of the human good or of justice necessarily assume a rhetorical form such that it is as assertion and counterassertion, rather than as argument and counterargument, that rival standpoints confront one another. . . . [P]ersuasion replaces argument. . . . Standpoints are construed as the expressions of attitude and feeling and often enough come to be no more than that.[31]

In this situation, MacIntyre argues, the state becomes primarily the provider of goods and services, and the arbitrator of differences. It is the means to the achievement of our preferences. Although to my knowledge he never mentions John Courtney Murray, he seems to agree that the modern state is incapable of exercising the role of a moral agent seeking a common human good. Indeed he goes far beyond Murray in contending that neither can the responsibility for the "total common good" be allotted to society.

This is part of the reason why MacIntyre has always vigorously separated himself from the "communitarians" with whom he is often identified. Communitarians recognize the need—in a society where none of the contending interests can claim to override the claims of others, and where resolution of conflicts cannot require that individuals give up their preferences as simply wrong, inadmissible—for some overriding allegiance to the system itself, to the community as a whole. It is proposed that we retrieve the common values that we can find in our tradition and give an overriding common allegiance to them. MacIntyre's question is: "what good reasons could an individual find for placing himself or herself at the service of the public good rather than of other goods?"

Given his description of the liberal state and its public arena, it is consistent of him to side with contemporary liberals (and with Murray) against the communitarians on the grounds that the attempt to retrieve common values is only going to recover what Richard Rorty calls what "we" think or what Murray called "commonly accepted standards of public morality."[32] Indeed he believes that the attempt to make the liberal state an all-embracing community opens the door to totalitarianism.

These analyses and the perceptions on which they are based are not as singular as they may at first seem. Not only can we, I think, come to recognize a kind of self-portrait therein, but others have remarked on the same phenomena. In *Centesimus Annus*, John Paul II observes that there appears to be a kind of

> crisis within democracies themselves, which seem at times to have lost the ability to make decisions aimed at the common good. Certain demands that arise within society are sometimes not examined in accordance with criteria of justice and morality, but rather on the basis of the electoral or financial power of the groups promoting them. With time, such distortions of political conduct create distrust and apathy, with a subsequent decline in the political participation and civic spirit of the general population, which feels abused and disillusioned. As a result, there is a growing inability to situate particular interests within the framework of a coherent vision of the common good. The latter is not simply the sum of particular interests....[33]

And four years later, in *Evangelium Vitae*, insisting on the relation between democracy and moral values, he writes:

The basis of these values cannot be provisional and changeable "majority" opinions, but only the acknowledgment of an objective moral law which . . . is the obligatory point of reference for civil law itself. If, as a result of a tragic obscuring of the collective conscience, an attitude of skepticism were to succeed in bringing into question even the fundamental principles of the moral law, the democratic system itself would be shaken in its foundations and would be reduced to a mere mechanism for regulating different and opposing interests on a purely empirical basis.[34]

The problem is not democracy as a political form, which John Paul strongly supports—it is rather that separation of freedom from the truth which characterizes the "culture of liberalism" and sets the ground rules for political discussion. "Freedom," he says, "attains its full development only by accepting the truth."[35] Indeed, as a bishop at the Vatican Council thirty years earlier, Karol Wojtyla had criticized early drafts of the Declaration on Religious Freedom for just such a separation.[36]

One way to glimpse the problem of the relation of freedom and truth for democracies here is to recall John Stuart Mill's argument for freedom of discussion in his *Essay on Liberty*. We need to listen to all viewpoints, he says, because we can never be sure that the opinion we think to be true is true, and if we don't listen to opposing positions we will never have the opportunity to exchange what may be our erroneous view for the true view.[37] That sounds persuasive to our ears (it has become the conventional wisdom) until we ask ourselves: if we can't ever be sure that the opinion we hold is the true one, how will we know that the exchange won't go in the other direction and we will end up having exchanged our true opinion for a false one?[38]

IV

It should now be apparent why I began with Maritain's concerns about "merely governmental" world government. Not only, it seems to me, does that form of international authority likely lie ahead of us, it is the form of authority that has already come to exist in modern liberal democracy. We no longer form one political community, sharing a sense of one human good which we seek together and which we argue about within a common set of moral principles. (Indeed, arguing is how a community articulates that sense.) Many of us no longer find an essential part of our identity in our being part of one political society for whose good we strive, despite the images and symbols drawn from the history of our nation.

That has not, in my view, been the case for all of our history (and I speak of the United States here since I know that best). In the nineteenth century, in one of the most closely followed political debates in the country, Lincoln was able to assert—along with many "political" and constitutional arguments—that it was simply wrong for one human being to own another.[39] But that was over a century ago, and I do think that MacIntyre's analysis of the arena of public discussion is now largely on the mark.

John Courtney Murray perceived this change in the nature of existing government and hence saw the need to remove the responsibility for moral evaluations from the jurisdiction of the state. That meant rejecting the traditional (thesis/hypothesis) position because that traditional position rested on the normative conception of the state as a moral agent responsible for seeking the common good. Murray thought that the common good was still a legitimate goal for society to pursue. But there are unresolved problems with the form of disengagement between state and society that he tried to articulate and defend.

MacIntyre is more radical. For him, not only is the modern state not structured, not competent to decide questions about human good, but neither is the society within a liberal democracy. The fact that the same terms may be used doesn't mean that Aristotle and John Stuart Mill were talking about the same thing when they talked about "political society."

Assume, for the moment, that these thinkers were attuned to "the signs of the times" and that Maritain's concerns about merely governmental government were valid. Where does that leave the social teaching of the Church? How does the Church relate its teaching to political societies incapable of public moral discourse because they are without a shared moral common good and so are no longer political societies in the traditional sense?

It doesn't seem to me that it changes anything radically. Clearly, recent popes have seen no inconsistency in speaking of a universal common good of all humanity[40] even though no political society now exists that corresponds to it and no world government has jurisdiction over it. Maybe we will have to live with merely governmental government for some time on both the national and, possibly one day, the international level. But encyclicals can—and must—still address questions of justice and of right and wrong and continue to assess and teach morality without having to assume governments to be more than merely governmental. As Maritain never tired of pointing out, it is possible to agree about things to be done without necessarily agreeing on the reason to do them. And the Church can try to bring to the consciences of its hearers the perception of what demands simply being human makes. Would the structures and public arenas of democracies allow those sparks in consciences to turn into flame? Only God knows.

Chapter 1

1. Demetrius, *On Style*, trans. W. R. Roberts (Cambridge, Mass.: Harvard University Press, 1982), bk. 4, sec. 222.

2. Strauss qualifies this statement by distinguishing classical from modern philosophers, the latter believing that, over time, education and the diminishment of religion will result in a larger number of esoteric readers.

3. *Phaedrus*, 274c–d.

4. Alexis de Tocqueville, *Democracy in America* (New York: Mentor, 1984), pt. 2, bk. 1, chap. 1, p. 146.

5. To use Lincoln's term from the Gettysburg address.

6. For brief delineations of Strauss's position, see the introduction and chapter 2 of his *Persecution and the Art of Writing* (Glencoe: Free Press, 1952), and "On a Forgotten Kind of Writing," in *What Is Political Philosophy?* (Glencoe: Free Press, 1959), 221–32. A helpful overview is Paul Bagley's "On the Practice of Esotericism," *Journal of the History of Ideas* 53, no. 2 (April–June 1992): 231–47, although after a brief discussion of Aristotle's mention of exoteric discourses, most of his examples are from Renaissance and modern writers.

7. Twice in the *Nicomachean Ethics*, twice in the *Eudemian Ethics*, twice in the *Politics*, once in the *Physics*, once in the *Metaphysics*. For a listing of the loci and a discussion see Ross's edition of the *Metaphysics* at 13.1.1076a28.

8. So, for example, Aristotle in the *Politics* says that the Cretans do not involve themselves in external rule or foreign rule—*exoterikes arches* (2.10.1272b20).

9. Aristotle, *Eudemian Ethics*, trans. Harris Rackham (Cambridge, Mass.: Harvard University Press, 1972), 1.8.1217b24.

10. Cicero, *De Finibus* (Cambridge, Mass.: Harvard University Press, 1983), bk. 5, sec. 5, no. 12. He also uses the Greek term *exoterikous* once in a letter to Atticus, to refer to the writings that Aristotle so named. See *Letters to Atticus*, trans. David Bailey (Cambridge, Mass.: Harvard University Press, 1999), vol. 1, no. 89, p. 336.

11. Plutarch's life of Alexander the Great in *Plutarch's Lives* (Cambridge, Mass.: Harvard University Press, 1986), 7:1–4.

12. Lucian, *Bion Prasis*, trans. A. M. Harmon (New York: Macmillan, 1915), 2:26. There is no earlier use of "esoteric" to designate a kind of discourse in either Greek or Roman writers.

13. Aulus Gellius, *Attic Nights*, trans. John C. Rolfe (London: Heineman, 1927), 3:433.

14. Letter 135, in *Letters of St. Augustine*, trans. Wilfrid Parsons, Fathers of the Church, vol. 20 (Washington, D.C.: Catholic University of America Press, 1953).

15. John of Salisbury, *Policraticus*, trans. C. J. Nederman (Cambridge, UK: Cambridge University Press, 1990), bk. 7. The terms are probably derived from Aulus Gellius.

16. What we could call acroatic, using the terminology Plutarch borrows from philosophers. Origen, *Contra Celsum*, trans. Henry Chadwick (Cambridge, UK: Cambridge University Press, 1965), bk. 1, secs. 7–8; bk. 3, sec. 46. See the discussion in Henri Crouzel, *Origene et la connaissance mystique* (Brouges: Desclee de Brouwer, 1961), 162–65. For a good discussion of the same issue in Clement, compare Ernest Fortin, "Clement of Alexandria and the Esoteric Tradition," in *Studia Patristica* IX (Berlin: Akademie-Verlag, 1966), 41–56.

17. St. Augustine, *City of God*, trans. Henry Bettenson (London: Penguin, 1987), bk. 8, chap. 4, p. 304. On Apuleius compare bk. 9, chap. 8, p. 353: "he made clear, to the thoughtful readers."

18. Ibid., bk. 5, chap. 9, p. 190.

19. Ibid., bk. 4, chap. 31, p. 174. See also bk. 6, chaps. 4–5, pp. 232–36, where Augustine says Varro gives "subtle hints" and leaves things "to be inferred by the intelligent reader."

20. St. Augustine, *Against the Academics*, trans. J. J. O'Meara (Westminster, Md.: Newman Press, 1950), bk. 3, chap. 17, no. 38. See also Augustine's letter 118 to Dioscuros.

21. St. Augustine, *Confessions*, trans. J. K. Ryan (New York: Doubleday, 1960), bk. 3, chap. 5, no. 9.

22. Ibid., bk. 6, chap. 5, no. 8.

23. St. Augustine, *City of God*, bk. 4, chap. 33.

24. Luke 24:27.

25. St. Augustine, *On Christian Doctrine*, trans. Durant Robertson (New York: Liberal Arts, 1958), bk. 4, chap. 9, no. 23.

26. Ibid.

27. Boethius, *De Trinitate*, in *Theological Tractates*, trans. H. F. Stewart, E. K. Rand, and S. J. Tester (Cambridge, Mass.: Harvard University Press, 1928), 5.

28. See, for example, *Confessions*, bk. 2, chap. 31, no. 42, and the present author's "Structure and Meaning in St. Augustine's *Confessions*," in *The Augustinian Tradition*, ed. G. B. Matthews (Berkeley: University of California Press, 1999).

29. St. Thomas Aquinas, *Expositio super librum Boethii De Trinitate*, q. 2, a. 4. Aquinas cites here the text from Augustine's *On Christian Doctrine* quoted above. Compare Plato's *Phaedrus* 275d–277c.

30. St. Thomas Aquinas, *Summa Theologiae* I, q. 1, a. 9.

31. Ibid. II-II, q. 8, a. 1.

32. Ibid. III, q. 42, a. 3.

33. John Paul II, *Fides et Ratio* (Washington, D.C.: United States Catholic Conference, 1999), sec. 11.

34. Compare "On a Forgotten Kind of Writing," in *What Is Political Philosophy?*

35. *Summa Theologiae* II-II, q. 110, a. 3.

36. St. Augustine, *On Christian Doctrine*, bk. 4, chap. 9, no. 23. This rule applies to oral teaching of one or a few, not to writing, for reasons already alluded to.

37. I Corinthians 3:1–2.

38. Strauss, *Persecution and the Art of Writing*, 17.

39. Although Aquinas uses the terminology of latent and exterior (as cited earlier), he also speaks of *occultum*/hidden and *publicum*/open. I have tried to consistently use the latent/manifest language to underline the difference from the philosophical tradition.

40. Compare, for example, the present author's article on "The Disclosure of Hidden Providence," in *A Reader's Companion to Augustine's "Confessions"* (Louisville: Westminster John Knox Press, 2003).

41. St. Augustine, *Confessions*, bk. 12, chap. 18, no. 27, and bk. 12, chap. 31, no. 42. So different readers can take away different understandings, as he has said of Scripture before (see above, notes 18 and 19).

42. Strauss, *Persecution and the Art of Writing*, 19.

43. "St. Thomas Aquinas," in *History of Political Philosophy*, ed. Leo Strauss and Joseph Cropsey (Chicago: Rand McNally, 1972), 225.

44. Compare M. D. Jordan, *The Alleged Aristotelianism of Thomas Aquinas* (Toronto: Medieval Institute, 1992), 5–6.

45. Robert Henle, *St. Thomas and Platonism* (The Hague: H. Nijhof, 1956), xxi.

46. There are passages in Aristotle that might have offered the opportunity for comment on the topic, but they occur in loci that Aquinas did not comment on. For example, *Politics* 3.13.1284a26–36.

47. See notes 26 and 27 above.

48. St. Thomas Aquinas, *Sententia super de Anima*, bk. 1, lect. 8. Compare his comments on Socratic dialogues in *In Libros Politicorum Aristotelis Expositio* II, lect. 6.

49. Ernest Fortin, *Dissent and Philosophy in the Middle Ages* (Lanham, Md.: Lexington Books, 2002), 144. The French original was published in 1981.

Chapter 2

1. J. J. O'Meara, *The Young Augustine: The Growth of St. Augustine's Mind up to His Conversion* (London: Longmans, Green, 1954), 13, 44; H. Marrou, *St. Augustin et la fin de la culture antique* (Paris: E. De Boccard, 1958), 1.

2. *Civ.*, respectively: 8.4, 5.9, 4.3 and 6.4, and 9.9. Compare *On Christian Doctrine*, trans. D. W. Robertson (New York: Liberal Arts Press, 1958), 2.6.8: "no one doubts that things are perceived more readily through similitudes and that what is sought with difficulty is discovered with more pleasure." Cf. ibid. 4.8.22. And of course, Augustine makes similar remarks in the *Confessions* about the popular and the obscure understanding of the Academics: 5.10.19 and 5.14.25.

3. *On True Religion*, trans. J. H. S. Burleigh, in *Augustine: Earlier Writings* (Philadelphia: Westminster Press, 1953), 17.33. Compare, out of many similar comments: "The obscurity itself of the divine and wholesome writings was a part of a kind of eloquence through which our understandings should be benefitted not only by the discovery of what lies hidden but also by exercise" (*Doctr. chr.* 4.6.9).

4. *Confessions*, trans. Maria Boulding (Hyde Park, N.Y.: New City Press, 1997), 6.5.8. Cf. similarly 3.5.9, 12.27.37. (References in the text to loci where no title is cited will be to this translation.)

5. *Conf.* 12.31.42.

6. Aquinas, *The Trinity and the Unicity of the Intellect*, trans. R. E. Brennan (St. Louis: Herder, 1946), Q. Two, art. 4.

7. This is a standard or common view. E.g., "the structural parallel between Rousseau's *Confessions* and Augustine's *Confessions* has at its center the 'conversions' recounted in Book 8 of each work. The conversion represents a radical turning point for both Augustine and Rousseau." Ann Hartle, *The Modern Self in Rousseau's "Confessions": A Reply to St. Augustine* (Notre Dame, Ind.: University of Notre Dame Press, 1983), 136.

8. *Conf.* 5.1.1.

9. *Conf.* 5.8.14. Cf. 5.8.15: "You knew all along, O God, the real reason why I left to seek a different country, but you did not reveal it either to me or to my mother."

10. *Conf.* 5.13.23. The phrase succinctly expresses the paradox of God's hidden providence.

11. As he comments about the books of the Platonists, "No one there hears a voice calling, come to Me" (*Conf.* 7.21.27).

12. Cf. *On the Usefulness of Belief*, trans. J. H. S. Burleigh, in *Augustine: Earlier Writings* (Philadelphia: Westminster Press, 1953), 16.34: "If the providence of God does not preside over human affairs, there is no need to worry about religion," and ibid. 8.20 and 13.29.

13. Cf. the opening sentence of *Conf.* 5.8.14.

14. Although he would remain publicly a member of the sect "until some preferential option presented itself" (*Conf.* 5.7.13).

15. The numbering of the paragraphs, of course, dates from the Maurist edition of 1679, but they indicate approximately the respective distances.

16. The Latin says "the Catholic Church commended to me by my parents."

17. "[P]opularly thought" is another reference to the two levels of meaning in a teaching. For a discussion by Augustine of why the Academics concealed their true theory, cf. *Acad.* 1.7.14ff.

18. He speaks later of the "keen attention I had directed toward Mani's writing," and gives examples of errors in Mani's books (*Conf.* 5.7.12–13).

19. Aristotle, *Categories*, trans. E. M. Edghill, in *Basic Works of Aristotle*, ed. R. McKeon (New York: Random House, 1941), chap. 5, 4a10.

20. *Conf.* 4.16.29. These comments of Augustine about "simple and changeless" foreshadow a problem that will dominate Book Eleven: how then can we tell a story, as Genesis does, of what God did on the successive days of creation?

21. It is interesting that there is no mention of the name Christ from the time he encounters the Manichees (*Conf.* 3.6.10) until he lands in Italy (*Conf.* 5.9.16).

22. See, for example, Cicero's presentation of the Epicurean position in *De finibus*, Book One. (For pleasure as the greatest good, 1.12.40ff.; for friendship, 1.20.65ff.) Augustine knew of Lucretius, the chief Roman expositor of Epicureanism, but cites him rarely. It seems likely that Cicero is his major source.

23. He had earlier commented that "when I wanted to think about my God I did not know how to think otherwise than in terms of bodily size, for whatever did not answer to this description seemed to me to be nothing at all. This misapprehension was the chief and almost sole cause of the error I could not avoid" (*Conf.* 5.10.19).

24. First John 2:16. Augustine refers to this triad repeatedly in the *Confessions*, e.g., "These are the chief kinds of sin, which sprout from a craving for

domination, or for watching shows, or for sensory pleasure" (*Conf.* 3.8.16). Cf. the similar analysis in Cicero, *Off.* 1.4.11–13.

25. Plato, *Resp.* 435ff. This tripartite division of the soul in Plato is adopted by the Platonists, e.g., Plotinus, *Enn.* 1.1.5–6.

26. In Book Ten, where he is reflecting on the three concupiscences, Augustine comments on "the temptation to win veneration and affection from others, and to want them not for the sake of some quality that merits them, but in order to make such admiration itself the cause of my joy. It is no true joy at all, but leads only to a miserable life and shameful ostentation" (*Conf.* 10.36.59).

27. For example, *Conf.* 3.1.1–3, 3.3.6; 4.2.2, 4.13.20; 5.13.23; 6.10.17, 6.15.25.

28. He describes his state at this point as "enslavement to worldly affairs," hardly a desire or concupiscence.

29. John Henry Newman, *An Essay in Aid of a Grammar of Assent* (Notre Dame, Ind.: University of Notre Dame Press, 1979), 49–92.

30. This communal end of his journey is signaled in the last lines of the last narrative book by the reference to his "fellow citizens in the eternal Jerusalem" and his request to his readers to remember his mother and father in their prayers (*Conf.* 9.13.37).

31. The order of naming: Alypius, Nebridius, and Romanianus in Book Six; Vindicianus and Firminus in Book Seven; Simplicianus, Verecundus, and Ponticianus in Book Eight; Adeodatus, Evodius, Monica, and Patricius in Book Nine.

32. *Util. cred.* 13.28 and 16.34.

Chapter 3

1. I pass over the single lost work of his written in Carthage before his conversion, *De pulchro et apto. Conf.* 4.13.20.

2. *Conf.* 9.6.14: adiunximus etiam nobis puerum Adeodatum, ex me natum carnaliter de peccato meo, tu bene feceras eum; annorum erat ferme quindecim, et ingenio praeveniebat multos graves et doctos viros … quod enim et nutriebatur a nobis in disciplina tua, tu inspiraveras nobis, nullus alius: munera tua tibi confiteor. Est liber noster, qui inscribitur de Magistro; ipse ibi mecum loquitur, tu scis illius esse sensa omnia, quae inseruntur ibi ex persona conlocutoris mei, cum esset in annis sedecim.

3. How much of the year's delay was due to Monica's death and how much to the threatening naval force of Maximus is uncertain. Cf. O. Perler, *Les voyages de saint Augustin* (Paris, 1969), pp. 147–49.

4. *Retr.* 1.12. Note that in this brief description done, one assumes, after consulting the text, there is no mention of Adeodatus by name. "We"—meaning Augustine and someone else—"dispute and . . ."

But this is appropriate for a literary-rhetorical description of the text as distinguished from a historical one. Thirty years have passed since the death of his son. Still, Brown cites a late passage which could be read as reflecting a father's pain over the death of a young son. P. Brown, *Augustine of Hippo.*

5. G. Weigel in the Corpus Scriptorum edition of the text (CSEL 77, 1, p. XXIX) says "about the year 390." H. I. Marrou, *St. Augustin et l'augustinisme* (Paris, 1956), p. 21, gives 389 for both the death of Adeodatus and the composition of *De Magistro.*

6. G. Wijdeveld, *Aurelius Augustinus de magistro, ingeleid, vertaald en toegelich door . . .* (Amsterdam, 1937).

7. He also mentions the unliterary character of the first part, seeming mistakes in the recapitulation by Adeodatus, and the differing syntactical nature of the speeches in the first and third parts. In addition to others to be noted later, cf. Peter Brown, *Augustine of Hippo* (London, 1967), p. 120: "Dialogues which betray amateur philosophers at work can be most painful reading. There are digressions, inconsequential trains of thought and a general misuse of argument. . . . It is easy to dismiss such works as immature."

8. Cf. the discussion of Wijdeveld's arguments in G. Madec, introduction to *Œuvres de St. Augustin,* vol. 6 (Paris: Desclée de Brouwer, 1976), pp. 12–16.

9. At ego puto esse quoddam genus docendi per commemorationen, magnum sane, quod in nostra hac sermocinatione res ipsa indicabit.

10. Cf. the judicious and comprehensive discussion in G. Madec, "L'historicité des *Dialogues* de Cassiciacum," *Revue des Etudes Augustiniennes* 32 (1986): 207–31.

11. B. R. Voss, *Der Dialog in der frühchristlichen Literatur* (München, 1970), p. 198.

12. *Art. cit.,* p. 230.

13. E.g., 11.36: Quod si dixeris, . . . Respondebo . . .

14. The prime example, for me, of such merely apparent disorder in a dialogue is the *De ordine.*

15. Erwin Schadel, *De magistro: Einführung. Übersetzung und Kommentar* (Bamberg, 1975), p. 40.

16. 2.4. Schadel also cites 13.44, which refers to a discussion about a Punic word.

17. G. Bardy, *St. Augustin, l'homme et l'œuvre* (Paris, 1948), p. 149. G. Bonner, *St. Augustine of Hippo* (London, 1963), p. 109.

18. R. A. Markus, "St. Augustine on Signs," *Phronesis* 2 (1957), p. 69. Reprinted in *Augustine: A Collection of Critical Essays*, ed. R. A. Markus (Garden City, N.Y., 1972). Despite the quotation, this is not correct. Nor is the preceding sentence correct: "This [Interior Teacher] is the teacher whose activity is presupposed by all learning." There can be genuine teaching and learning about spatio-temporal things.

19. *Retractationes*, 1.12: "in quo disputatur et quaeritur, et invenitur, magistrum non esse, qui docet hominem scientiam, nisi Deum . . ."

20. *Œuvres de Saint Augustin*, vol. 6, trans. F. J. Thonnard (Paris, 1941), cf. pp. 15 and 103. Similarly, G. Madec, "Analyse du *De magistro*," in *Revue des Etudes Augustiniennes* 21 (1975): p. 63.

21. St. Augustine, *The Greatness of the Soul* and *The Teacher*, trans. and annotated by J. M. Colleran (Westminster, Md., 1950), pp. 115, 116. See also R. A. Markus, *art. cit.*, p. 65: "The work, dated about 389, is a dialogue, genuine and historical as Augustine claims in the *Confessions*, between himself and his son Adeodatus." Markus adds in a note, ". . . it is difficult, in reading the record of this conversation, not to take Adeodatus's side time and again in his refusal to acquiesce in some of his father's more palpable sophistries."

22. *Confessions* 9.6.14, quoted in Colleran, *op. cit.*, p. 115. I shall generally follow Colleran's translation of the *De magistro* for quotations.

23. *Retractationes*, 1.12: "Per idem tempus scripsi librum cujus est titulus, de Magistro. . . ."

24. *Art. cit.*, p. 67. Markus describes the first part of the dialogue as "a bewildering and often sophistical discussion."

25. Namely, in 5.14. Cf. M. Sirridge, "Augustine: Every Word is a Name," *New Scholasticism* 50 (1976): p. 186n. This is a first-rate article on the semantics of one of the arguments in the first division of the *De magistro*.

26. Cf. Christopher Kirwan, *Augustine* (London: Routledge, 1989) for a careful discussion of the logic and semantics involved; in particular p. 52: "the word 'because' is *used* to refer in these claims [of Augustine in *De magistro* 5.13] and in that use it is a name." See further for analyses of this aspect of the dialogue, A. Mandouze, "Quelques principes de 'linguistique Augustinienne' dans le De Magistro," in *Forma futuri, Studi in onore del Cardinale Michele Pellegrino* (Torino, 1975), pp. 790–95; and J. Collart, "Saint Augustin grammairien dans le *De Magistro*," *Revue des Etudes Augustiniennes* 17 (1971): pp. 279–92.

27. H. I. Marrou, *Saint Augustin et la fin de la culture antique* (Paris, 1936), p. 75. In later editions, Marrou qualified this judgment by excepting some writings.

28. 12.40: "Velut si abs te quaererem hoc ipsum quod agitur, utrum nam verbis doceri nihil possit, et absurdum tibi primo videretur non valenti totum conspicere, sic ergo quaerere oportuit, ut tuae sese vires habent ad audiendum

illum intus magistrum . . . ;" Citations without title, either in the text or notes, will be to *De Magistro*. The pagination of the Corpus Christianorum series Latina edition, vol. 29 (Turnholti: Brepols, 1971) will be given in parentheses (CCL 198.48–52).

29. 2.4: "illud certe tibi attendere facile est, exposuisse te verbis verba, id est signis signa, eisdemque notissimis notissima. Ego autem illa ipsa quorum haec signa sunt, mihi si posses vellem ut ostenderes" (CCL 161.68–72). If language never escapes from self-reference, then there is no signifying of anything except other signifiers. That is why the thesis that genuine teaching is showing is fundamental for Augustine.

30. 3.6. I pass over the possible problem of ambiguity with such ostensive answers (a problem which Augustine raises). It should, however, be noted that the question of whether anything can be shown without signs is one to which Adeodatus gives alternately yes and no answers in the course of the discussion. Cf. 3.6 (compare 7.19), 10.29–30, 10.32. Of course, explaining the meaning of a word by pointing or performing does not at all imply the semantic thesis that the meaning of a word is the thing it refers to—although some epigones of Wittgenstein have attributed this thesis to Augustine.

31. 4.7: "Cum ergo de quibusdam signis quaeritur, possunt signis signa monstrari: cum autem de rebus, quae signa non sunt, aut eas agendo post inquisitionem si agi possunt, aut signa dando, per quae animadverti queant" (CCL 164.7–10). The spacing and numbering in the text is mine.

32. Ibid. (CCL 164.12–13).

33. Colleran relegates the *tripartita distributione* to a subsection of one of the seven sections into which he divides the dialogue and even converts it into a twofold division: *op. cit.*, p. 116. Carl Johann Perl, in annotations to his translation, notes the *tripartita* when it occurs in 4.7, but does not mention it again. Instead he finds three "Ziele": 10.33 (Die eigentlich belehrende Macht liegt stets in den Dingen selbst); 10.36 (den Vorgange des Lernens [psychologisch gesehen] ist … eine Frucht der Selbstbeobachtung); and 10.38 (Augustinus verneint zum letzenmal, das er es sei, der seinen Sohn lehrt). *Der Lehrer*, trans. C. J. Perl (Paderborn: Verlag Ferdinand Schöningh, 1959), pp. 90–91. M. F. Burnyeat divides the discussion into a first section (1.1–10.31) in which the wrong thesis is explored, a second which states the defensible thesis (10.32–35), and the "remainder" which justifies it. "Wittgenstein and Augustine *De Magistro*," *Proceedings of the Aristotelian Society*, supplement V (1987): p. 8.

34. Thus, e.g., for Madec, *art. cit.*, pp. 63–69, the order of consideration of the threefold division:

[1]: sections 7–21;
[2b]: sections 22–28;
[2a]: sections 29–30.

As far as I can see, Madec gives no reason for the inverted order. I have briefly discussed the issue of the *tripartita distributione* in "The structure of the *De Magistro*," *Revue des Etudes Augustiniennes* 35: 1 (1989), pp. 120–27.

G. Wijdeveld, *Aurelius Augustinus de magistro*, Amsterdam 1937, also compresses [2a] and [2b] into sections 22–32 of the text, in order to begin the second part with the *oratio perpetua*—again a two-part interpretation of the dialogue overriding the threefold division.

35. Thonnard, *op. cit.*, titles this first division "lorsque la demande porte sur certain signes, on peut les montrer par d'autres signes." More explicitly: if we are to *show* signs by signs and not merely talk about them, there must be mutual signification and reflexivity.

36. J. H. S. Burleigh in *Augustine: Earlier Writings*, trans. J. H. S. Burleigh (Philadelphia: Westminster Press, 1953), p. 65. C. J. Perl, *op. cit.*, p. xviii: "Danach ist alles Vorhergegangene nur Vorspiel gewesen . . . wir sind hier blos auf Hypothesen angewiesen." Augustine does speak of "playing" (*ludendi*) with Adeodatus, but that refers to the beginning of the second division, not to what has gone before (8.21–22).

37. Markus, *art. cit.*, p. 67.

38. Sameness of extension here requires showing that every word is a name (clearly, every name is a word). For a discussion and defense of this paradoxical thesis, see Mary Sirridge, *art. cit.*, and compare Frege's argument that while normally a name is the name of its referent, in some contexts it can name its meaning.

39. Why would a language have two different words with the same meaning and extension? Wouldn't one of the words tend to disappear from usage? To get an example of two words with the same extension and meaning, Augustine goes to another language: here, Greek.

40. 8.22: "Age jam ergo illam partem consideremus, cum signis non alia signa significantur, sed ea, quae significabilia nominamus" (CCL 180.25–181.1). This is the second occurrence of "consideremus" in the dialogue; the first was noted above (4.7). This second part has caused the most difficulties for those interpretations which assume that the threefold division is completed before the *oratio perpetua* begins.

41. Note that for this to be understood as a question, the other words ("utrum . . . sit") have to be taken as signifying. Otherwise, Augustine points out to Adeodatus, there would only be a string of syllables.

42. Markus, *art. cit.*, p. 67.

43. 8.23 *in fin*: "Nam quae loquimur, ea significamus, non autem res, quae significatur, sed signum, quo significatur loquentis ore procedit, nisi cum ipsa signa significantur, quod genus paulo ante tractavimus" (CCL 183.106–109).

44. Cf. Madec, *art. cit.*, p. 67.

45. 9.28 *in fin*: "Quare jam illud magis magisque discutiamus, quale sit genus rerum quae sine signis monstrari posse dicebamus per se ipsas …" (CCL 188.115–117).

46. Peter Hart Baker is wrong to say that at 10.31 Augustine summarizes "the whole course of the dialogue thus far." What is summarized here is only what has been discussed in the second part of the dialogue, i.e., since the previous summary by Adeodatus in 7.19–20. Cf. Peter Hart Baker, "Liberal Arts as Philosophical Liberation: St. Augustine's *De Magistro*," in *Arts liberaux et philosophie au Moyen Age* (Montreal and Paris, 1969), p. 472.

47. 10.32 *in fin*: "Nam ut hominum omittam innumerabilia spectacula in omnibus theatris sine signo ipsis rebus exhibentium; solem certe istum lucemque haec omnia perfundentem atque vestientem, lunam et caetera sidera, terra et maria, quaeque in his innumerabiliter gignuntur, nonne per seipsas exhibet atque ostendit Deus et natura cernentibus?"

48. Louis H. Mackey misses the significance of the possessive pronoun here, and with it the role of the first division: he writes that Augustine "suggests that if we think about the matter more carefully, we may find that 'there is nothing which is learned by means of signs (*fortasse nihil invenies, quod per sua signa discatur*).'" "The Mediator Mediated: Faith and Reason in Augustine's 'De Magistro,'" in *Franciscan Studies*, vol. 42, annual XX, 1982, p. 135.

49. It occurs once at the end (10.45) but there it refers to external events as signs of God's providence.

50. Hence the common but misleading assertion that Augustine claims that all learning presupposes the Interior Teacher (cf., e.g., note 1 supra). Wherever something can be *shown* by someone, and not just told, teaching and learning can occur.

51. 10.38: "De universis autem, quae intelligimus non loquentem, qui personat foris, sed intus ipsi menti praesidentem consulimus veritatem, verbis fortasse ut consulamus admoniti" (CCL 195.44–196.46). This is the opening sentence of the "Interior Teacher" section of the dialogue.

52. Indeed, one has the sense that Augustine thinks communication falls short of its goal of shared understanding much more often than we think.

53. Cf. Augustine's response to Adeodatus in 1.1: "I see what you are thinking" (*video quid sentias*).

54. 14.45: "Nam quis tam stulte curiosus est, qui filium suum mittat in scholam, ut quid magister cogitet discat?" (CCL 202.305).

55. It is worth remarking that Adeodatus is not shown that Christ is the Interior Teacher: in his summary, he says that what his father said has been confirmed by "that hidden oracle" (*secretum illud oraculum*) within us. One can

only believe, on the basis of Scripture, that the Interior Teacher is Christ. Reason, which is the authority in the dialogue (5.15), as in the classical models of philosophical dialogue, must be supplemented by belief if the truth is to be attained. Perhaps this is why the *De Magistro* is Augustine's last dialogue.

56. There are a number of reasons why this seems to be the structure of the dialogue which Augustine intended. First, this reading sets apart the uninterrupted discourse of Augustine (10.32–14.45) by itself as forming a single coherent division of the subject, as contrasted with those interpretations which take the fundamental division to occur midway through it with 10.38, the introduction of the thesis of the Interior Teacher. Second, the *oratio perpetua* clearly exemplifies the third part of the threefold division [2b], namely, teaching about things signified by giving signs which direct attention to the signifiables. Third, the conclusion of 10.32 is clearly the end of the second division [2a] about what can be shown without signs. (This would appear to be what led Madec to invert the order of [2a] and [2b] in his analysis.) Fourth, it takes account of the indication of the *consideremus* as occurring only at the *incipit* of each of the divisions. (There are, if I am not mistaken, nine other occurrences of forms of considerare: considera, 3.5; considerare, 4.7 and 6.17; consideratione, 8.23; consideres, 9.29; considerans, 10.29; consideratis, 10.31; considerant, 14.45; and consideretur, 14.46.) To give any significance to this observation is to attribute to Augustine a care in composition of which I believe he was quite capable.

57. Is me autem aliquid docet, qui vel oculis, vel ulli corporis sensui, vel ipsi etiam menti praebet ea quae cognoscere volo (11.36).

58. The clarification of the meaning of a word is thus to be sought in one of three regions: 1) the "affectionem animi" or what is located "in animo" (2.3); 2) the things of the spatio-temporal world; 3) the "intelligibilia" (12.39).

59. And so perhaps as an image of God. Compare the Prologue to *De Doctrina christiana*, on the relation of the human arts to God's entrusting of interpreting the Scriptures to man. I am grateful to Mark Jordan for reminding me of this, as well as for reading the manuscript carefully and making helpful suggestions.

60. Although I use the language of gestalt psychology here, the notion of near and remote, of salient and hidden, are common in Augustine's discussions of *memoria*. Cf., e.g., *Confessions* 10.8.12, 10.10.17 *et passim*.

61. 10.31 *in fin*: "Nam difficillimum omnino est non perturbari, cum ea, quae prona et procliua adprobatione tenebamus, contrariis disputationibus labefactantur et quasi extorquentur e manibus. Quare, ut aequum est, bene consideratis perspectisque rationibus cedere, ita incognita pro cognitis habere periculosum; metus est enim ne, cum saepe subruuntur, quae firmissime statura et mansura preasumimus, in tantum odium vel timorem rationis incidamus, ut ne

ipsi quidem perspicuae veritati fides habenda videatur" (CCL 190.71–79). Compare the similar warning against "misology" by Socrates in the *Phaedo* 89d.

62. 12.40: "Nam quod saepe contingit, ut interrogatus aliquid neget atque ad id fatendum aliis interrogationibus urgeatur, fit hoc imbecillitate cernentis, qui de re tota illam lucem consulere non potest; quod ut partibus faciat, admonetur, cum de istis partibus interrogatur, quibus illa summa constat, quam totam cernere non valebat" (CCL 198.40–45). Compare the contrast between opinions implanted by rhetoric and knowledge implanted by dialectic, in the *Phaedrus*. This is one of the reasons why philosophy cannot be conveyed as information, i.e., separated from the inquiry which yields its conclusions.

63. ... nihil esse aliud discere ista ... nisi ea, quae passim atque indisposite memoria continebat, cogitando quasi colligere ... et cogenda rursus, ut sciri possint, id est velut ex quadam dispersione colligenda. *Confessions* 10.11.18. He goes on to relate bringing together (*cogo*) and thinking (*cogito*).

64. Everything that I understand, I know, but it is not the case that everything that I know, I understand. Cf. 11.37: Omne autem quod intelligo, scio ...

65. 13.41–44. Compare his remarks on the same problems in *De utilitate credendi* 4.10–11.

66. Neither pointing nor proper signs can make present, but pointing does have an advantage over words: you don't have to know the thing signified already in order to know that pointing is a sign (not a proper sign, sua signa, but a sign of the showing itself), because it is part of that natural language common to all peoples (tamquam verbis naturalibus omnium gentium, *Conf.* 1.8.13).

67. So Perl, *op. cit.*, says that it is "Selbstbeobachtung" which yields intelligible truths, and Gerard O'Daly says that we grasp them through "introspection." G. O'Daly, *Augustine's Philosophy of Mind* (London: Duckworth, 1987), p. 176.

68. Many problems about the theory of illumination in the *De Magistro* have been discussed at length (mainly the locus of the things known vis-à-vis God), but very little has been said about a most serious epistemological difficulty which appears here, namely, the lack of any relation between *intelligibilia* and things in the world, including signs. Plato links the two worlds by *chorismos*, participation of appearances in the Forms, and Aristotle derives knowledge of the essence from the physical thing, but Augustine here does not discuss the relation of the two worlds. But if language (signs) belongs to this world, how does it "hook up" with the other?

69. I have in mind here a remark by the deviser of a computer program for playing checkers. When the computer played (very well indeed) against checker champions, several of them commented independently that their computer opponent lacked any style of play, although it played very rationally.

70. Hence Augustine is not speaking ironically when he says after the elegant summary by Adeodatus (7.19–20), "I must acknowledge to you that I now see these distinctions more clearly than when the two of us resorted to inquiry and discussion to dig them out of ever so many hiding places" (8.21). Knowing where we are going does not require knowing every step of the way, and in dialogical inquiry, both parties can and usually do profit, even if one of them leads.

71. This view continues in Thomas Aquinas: "the act whereby we apprehend the truth about something . . . is not within our power, for it takes place in virtue of some light, natural or supernatural." *Summa Theologiae* I-II, q. 17 a. 6. In our time, it is of course Heidegger who has retrieved this Platonic teaching and characterized truth (*aletheia*) as disclosure, as opening up beings to our comprehension.

Chapter 4

1. *Phaedrus*, 274c.

2. 1 Cor. 1:25.

3. Rom. 1:19–20.

4. James J. O'Donnell, in his edition of *Confessions* (Oxford: Oxford University Press, 1992), 1: xliii.

5. Cf. *De utilitate credendi* 7.16: "must we not diligently seek from its teachers that [religion] that we hope to find" (*quod non apud ejus magistros eam diligenter investigamus*). Numbered references in the text, without other indication, will be from this work.

6. "bonis praeceptoribus catholicae Christianitatis te pia fide." Ibid. 18.36. As he shows at length in *De magistro*, the teacher—strictly speaking—is one who shows us what is so.

7. *Contra epistulam Manichei*, 6.

8. *Epist.* 120.3.

9. *Leviathan*, xliii, 8. Cf. vii, 7.

10. William James, *Varieties of Religious Experience* (New York: New American Library, 1958), 32.

11. *Confessions* 5.3.6.

12. See Hebrews 11:6.

13. See *De vera religione* 3.4.–4.7.

14. Norman Kretzmann, "Faith Seeks, Understanding Finds," in *Christian Philosophy*, ed. Thomas P. Flint (Notre Dame, Ind.: University of Notre Dame Press, 1990), 12, 16–17, 18.

15. *Retractationes* 13.3.

16. *De magistro* 11.37.

17. *Confessions* 10.11.18.

18. Myles F. Burnyeat, "Wittgenstein and Augustine *de Magistro*," *Proceedings of the Aristotelian Society*, supplementary volume for 1987, 29.

19. Galileo Galilei, *Dialogue on the Two Chief World Systems*, trans. Stillman Drake (University of Southern California Press, 1962), 51.

20. *De trinitate* 15.2.2.

21. C.S. Peirce, "The Fixation of Belief," in *Philosophical Writings of Peirce*, ed. Justus Buchler (New York: Dover Publications, 1955), 10.

22. *Summa theologiae* 2.2.2.1.

23. *De praedestinatione sanctorum* 2.5.

24. *In Joannis evangelium tractatus* 29.6. Cf. *Sermones* 126.1.1.

Chapter 5

1. It is curious that the trilogy of dialogues, explicitly linked together by Cicero himself (cf. *De Fato* 1.4, *De Divinatione* 2.1.1–3) has not been published together in an English translation for a century, although there have been several versions of the *De Natura Deorum* and *De Divinatione* separately (only a part of *De Fato* has come down to us). *De Natura Deorum* will henceforth also be abbreviated as DND, and *De Divinatione* as DD.

2. Velleius, the Epicurean spokesman in DND, considers the primary ground or reason for the alleged universal acknowledgment of the gods to be a *prolepsis* or innate preconception of the gods, and the experiences of dreams and visions to be the ground for considering the gods to have human forms, to be "quasi-corporeal" (DND 1.16.43–1.18.49).

3. DND 2.5.13. Xenophon's Socrates develops this argument in *Memorabilia* 4.3.3–14.

4. David Hume, *The Natural History of Religion* (Stanford, 1967), pp. 27, 42, 47.

5. 5 DND 2.2 and 2.3.

6. Of course, divination can have a much broader, non-religious meaning and include astrology, water divining by a dowsing rod, tarot cards, and so forth. Cicero's concern is with its practice as a part of the *ius divinum* of Roman religion.

7. One example among many others: Brian Davies, *Introduction to Philosophy of Religion* (Oxford, 1982), which despite its title is exclusively devoted to natural theology.

8. Thus the conclusion of DD: cf. 2.148–50.

9. F. Copleston, *A History of Philosophy*.

10. "Except for Homer, the authors of great books who come later in the course of the Great Conversation enter into it themselves as a result of reading the earlier authors. Thus, Plato is a reader of the Homeric poems and of the tragedies and comedies; and Aristotle is a reader of all of these and Plato, too. Dante and Montaigne are readers of most of the Greek and Roman books, not only the poetry and history, but the science and philosophy as well. . . ." R. Hutchins, *The Great Conversation*, vol. I of *Great Books of the Western World* (Chicago: Encyclopedia Britannica, 1952), pp. 78–79. "The set is almost self-selected, in the sense that one book leads to another, amplifying, modifying, or contradicting it." Ibid., pp. xvi–xvii. Mortimer Adler, co-editor of the set, says in his autobiography that he later came to regret omitting "Cicero, Calvin, Leibniz and Moliere." *Philosopher at Large* (New York: Macmillan, 1977), pp. 240–41. Cf. his comments on Cicero, ibid., pp. 47–48.

11. Augustine, *Contra Academicos* 1.8: "Cicero . . . a quo in latina lingua philosophia et inchoata est et perfecta."

12. See the chapter on Cicero's influence in the very helpful book of Paul MacKendrick, *The Philosophical Books of Cicero* (New York: St. Martin's Press, 1989). Cardinal J. H. Newman referred to him as "mens magna in corpore magno."

13. "[*De Fato*] is technical, dense, intense, full of subtle dialectical twists and turns . . . and devoted to an abstruse metaphysical topic. It conveys the interplay of ingenious minds arguing and putting fresh and unexpected lines of thought to each other better than any of Cicero's other philosophical writings, even though it is formally presented not as dialogue but as the continuous discourse of a single speaker. It is the Ciceronian treatise philosophers most enjoy reading." M. Schofield, "Cicero For and Against Divination," *Journal of Roman Studies* 76 (1986): p. 50.

14. Such an approach to his texts is not wholly without ground: fragments of previous writers are there. Cicero notoriously comments in one of his letters to his friend Atticus that what he writes "are only *apographa* [copies] which take little work, I only contribute the words and I have lots of them" (*Ad Att.* 12.52.3). But he also writes elsewhere: "we do not just act as translator, but, preserving what is said by those we esteem, we add our own judgment and re-arrangement" (*De Finibus* 1.2.6), and "I shall follow the Stoics; as usual, not as a mere commentator, but drawing from them at will, according to my own judgment, as much or as little as I need, and treating it in my own way" (*Ad Att.* 16.1.6, cited in MacKendrick, *op. cit.*, p. 234). The judgment of one editor of the *De Fato* is harsh but not inaccurate: "Toutes les études, souvent très pénétrantes, qui ont

été écrites sur la composition et la suite des idées dans le traité *du Destin*, sont viciées par l'arrière-pensée qui les domine de chercher, par ce moyen, la source grecque dont s'est inspiré Cicéron." A. Yon in *Traite du Destin*, Budé ed. (Paris, 1944), p. xvii.

15. P. MacKendrick, *op. cit.*, p. 6, says that "no Greek had tried the dialogue form since Aristotle" but this is a bit too strong, since Plutarch cites what seems to be a fragment of a dialogue by Epicurus (cf. *Adv. Colotes* 129, 131) and Cicero himself refers to the dialogues of Heraclides of Pontus, a contemporary of Aristotle (e.g., *Ad Atticus* 13.19). Nonetheless, it is striking that the dialogue form seems to recede from view after Aristotle first transformed it and then apparently abandoned it in his later years.

16. Of course the middle dialogues do often come to an at least tentative doctrine, and in the late dialogues (*Laws*, *Timaeus*) continuous speech by one character is dominant.

17. So Werner Jaeger declares that "while Plato in his later days was tending to replace dialogue by dogmatic lecture, Aristotle [in his dialogues] set speech against speech, thus reproducing the actual life of research in the later Academy." *Aristotle: A History of His Development* (Oxford, 1948), p. 28.

18. In a recent book, an interviewer of Paul Ricoeur, the contemporary French philosopher, objects to Ricoeur because "he gave too much credit to others . . . and spent too much time carefully working through their positions. He [Ricoeur] said he understood my criticism, but he owed a debt to those he had read, both contemporary and historical authors, and thought he should pay them and their work its just due. He said almost every philosopher has had a piece of the truth and none of them has had it all. He felt he should sort through their positions before he advanced his own." Charles Reagan, *Paul Ricoeur* (Chicago, 1996), p. 60.

19. *Topics* 1.1 (100a25–100b23). Compare Xenophon's description of the inquiries of Socrates as beginning from what was commonly assented to (*Memorabilia* 4.6.15).

20. *Rhetoric* 1.1 (1354a1–2), 1.2 (1356a30–34). The first two chapters of the *Rhetoric* develop the similarities and differences of rhetoric and dialectic at length. Neither of them is a science (*episteme*), in part because neither of them begins from premises that are true and primary or premises derived from true and primary premises. Cf. *Posterior Analytics* 1.2 on the conditions required for scientific demonstration. Cicero characterizes the difference of rhetoric and dialectic in *Academica* 1.8.32.

21. On the basic division of Cicero's method for philosophy into a) the discovery of premises and arguments, dealt with in his *Topica*, and b) the judging of premises and arguments by seeing what follows from them—namely,

through dialectic—see inter alia, M. Buckley, "Philosophic Method in Cicero," *Journal of the History of Philosophy* 8 (April 1970): pp. 143–54, and R. McKeon, "The Methods of Rhetoric and Philosophy: Invention and Judgment," in *The Classical Tradition*, ed. L. Wallach (New York: Cornell, 1966), pp. 365–73.

22. *Rhetoric* 1.1 (1355a25–30).

23. Skillful rhetoricians should learn how to argue either side of a topic, not in order to be able to persuade people of what is wrong, but in order to be able to anticipate arguments from the other side and so be prepared to answer them. Ibid. (1355a30–38).

24. *Topics* 1.2 (101a35–37). "In fact, the true and that which resembles it [*to te gar alethes kai to omoion to alethei*] are perceived by the same power. . . . hence one who is skillful at aiming at the true will be able to do the same with what resembles it." *Rhetoric* 1.1 (1355a14–18).

25. "Aristotle was the first to institute the method of arguing both sides on each question, not always arguing against every position like Arcesilas, but to bring forward whatever could be said pro and con" (*De Finibus* 5.4.10). Cf. *De Oratore* 3.21. On the short question-and-answer versus the continuous speech as the two methods of philosophical inquiry, cf. *De Finibus* 2.5.17.

26. "I follow Aristotle's practice: the conversation of the others is so put forward as to leave him the principal part [principatus]" (*Ad Atticum* 13.19).

27. "I have chosen particularly to follow . . . the practice of Socrates in trying to conceal my own private opinion . . ." (*Tusculan Disputations* 5.4.11); "this method in philosophy of speaking against all things and making no positive judgments openly [*aperte*] . . . was begun by Socrates . . ." (DND 1.5.11).

28. E.g., *Metaphysics* 1, *Physics* 1, *De Anima* 1, *Politics* 2, etc.

29. *Republic* 393c.

30. Cf. DD 2.1.1–4 for Cicero's enumeration of his philosophical dialogues. Note that critique is not merely negative.

31. "For even though many difficulties hinder every branch of knowledge, and both the subjects themselves and our faculties of judgment involve such a lack of certainty that the most ancient and learned thinkers had good reason for distrusting their ability to discover what they desired, nevertheless they did not give up, nor yet will we . . . ; and the sole object of our discussions [*disputationes*] is by arguing on both sides to draw out and give shape to some result that may be either true or the nearest possible approximation to it [*id quam proxime accedat*]" (*Academica* 2.3.7). Cicero thinks of this process of thesis and critique as having its roots in the Socratic paradigm: "after the would-be listener had expressed his view, I opposed it. This, as you know, is the old Socratic method of arguing against your adversary's position; for Socrates thought that in this way the probable truth [*veri simillimum*] was most readily discovered" (Ibid. 1.4.8 [Loeb]).

32. *Tusculan Disputations* 2.3.9. Referring to dealing with both sides of a question, Aristotle says, "No other of the arts draws opposite conclusions: dialectic and rhetoric alone do this. Both these arts draw opposite conclusions impartially" (*Rhetoric* 1.1 (1355a35–6), trans. W. R. Roberts).

33. E.g., *Tusculan Disputations* 1.4.8, DND 1.5.11. Cf. note 30.

34. See the discussion of this point in Pierre Grimal, "Ciceron, fut-il un philosophe?" *Revue des études anciennes* 64 (1962): pp. 117–26. "Mais que l'on y prenne garde: l'exemple de Cicéron nous enseigne qu'il ne s'agit jamais d'élaborer, par des emprunts, une doctrine composite, mais d'appuyer sur des raisonnements classiques, éprouves, des intuitions originales" (Ibid., p. 125).

35. Gregory Vlastos has stressed that Socrates used the elenchus not only to refute his opponents but to "find positive support for those strong doctrines of his on whose truth he based his life." "The Socratic Elenchus," *Oxford Studies in Ancient Philosophy* 1 (1983): p. 46. Mary Beard argues that one should take seriously Cicero's claims that followers of the Academy put forward no conclusion (*iudicium*) of their own. "Cicero and Divination: The Formation of a Latin Discourse," *Journal of Roman Studies* 76 (1986): p. 35.

36. Referring to a speech to be made on an agrarian law, he writes: "I shall follow the fashion of the Socratic schools in giving both sides of the question, ending, however, as they do, with the one which I prefer" (*Ad Atticum* 2.3 [Loeb]). To give hermeneutic weight to this statement is to disagree with Malcolm Schofield's observation about ending DD with no rejoinder to Cicero's critique: "But the absence of a reply is surely simply a function of Cicero's standard and natural expository procedure in his philosophical dialogues: first he presents the arguments for a thesis, then those against. The spokesman *pro* is *never* given the right of reply: to assume that this indicates Cicero's view of the merits of his case would be like thinking that whichever side in court is permitted the last word is deemed to have won." "Cicero for and against Divination," *Journal of Roman Studies* 76 (1986): p. 57n. Cf. *Tusculan Disputations* 1.4.8, DND 1.5.11.

37. DND 1.4.7–9.

38. DD 2.1.1–3. These dialogues cover the three basic fields of what may be called "topical philosophy" (as distinguished from epistemic or scientific philosophy) which Aristotle names in the *Topics*: logical, ethical, and physical (105b19). The division became standard in the Hellenistic period. Cicero adds to the enumeration of these seven dialogues a listing of seven other works of his which discuss or touch on philosophical subjects. Thus, for example, St. Augustine distinguishes the *De Republica* from Cicero's "philosophical writings" in *City of God* 5.13.

39. For a brief and clear description of these and other practices, cf. R. M. Ogilvie, *The Romans and Their Gods in the Age of Augustus* (Norton, 1970).

40. DND 3.2.5: Cumque omnis populi Romani religio in sacra et in auspicia divisa sit, tertium adjunctum sit si quid praedictionis causa ex portentis et monstris Sibyllae interpretes haruspicesve monuerunt (Loeb). Compare *De Legibus* 2.20, 2.30; *De Haruspicum Responsis* 18.

41. The *haruspicia* or "readings" of the liver of animals slaughtered for sacrifice, which required the special interpretive skill of a haruspex, were a supplement to auspices.

42. Augurs had nothing to do with interpreting prodigies or with the oracular sayings of the Sibylline pages: these were the responsibility of the haruspices and the *quindecimviri*, on request of the Senate (DND 2.4.12). Cf. in addition to Ogilvie, *op. cit.*, Jerzy Linderski, "Cicero and Roman Divination," *La Parola del Passato* (1982).

43. There were about 115 such holidays (*dies nefasti*) annually, when no business could be conducted.

44. *De Domo Sua* 1.1 (Loeb).

45. However, it seems too much to claim, as does Erich Frank, that "however the philosopher conceives the nature of the gods, their existence remains unquestioned." *Philosophical Understanding and Religious Truth* (Oxford University Press, 1945), p. 49n22. Cotta explicitly confesses to doubts about whether any gods exist (DND 1.22.61), Balbus explicitly undertakes to prove their existence (DND 2.9.23), and of course philosophers who denied the gods' existence are mentioned a number of times.

46. *Metaphysics* 12.8. For an interesting analysis of Aristotle's conception which construes the prime mover as more like a religiously accessible god, cf. T. De Koninck, "Aristotle on God as Thought Thinking Itself," *Review of Metaphysics* 47 (1994): pp. 471–516.

47. DND 1.2.3–4. As Friedrich Solmsen states it, rather too sharply, "For Cicero religio is a political, not a private problem." *Classical Weekly* 37 (1944): p. 160. It is probably safe to say that no philosopher before the twentieth century discussed religion without taking account of its political role.

48. DND 1.2.3.

49. Ibid. 1.6.14, 1.1.1 ("et ad cognitionem animi pulcherrima et ad moderandam religionem necessaria.") Compare David Hume, who begins his treatise on the history of religiousness by saying that there are two central questions about religion, "that concerning its foundation in reason, and that concerning its origin in human nature." *The Natural History of Religion*, p. 21.

50. Of Velleius and Balbus virtually nothing is known outside of Cicero's text. Cotta, however, was a consul in 75 B.C. and had been elected a priest before the dramatic date of the dialogue. It seems likely that he was chosen as critic in part at least for this reason.

51. DND 1.20.53. Hans Blumenberg notes that Cicero has Velleius state the Epicurean position with precision: he uses the ablative case to describe how things are produced by nature, by natural processes, in contrast to characterizing the Stoic position that nature (nominative case) is itself a generative source. *The Legitimacy of the Modern Age* (MIT Press, 1983), p. 610n21. The most complete ancient explication of Epicurus' theory is of course the famous poem by the contemporary of Cicero, Lucretius' *On the Nature of Things.*

52. Compare the position of Richard Rorty, a contemporary "Epicurean" with respect to the cultural dimension as well as the natural. Rorty writes that language is not constrained by the truth about the world, that we should give up the view that it is, and so regard cultural changes in vocabularies as contingent events: we should "see language as we now see evolution, as new forms of life constantly killing off old forms—not to accomplish a higher purpose [i.e., pursuing the truth], but blindly . . . [we need to] "get to the point where . . . we treat *everything*—our language, our conscience, our community—as a product of time and chance." *Contingency, Irony, and Solidarity* (Cambridge University Press, 1989), pp. 19, 22.

53. Descartes, *Meditations* IV; Wm. James, *Varieties of Religious Experience* XVIII. Of course in the Hindu tradition, this is the unique route to rationally grounded religiousness.

54. The attribution of significance to the universal assent to the existence of gods goes back at least to Plato, *Laws* X 886a (where it is not given much weight).

55. These representations of the gods are perceived only by thought, not by the senses (DND 1.37.105) and are derived from a continuous stream of images which flow from the gods, too faint and tenuous to be sensed, but detected by the mind. Cf. DND 1.16.43–17.45, 19.49, 37.105, 41.114. There is dispute about how some of these passages should be understood: cf. the editorial commentaries of Pease and van den Bruwaene, *ad loc.* For a general discussion of the notion of a *prolepsis* or preconception, cf. M. Schofield, "Preconception, Argument and God," in *Doubt and Dogmatism,* ed. M. Schofield, M. Burnyeat, and J. Barnes (Oxford, 1979).

56. Diogenes Laertius in his life of Epicurus claims that although the latter wrote more than three hundred rolls (books), "There is not in them one single citation from another author: it is all Epicurus' own words." *Lives of the Eminent Philosophers* 10.26.

57. The only apparent exception to this rule is Protagoras, who is mentioned here and elsewhere in the dialogue as an agnostic, one who claims not to be able to decide whether there are gods or not. But an agnostic position could be counted as not disallowing non-anthropomorphic gods. It is curious that the

one who is called elsewhere in the dialogue the parent and the chief of philosophy (namely, Socrates) appears in the doxography only as the spokesman for the views of Xenophon and that he is placed in the very middle position, fourteenth of twenty-seven, so that the list divides into even numbers of pre-Socratics and post-Socratics.

58. The closest a Platonic text seems to come to this is to mention the possibility that the mover of the sun (and the movers of the other heavenly bodies) is a soul naked of (or separated from) body (*psile somatos ousa*), *Laws* X 899a. The demiurge of the *Timaeus*, responsible for the making of the universe, is not called *asomatos*, as Pease observes *ad loc*. Yet A. E. Taylor is right to name Plato as the creator of natural theology and the tenth book of the *Laws* the origin of philosophical theism as a doctrine claiming to be capable of demonstration. Cf. *Plato: the Man and his Work* (London, 1952), pp. 492–93.

59. This is the Epicurean interpretation of the self-sufficiency which was generally thought to be characteristic of divinity. It was standard among Epicureans to hail their founder, Epicurus, as a god (i.e., as having led a godlike life), which suggests that happiness thus defined is not threatened by mortality, a famous Epicurean thesis. On Epicurus as divine, cf. inter alia Lucretius, *De Rerum Natura* 5.1–8, 5–54; DND 1.16.43. As Blumenberg observes, "similarity of form suggests the possibility of the same eudaimonia," *op. cit.*, p. 167. On Cotta's criticism of the Epicurean conception of the gods' happiness, compare Aristotle, *Nicomachean Ethics* 10.8, 1178b8ff.

60. DND 1.30.85, 44.123. At the beginning of Book Three, Cotta returns to this charge (3.1.3).

61. It is a puzzle which will never be solved: why virtually no treatises by Stoic philosophers prior to Cicero's time have come down to us intact. By all accounts (e.g., Diogenes Laertius), some of them were prolific writers, but we know them only as they are cited by others like Cicero. This is of course largely true of Hellenistic philosophy as a whole. The fragments of Stoic treatises cited or quoted by others are collected in *Stoicorum Veterum Fragmenta*, edited by H. von Arnim (henceforth SVF).

62. SVF 2.1049, from Plutarch *de. comm. not.* 31.1075a, c. Cf. the discussion in Josiah Gould, *The Philosophy of Chrysippus* (SUNY, 1970), p. 155–56. Plutarch expresses this by saying that at the time of the conflagration (*ekpyrosis*) all of the gods [= parts of the universe] are destroyed except Zeus. I think of Van Gogh as the painter of Stoicism, because nature in his landscapes and garden scenes is always throbbing with life—including the earth and sky and sun and stars.

63. This descent into superstition sets the stage for Cotta's criticism which repudiates not just the excesses but the whole multiplication of divinities. As

Hume remarks, Cotta "refutes the whole system of mythology by leading the orthodox gradually, from the more momentous stories, which were believed, to the more frivolous, which every one ridiculed: From the gods to the goddesses; from the goddesses to the nymphs; from the nymphs to the fawns and satyrs." *Op. cit.*, p. 65.

64. Paul Ricoeur analyzes this Hegelian contrast in a positive way: cf. "The Status of *Vorstellung* in Hegel's Philosophy of Religion," in *Meaning, Truth, and God*, ed. L. S. Rouner (Notre Dame, Ind.: University of Notre Dame Press, 1982).

65. This embodied-divinity position may seem only a historical curiosity, but in fact it continues to exercise an attraction for many people today, including scientists as well as theologians. The British cosmologist Fred Hoyle reviews the evidence and argues to the conclusion that "God is the universe: God = universe." F. Hoyle and N. C. Wickramasighe, *Evolution from Space* (New York: Simon & Schuster, 1981), p. 143. Compare G. Kaufman, *Theology for a Nuclear Age* (Philadelphia, 1985), p. 43 and S. McFague, *The Body of God* (Fortress, 1987).

66. DND 1.8.19.

67. DND 3.9.24, 11.28. Nature in this sense—that is, as an alternative to inferring divine causality—is also invoked at 3.10.26 and 11.27. Cotta accepts, in other words, the appearance of order, but denies that it need be attributed to design. The mistake of Zeno (the founder of the Stoic school), he says, was not to recognize the distinction between reason and nature as sources of order.

68. E.g., Leonardo Taran, "Cicero's Attitude Towards Stoicism and Skepticism in the *De Natura Deorum*," in *Florilegium Columbianum*, ed. K. Selig and R. Somerville (New York: Italica Press, 1987), pp. 20–21. I am inclined to think that Cotta speaks for Cicero when he exclaims that such crucial questions as the existence of gods should not be decided by the beliefs of the foolish (*opinione stultorum*) (DND 3.4.11). When Quintus defends divination in DD (1.6.11) by appealing to universal consensus, Cicero declares that nothing is so common as lack of sense (DND 2.39.81). Cf. *Tusculan Disputations* 4.24.54.

69. DND 2.9.23. Balbus himself later refers to such stories of gods intervening in battles as superstitious and foolish (DND 2.28.70).

70. For an interesting defense of divination against Cicero's arguments in DD, cf. N. Denyer, "The Case Against Divination," *PCPS*, n.s., 31 (1985): 1–10. See also M. Beard, "Cicero and Divination: the Formation of a Latin Discourse," *Journal of Roman Studies* 76 (1986), pp. 33–46, and M. Schofield, "Cicero For and Against Divination," ibid., pp. 47–65. For a contrary and more widely accepted view, cf. J. Linderski, "Cicero and Roman Divination," *La Parola del Passato* (1982): pp. 12–38.

71. Plato, *Apology* 41d. Xenophon's Socrates seems to defend a stronger version of particular providence than Balbus does here. Cf. *Memorabilia* 1.4. The Stoic Chrysippus sometimes sounds like Job's so-called comforters in justifying misfortune as punishment. Cf. Gould, *op. cit.*, p. 157–58.

72. Actually a fairly large lacuna in the received text occurs just as Cotta is about to begin his criticism of the notion of providence, so we do not know how long it originally was. But even in the extant text, it covers a fourth of his discussion of the Stoic position.

73. On the other hand, in the *Academica* (2.38.121) Cicero finds the idea that a god pays any attention to an individual a source of anxiety and concern.

74. DD 1.5.8. Arthur Pease comments that if DND were "written with the intention of gaining converts for any other system than that of Academic scepticism, its plans have been most ill arranged, its details most unsuccessfully executed." "The Conclusion of Cicero's *De Natura Deorum*," *Transactions of the American Philological Association* 44 (1913): pp. 32–33.

75. Haec cum essent dicta, ita discessimus ut Velleio Cottae disputatio verior, mihi Balbi ad veritatis similitudinem videretur esse propensior (DND 3.40.95).

76. As mentioned above, when he writes DD, Cicero puts in the mouth of his brother Quintus—his interlocutor in the dialogue—the judgment that Cotta's criticism in DND is subversive of all religion, to which Cicero (the persona in the dialogue) responds that the criticism was only intended to refute the Stoics. But one must observe that many have read it with Quintus' eyes (e.g., Lactantius, St. Augustine, and David Hume).

77. The secondary literature on this issue is extensive (not accidentally, it rivals that on the last sentence of Hume's *Dialogues Concerning Natural Religion*). Indeed the distinction of these three interpretations from the existing literature goes back to Pease's essay in 1913, "The Conclusion of Cicero's *De Natura Deorum*," *Transactions of the American Philological Association* 44 (1913): pp. 25–37.

78. See the quotation supra at note 44. Cf. also note 47.

79. So claims L. Taran, *art. cit.*, pp. 20–21.

80. 1.13.30. Hume paraphrases this claim in an ironic fashion at the beginning of the *Dialogues*.

81. *Op. cit.* 1.16.36. In DND 1.1.2, Cicero says all are led to this belief by nature (duce natura venimus).

82. Similarly, virtue is a good and vice is an evil whether the gods exist and reward or punish or whether they don't. But only the thoughtful and self-disciplined person may be capable of carrying out this realization in the course of life. Hence it is needful to keep in view the role of belief in reward and pun-

ishment for most people. Cf. F. J. Crosson, "Religion and Natural Law," *American Journal of Jurisprudence* 33 (1988): pp. 4–6.

83. Cf. DD 2.3.8, 20.45, 35.74 (esse divinationem nego).

84. DND 1.36.100: there must exist some outstanding and excellent nature which brought about, moved, guided, and governed these things (suspicate essent aliquam excellentem esse praestantemque naturam quae haec effecisset moveret regeret gubernaret); ibid. 2.2.4: [what can be so clear and manifest as that] there is some most excellent intelligent power through which these things are guided (esse aliquod numen praestantissimae mentis quo haec regantur). On *quo* here as an ablative of means rather than agency, cf. Pease's note in his edition of DND *ad loc.* Cotta responds to this argument of Balbus at DND 3.4.10.

85. *Op. cit.* 1.28.70: haec igitur et alia innumerabilia cum cernimus, possumusne dubitare quin iis praesit aliquis vel effector, si haec nata sunt, ut Platoni videtur, vel, si semper fuerunt, ut Aristoteli placet, moderator tanti operis et muneris. Cf. also *Academica* 2.38.119. The language Cicero uses here is reprised in Hume's *Dialogues*, where Philo—who like Cotta criticizes unrelentingly the design argument—concedes that the appearance of order in the universe strikes us with "irresistible force" and asks, after sketching some examples of order, "who can now doubt of a supreme intelligence?" *Dialogues Concerning Natural Religion*, ed. N. K. Smith (Indianapolis, Ind.: Bobbs-Merrill, 1976), pp. 202, 215. Philo immediately adds, however, that there are such doubters.

86. The most interesting and persuasive discussion of this aspect of DND is that of Philip Levine, "The Original Design and the Publication of the *De Natura Deorum*," *Harvard Studies in Classical Philology* 62 (1957): pp. 7–36. Levine argues that Cicero cannot have intended to present the Academic position as atheistic, though that would be the implication (as Quintus observes) if the last sentence were not added. Levine goes on to argue that the extraordinary demotion of the role of the Cicero persona in the dialogue—contrary to his being the primary speaker in all of the other seven philosophical dialogues and to his own declared intention in his letters—suggests that Cicero revised the dialogue (there is internal evidence of revision) to replace the role which he originally gave himself with that of Cotta. Like Cicero, Cotta holds a religious office, was a consul, declines to give his own opinion (cf. 1.5.10 with 2.1.2–3), and combines rational skepticism about religion with firm adherence to traditional religious practices.

87. At least five times in the third book Cotta asserts this to be the proper attitude toward the religious institutions established by the founders: 3.2.5,6,7,9, 17.43.

88. DND 3.4.9, 2.6, 3.7, etc. Certainly Balbus, although he refers to the traditions—notably at DND 3.40.94—always offers arguments and never appeals, as Cotta does, to belief in the *maiores* as a ground for religiousness.

89. DD 2.33.70. He asserts unambiguously also at 2.12.28 and 35.75 that political usefulness is a fundamental reason for preserving such practices. If I am not mistaken, he always formulates positive assertions (we believe, we accept, etc.) in the plural and not in the singular. However, he does deny in the first person singular the reality of divination, as noted previously.

90. DD 2.72.148. As Cotta says, "what could be less appropriate for a philosopher [than to deny the existence of gods]?" DND 3.17.44.

91. *Physics* VII 2. See the discussion in F. Solmsen, *Aristotle's System of the Physical World* (Cornell, 1960), pp. 192–95. Peter Geach, in giving an explanation of Frege's term *Wirklichkeit*, says "x is actual if and only if x either acts, or undergoes change, or both." *God and the Soul* (London, 1969), p. 65. (This language of course allows for a broadening of the Aristotelian conception of efficient cause.)

92. At DND 1.42.118, Cotta denounces the view that the stories which ground the institutions of religion are merely an invention of some prudent men for securing political power over the many. As usual his language (i.e., Cicero's) is careful: he denounces the view that such stories are totally (*totam*) fictions. This issue is related to the discussion (at 1.7.16) about the absence of a Peripatetic philosopher in the discussion. Balbus says that Peripatetics think that there is no sharp distinction between what is right and what is expedient. One of the underlying issues in the dialogues is what the political utility of religion (asserted by Cicero in DD 2.12.28, 33.70, 35.75) might justify.

93. Cf. DND 1.51.116, *De Inventione* 2.53.161, 2.22.66.

Chapter 6

1. *Confessions*, trans. J. K. Ryan (New York: Image, 1960), 5.8.15; 5.13.23.

2. *Apologia pro vita sua* (New York: Norton, 1968), p. 82. Subsequent page references for the *Apologia* will be given in parenthesis in the text.

3. It bears underlining that this moment and its sequent are characteristic of the uncompromisingly intellectual nature of both men. Newman repeats many times that he could not follow his feelings or his imagination but had to follow his reason. Feeling could point the way, but reason had to wait to see that the ground was sure. Book Seven of the *Confessions*, the longest of the narrative books, deals with Augustine's resolution of his intellectual problems, and Chapter Four of the *Apologia*, the longest of the narrative chapters, recounts the resolution of Newman's. (Similarly, the post-narrative sections of each work consolidate the intellectual grounds of the whole process.)

4. Reprinted in *Church of the Fathers* (London: Burns & Oates, 1868).

5. *Apologia*, 98–99. Responding much later, in a letter of 6.26.64, to the query of why the "Securus . . ." had had such an impact, he wrote: "The history of the 5th century showed me that the argument which I had used for Anglicans—was wrong. Then St. Augustine's words came as the key, or rather as an expression or aphorism, of the state of the case." *Letters and Diaries of J.H. Newman* (London and New York: Th. Nelson, 1961–80), v. XXI, p. 135.

6. See "Structure and Meaning in St. Augustine's *Confessions*," *Proceedings of the American Catholic Philosophical Association*, vol. 63 (Washington, D.C.: American Catholic Philosophical Association, 1989): 84–97.

7. Augustine describes his departure for Rome as if, having circumvented his mother, he sailed alone. But in fact, as he later indicates, Nebridius and his mistress and son were not left behind.

8. The thought that the Academic (skeptical) position is best comes at the end of Book Five, as he realizes that he can no longer believe that Manicheism is true.

9. *Confessions*, 5.14.25.

10. *Confessions*, 8.12.29.

11. E.g., F. L. Cross called it "probably the greatest autobiography in the English language." F. L. Cross, *John Henry Newman* (London, 1933), p. 132. "It is," Newman wrote to a correspondent, explaining why the *Apologia* had not dealt with his undergraduate years, "a 'history of my religious opinions,' and I had no change in them when I was an Undergraduate . . . [hence] it did not bear on my subject." *Letters and Correspondence of John Henry Newman*, ed. Anne Mozley (London: Longmans, Green, 1891), vol. I, p. 5. The fact that he later published an "Autobiographical Memoir" dealing with the years up to 1833 does not entail, pace Houghton, that "he was ready to accept the *Apologia* as an adequate account of his life from 1833 to 1845." Walter E. Houghton, *The Art of Newman's Apologia* (Yale, 1945), p. 68.

12. Contrary to Martin Svaglic's view (cf. note infra), the anachronistic location of the story of Tract 90 is not some editorial slip in revising chapters. In a letter of 5.2.64 thanking a correspondent for sending copies of Newman's letters from that earlier period, he writes, "I have not begun Part 5 yet, which is from 1839 to 1845 (*except* the Number 90 matter) . . ." *Letters and Diaries*, vol. 21, p. 106. Newman's emphasis.

13. I have in mind here Froude's motto for the Lyra Apostolica, namely, Achilles' "You shall know the difference, now that I am back again" (40), and Newman's later wry comment acknowledging the "force and effectiveness of the genuine Anglican theory . . . [as] proof against the disputants of Rome; but still like Achilles, it had a vulnerable point . . ." (126).

14. *Apologia*, pp. 61 and 64: the first mention of the *Via Media* in the narrative, if I am not mistaken.

15. "[At the time of the publication of Tract 90] I was not confident about my permanent adhesion to the Anglican creed; but I was in no actual perplexity or trouble of mind..." (13).

16. Although he "could not hold office in its [the Church of England's] service, if I were not allowed to hold the Catholic sense of the Articles . . . I could not go to Rome" (121).

17. E.g., John J. O'Meara, *The Young Augustine* (London: Longmans, 1965), p. 13: "The central point in the *Confessions* is the conversion."

18. Houghton, *op. cit.*, p. 109.

19. He also quotes from four letters to him in Chapter Four; one each in Chapters Two and Three.

20. He published a collection of his sermons from the 1830s, and planned a series of volumes on the Lives of the Saints, but was discouraged from proceeding by the counsel of Pusey et al. Cf. Ian Ker, *The Achievement of John Henry Newman* (Notre Dame, Ind.: University of Notre Dame Press, 1990), p. 282. And of course he worked on what became the *Development of Christian Doctrine*.

21. I believe this is the only publication from which he quotes in Chapter Four.

22. Houghton, *op. cit.*, p. 98. Martin Svaglic suggests that Tract 90 is discussed in this chapter because "the speculations on which it is based arose well before that date and thus belong to the period of confidence," adding in a note that perhaps Newman originally intended to run the chapter to 1841, but changed his mind [and forgot to relocate the account of Tract 90]. In any case, that seems an unsatisfactory reason since Newman says later that although he had long thought about the Articles and their Catholic interpretation, "the actual cause of my [writing Tract 90] in the beginning of 1841, was the restlessness, actual and prospective, of those who neither liked the Via Media nor my strong judgment against Rome" (71). For Svaglic's comments, cf. "The Structure of Newman's *Apologia*" in the Norton edition of the *Apologia* cited, p. 449.

23. Although linear in one dimension, it is in another dimension the exhibiting of a triumphing ascent culminating in a blow which deflects the searcher's way.

24. The metaphor is not wholly my own: in preparing for Tract 90, Newman comments that he was "engaged in an *experimentum crucis*" (108).

25. This reflects what seems to have been a strong part of his nature. "It is face to face, '*solus cum solo*,' in all matters between man and his God . . . the purest and most direct acts of religion [lie] in the intercourse between God and the soul" (154). "My own soul was my first concern, and it seemed an absurdity to my reason to be converted in partnership" (170). Cf. *cor ad cor loquitur*.

26. E.g., 8.8.41, 12.25.41, 7.28.43, 10.13.43, 4.9.44, 4.27.45.

27. A number of his early writings are addressed to Manichean friends whom he seeks to bring to Catholic Christianity—e.g., *De vera religione* to Romanianus, *De utilitate credendi* to Honoratus.

28. Cf. his letter to Jemima on the morning after his reception into the Church of Rome: "All this is quite consistent with believing, as I firmly do, that individuals in the English Church are invisibly knit into that True Body of which they are not outwardly members; and consistent, too, with thinking it highly injudicious, indiscreet, wanton, to interfere with them in particular cases . . . it must be put on the ground of discretion. If I said that I ought in duty to go away, I should be confessing I ought not to join the Church of Rome at all." *Letters and Correspondence*, p. 469.

Chapter 7

1. "Religion and Faith in Augustine's *Confessions*," in *Rationality and Religious Belief*, ed. C. Delaney (Notre Dame, Ind.: University of Notre Dame Press, 1979). I am grateful to Gary Gutting, whose critical comments helped me to formulate my thoughts about proof and presence more clearly.

2. Non est autem possibile fidei cognitionem esse falsam neque vanam, ut ex dictis patet in principio Libri. *Op. cit.* III, 40.

3. Ea enim quae naturaliter rationi sunt insita, verissima esse constat: in tantum ut nec esse falsa sit possibile cogitare. Nec id quod fide tenetur, cum tam evidenter divinitus confirmatum sit, fas est credere esse falsum. Quia igitur solum falsum vero contrarium est, ut ex eorum definitionibus inspectis manifestis apparet, impossibile est illis principiis quae ratio naturaliter cognoscit, praedictam veritatem fidei contrarium esse. Ibid., I, 7.

4. quaecumque argumenta contra fidei documenta ponantur haec ex principiis primis naturae inditis per se notis non recte procedere. Unde nec demonstrationis vim habent, sed vel sunt rationes probabiles vel sophisticae. Et sic ad ea solvenda locus relinquitur. Ibid. There is a species of reciprocity here, in that the same claim can be turned around to discriminate what only appears to be the implications of faith. Two factors can mitigate the reciprocity: a long-examined and traditionally accepted faith doctrine places the burden of proof on a challenge to it, and a *magisterium* speaking out of the community can set parameters for interpretation. Compare Newman's *Essay on the Development of Christian Doctrine*.

5. II-II, 2, 10c: All references are to the *Summa Theologiae* unless otherwise noted.

6. oportet ea saltem per fidem praesupponi ab his qui eorum demonstrationem non habent: Ibid., 1, 5, 3m; cf. 2, 10, 2m.

7. ad demonstrandum ea quae sunt praembula fidei, quae necesse est in fide scire, ut ea quae naturalibus rationibus de deo probantur, ut deum esse, deum esse unum et alia hujusmodi vel de deo vel de creaturis in philosophia probata, quae fides supponit. *In Boet. de Trinitate* II, 3c.

Deum esse unum prout est demonstratum, non dicitur articulus fidei sed praesuppositum ad articulos: cognitio enim fidei praesupponit cognitionem naturalem, sicut et gratia naturam. *de Veritate* 14, 9, 8m. . . . non sunt articuli fidei sed praeambula ad articulos. *Summa Theologiae* I, 2, 2, 3m.

8. For an examination of the changes which emerged in the seventeenth century in the conceptualization of this issue, cf. G. deBroglie, "La Vraie Notion Thomiste des 'praeambula fidei,'" *Gregorianum* (1953): pp. 345–89.

9. II-II, 2, 2c: credere Deo.

10. naturalis ratio dictat homini quod alicui superiori subdatur, propter defectus quos in seipso sentit, in quibus ab aliquo superiori eget adjuvari et dirigi. Et quicquid illud sit, hoc est quod apud omnes dicitur Deus. Ibid., 85, 1c.

11. Credere Deum non convenit infidelibus sub ea ratione qua ponitur actus fidei. Non enim credunt Deum esse sub his conditionibus quas fides determinat. Et ideo nec vere Deum credunt, quia ut Philosophus dicit, in simplicibus defectus cognitionis est solum in non attingendo totaliter. Ibid., 2, 2, 3m. For a discussion of this failure of reference, cf. Peter Geach, "On Worshipping the Right God," in *God and the Soul* (New York: Schocken, 1969), pp. 100–16.

12. cui cultus exhibetus non quasi actus quibus Deus colitur ipsum Deum attingant, sicut cum credimus Deo, crendendo Deum attingimus. Ibid., 81, 5c and 1c.

13. multa per fidem tenemus de Deo quae naturali ratione investigare philosophi non potuerunt, puta circa providentiam eius et omnipotentiam, et quod ipse solus sit colendus. Ibid., 1, 8, 1m.

14. Si autem aliqui fuerunt qui sic de divinis veritatem invenerunt demonstrationis via quod eorum aestimationi nulla falsitas adiungeretur, patet eos fuisse paucissimos . . . cognition autem praedicta multum incertitudinis habet: quod demonstrat diversitas scientiarum de divinis eorum qui haec per viam demonstrationis invenire conati sunt. SCG III, 39.

15. *Dialogue Concerning the Two Chief World Systems* (Berkeley: University of California Press, 1962), p. 51.

16. Sagredo, in *op. cit.* p. 59; cf. p. 57.

17. Ibid., pp. 52, 336.

18. Ibid., pp. 18, 37. The analogy of Gestalt perception, the switching of visual perspectives which Norwood Hanson invoked in *Patterns of Discovery*, is

thus not pertinent. Cf. the discussion in Thomas Kuhn, *The Structure of Scientific Revolutions* (Chicago, 1965), p. 85.

19. *On Certainty* (New York: Harper and Row, 1969).

20. N. Bourbaki, *Elements d'histoire des Mathematiques* (Paris: Hermann, 1960), pp. 42 ff., and Galileo, *op. cit.*, p. 336.

21. Cf. Jos. Dauben, "Georg Cantor and Pope Leo XIII," *Journal of the History of Ideas* 38 (Jan.–Mar. 1977): pp. 85–108.

22. *Loc. cit.* There may seem to be a kind of disanalogy here, since some believers accept the conclusion but reject a proof of any part of it. But it would appear that either they reject such and such a proof, *de facto*, or they reject the possibility in principle of a proof on the grounds that God is not a reality to which the notion of proof applies at all. Gabriel Marcel and Wittgenstein are examples of this position. This is a view radically different from Aquinas, which involves rejecting the "principle of charity" referred to above. We cannot pursue it further in this essay.

23. Per cognitionem autem fidei non fit res credita intellectui praesens perfecte: quia fides de absentibus est, non de presentibus . . . Fit tamen per fidem Deus praesens affectui. SCG III, 40.

24. quamdiu sumus in corpore dicimur peregrinari a Domino in comparatione ad illam praesentiam qua quibusdam est praesens per speciei visionem; . . . Est autem et praesens etiam se amantibus in hac vita per gratia inhabitationem. II-II, 28, 1, 1m.

25. II-II, 83, 17c; cf. 83, 1, 2m.

26. Qui credit, assensum praebet his quae sibi ab alio proponuntur, quae ipse non videt: unde fides magis habet cognitionem auditui similem quam visioni. SCG III, 40.

27. On union in love, cf. I-II, 26, 2; 28, 1 and 2.

Chapter 8

1. *Letters of David Hume*, 2 vols., ed. J. Grieg (Oxford: Oxford University Press, 1932), 1.106. Of course, apart from what might be thought of the character of an infidel, there were social and legal sanctions consequent upon the printing of blasphemous sentiments.

2. Hume originally entitled this chapter "Of the Practical Consequences of Natural Theology"; cf. Norman Kemp Smith's edition of the *Dialogues Concerning Natural Religion* (Indianapolis, Ind.: Bobbs-Merrill, 1976), 51n1. I shall subsequently refer to the *Dialogues* (DNR) by this edition, as has become common. The pagination appears to be the same in all the revisions and printings

from the first in 1935, reviewing which stimulated E. C. Mossner's article "The Enigma of Hume" and helped launch the contemporary interest in Hume's religious views. The best recent critical edition of the *Natural History* and the *Dialogues* is by A. Wayne Colver and J. V. Price (Oxford: Oxford University Press, 1976).

3. H. E. Root, in the "Editor's Introduction" to his edition of *The Natural History of Religion* (Stanford, Calif.: Stanford University Press, 1967), 11.

4. Just as in the only other dialogue Hume published—titled simply "A Dialogue"—at the end of the *Enquiry Concerning the Principles of Morals* (1752).

5. E.g., Montaigne, *An Apology for Raymond Sebond*; Descartes, *Discourse on Method*; etc.

6. This is also an implicit theme of the *De Natura Deorum*, that the god or gods of the (Epicurean and Stoic) philosophers, even if their existence were demonstrated, would not support the traditional religious practices.

7. The *Dialogues* were being composed in 1751, as we know from Hume's correspondence, and were revised by him several times before being published three years after his death; see Appendix C of N. K. Smith's edition on the stages of composition. On the composition and suppression of the first edition of the *Natural History* and its subsequent publication, see E. C. Mossner, "Hume's Four Dissertations: An Essay in Biography and Bibliography," *Modern Philosophy* 48 (1950): 35–57.

8. The careful reader will note that the ground is laid for criticism. Consider, for example, the beginning of Chapter 2, where Hume remarks that "to persons of a certain turn of mind, it may not appear altogether absurd, that several independent beings ... might conspire in the contrivance and execution of one regular plan; yet is this a merely arbitrary supposition, which, even if allowed possible, must be confessed neither to be supported by probability nor necessity." Having conceded this, however, he immediately proceeds to give a counterexample.

9. *The Natural History of Religion*, ed. H. E. Root (Stanford, Calif.: Stanford University Press, 1967), 21. (Henceforth NHR; subsequent page references to this work will be to this edition.) A similar distinction is made in the opening sentence of the classical work that most influenced Hume's writings on religion, Cicero's *De Natura Deorum*.

10. Hence James Collins considered Hume to be the first philosopher of religion in the modern sense of the term; see James Collins, *The Emergence of Philosophy of Religion* (New Haven, Conn.: Yale University Press, 1967).

11. Thus his account is what we would call psychological, like that of the Epicurean Velleius in the *De Natura Deorum*.

12. Hume never uses this term in NHR, nor does he use "polytheism" after Chapter 9.

13. Hume is very sparing with the term "Christianity"—which can include the established religion—and its variants in NHR: it occurs only three times, if I am not mistaken, and never in a favorable reference (except ironically): 45, 53, and 68n1.

14. To give this thesis greater plausibility—which it needs—Hume takes great care with his language. The thesis gains plausibility if we understand it to be claiming that there is a tendency for theism to supplement its worship of one invisible God by visible or representable mediators (angels, saints, the Virgin Mary): what Hume terms "idolatry." Hence in later revisions of the text, he carefully changes "idolatry" to "polytheism" in the early chapters, conjoins the terms in the middle chapters, and does not use the term "polytheism" after Chapter 9, but only "idolatry" and other synonyms.

15. Why should Hume bother to do this, if he did? It has to be remembered that his readers were divided not only into religionists and "bystanders" (57) whom he wanted to understand him in different ways but also into the vulgar and the few (a division largely but not completely coincident with the former). One way to reach his intended audience, if it consisted of careful, thoughtful readers, would be by employing the patterns of the work to emphasize some parts over others, just as some ancient writers used, e.g., chiasmic pattern for increment of meaning. Knowledgeable readers may expect that if an author's views are at variance with established institutions and beliefs, and there are social consequences for contravening them, then he will not say so directly; he may indicate his real views by the structure, by qualification, by irony, by modifying subsequently what had been stated earlier.

16. There is another curious pattern in the footnotes of the final edition revised by Hume. Listed sequentially, the number of footnotes in successive chapters is: 0-1-2-25-4-1-3-0-11-5-0-25-6-5-0. It happens that Chapters 4 and 12 have more footnotes than all the other chapters of each half of the treatise put together—they each have 25. It also happens that each of them announces views both unusual and central to Hume's argument: Chapter 4 that polytheism is not a form of theism, and Chapter 12 that theism is not superior to polytheism or idolatry in its reasonableness.

17. It is thus puzzling that Keith Yandell maintains that in NHR Hume argues for a natural "propensity to minimal theism," since Hume denies that polytheism is a form of theism, minimal or otherwise. It is also puzzling that in an essay that takes the NHR as central to understanding Hume he does not deal with polytheism, although the discussion of the latter outweighs that of theism in NHR. See K. Yandell, "Hume on Religion," in *Hume: A Reevaluation*, ed. D. W. Livingston and J. T. King (New York: Fordham University Press, 1976).

18. In fact, Hume suggests that it probably is the case that somewhere in this universe polytheism is true, that somewhere there has come into being "a species of intelligent creatures, of more refined substance and greater authority than the rest" (53, 36n2), there being no contradiction in such a conception. There is merely no ground for supposing that this has happened on our planet.

19. The counsel to suspend judgment seems at variance with the opening paragraph of NHR, which says no reflective enquirer can do so. (See James Noxon, "Hume's Concern with Religion," *Southwestern Journal of Philosophy* 7 [1976]: 71, as against Yandell, "Hume on Religion," 113, who cites the opening statement without remarking on the closing one.) The inconsistency might be mitigated by taking the later counsel as referring to suspending judgment about popular religions, i.e., superstitions, and the former as referring to the design argument. This construal defers the question of Hume's inconsistency about suspending belief to the *Dialogues* where the issue reappears.

20. The differences between believer and atheist are of course discussed freely today, but the sort of language that Hume commonly uses to refer to differences between the vulgar or the many and the few is considered inappropriate or "elitist."

21. Simon Blackburn, *Spreading the Word* (Oxford: Oxford University Press, 1984), 3. Contrast Augustine's definition of "word": Verbum uniuscuiuque rei signum, quod ab audiente possit intelligi, a loquente prolatum (*De Dialectica* 5.7.6).

22. E.g., Terence Penelhum, *Hume* (London: Macmillan, 1975), 171: ". . . beyond any question the greatest work on philosophy of religion in the English language."

23. He writes to Adam Smith in 1776, "On revising them [the *Dialogues*] . . . I find that nothing can be more cautiously and more artfully written" (*Letters*, 2.334). Smith appears to have had reservations about the artfulness, since he declined to assent to his friend's request to publish them after Hume died.

24. It was E. C. Mossner who launched this question; see note 2 above. I am grateful to my research assistant Barbara Sain for reviewing some 120 articles from this period on the subject of Hume's writings on religion. It is interesting that there has been an increase in attention to the dramatic and rhetorical aspects of the *Dialogues* in the secondary literature. See, e.g., Michael Morrisroe, "Rhetorical Method in Hume's Works on Religion," *Philosophy and Rhetoric* 2 (1969): 121–38, and "Hume's Rhetorical Strategy," *Texas Studies in Literature and Language* 11 (1970): 963–74; and A. G. Vink, "The Literary and Dramatic Character of Hume's *Dialogues Concerning Natural Religion*," *Religious Studies* 22 (1986): 387–96.

25. See the surveys in DNR 58–59; John Bricke, "On the Interpretation of Hume's *Dialogues*," *Religious Studies* 11 (1975): 2–3; and J. Noxon, "Hume's Agnosticism," *Philosophical Review* 73 (1964): 250ff.

26. In keeping with their personae, Cleanthes becomes aware (199) sometime before Demea does (213) that Philo has been playing a double role. But then Cleanthes has been alert from the beginning to the possibility of purposeful ambiguity in Philo's pious affirmations (132).

27. Consider the following, from NHR: "Were there a religion (and we may suspect Mahometanism of this inconsistence) which sometime painted the Deity in the most sublime colours, as the creator of heaven and earth; sometimes degraded him nearly to the level with human creatures in his powers and faculties; while at the same time it ascribed to him suitable infirmities, passions, and partialities, of the moral kind: That religion, after it was extinct, would also be cited as an instance of those contradictions, which arise from the gross, vulgar, natural conceptions of mankind, opposed to their continual propensity towards flattery and exaggeration. Nothing indeed would prove more strongly the divine origin of any religion, than to find (and happily this is the case with Christianity) that it is free from a contradiction, so incident to human nature" (45). Or from DNR: "What truth so obvious, so certain, as the being of a God, which the most ignorant ages have acknowledged ..." (128).

28. J. Bricke, "On the Interpretation of Hume's Dialogues," 17. W. Salmon, "A New Look at Hume's *Dialogues*," *Philosophical Studies* 33 (1978), thinks that the *Dialogues* are presented by Hume as a discussion of the nature, rather than the existence, of God. It is true that Pamphilus thus describes the issue (128) and Demea also at times (141, 142), but it is also clear—and asserted (e.g., 143, 146)—that the issue is whether or not a deity exists. This is one of the many points in which Hume's strategy is illuminated by comparing it with that of Cicero in the *De Natura Deorum*, a work that had far more influence on the *Dialogues* than did Newton, Clarke, or Butler. On the parallels between the two works, see J. V. Price, "Empirical Theists in Cicero and Hume," *Texas Studies in Literature and Language* 5 (1963): 255–64, and "Sceptics in Cicero and Hume," *Journal of History of Ideas* 25 (1964): 97–106.

29. See, e.g., Terence Penelhum, "Natural Beliefs and Religious Beliefs in Hume's Philosophy," *Philosophical Quarterly* 33 (1983): 166–81; and J. Noxon, "Hume's Agnosticism," 251. Contrast Stewart Sutherland, "Penelhum on Hume," *Philosophical Quarterly* 33 (1983): 182–86, who argues that it is Cleanthes who changes in Part 12.

30. In Hume's original version, Philo only adds to Cleanthes' critique a very mild "observation" about the psychology of those who are attracted by metaphysical arguments through confusing them with the a priori method of mathematics. Only in one of his last revisions did he broaden this.

31. I.e., one who aspires to demonstrate that the cause of the order of nature coincides with the God of religion—which requires, as Philo emphasizes, the inferring of particular providence and moral intent from the empirical data.

32. See note 27 above. That the propensity is not natural, however, appears from the opposition between "natural inclination" and "religious motives" (221).

33. 219, 220, 222, and 226.

34. Thus, "hypothesis of experimental theism" (165), "of design" (169), of the "soul of the world" (170), of the "Epicurean hypothesis" (182), and of course of the "religious hypothesis" (138, 216). See also 172, 174, 180, 183, and 200.

35. This is only the second time he has used the word "Christian" and the only one that could be taken as commendatory (160, 228).

36. When Hume is speaking in his own voice (NHR 42) he quotes Francis Bacon's well-known remark as "A little philosophy makes men atheists: A great deal reconciles them to religion." But his Cleanthes quotes the same passage as "a little philosophy makes a man an atheist: A great deal converts him to religion" (DNR 139). In Bacon's original essay, "Of Atheism," the text runs: "It is true, that a little philosophy inclineth man's mind to atheism; but depth in philosophy bringeth men's minds about to religion"; see *The Works of Francis Bacon* (London: Longmans, 1861), 6.413.

37. Many, perhaps most, commentators deny this, e.g., John Bricke, "On the Interpretation of Hume's *Dialogues*."

38. 219. J. V. Price in his edition of the *Dialogues* puts this note in the text on the ground that "Hume, in preparing a final draft of the work, was conscious of the incongruity of a discursive note in a dialogue"; *Dialogues Concerning Natural Religion*, 251. Stanley Tweyman has noted (*Scepticism and Belief in Hume's Dialogues Concerning Natural Religion* [Dordrecht: Nijhoff, 1986]) that Part 12 of the *Enquiry Concerning Human Understanding* prescribes the antidote to dogmatism that is administered to Cleanthes.

39. Cf. the often-cited incident related by Diderot to Samuel Romilly in which Hume is said to have told Baron d'Holbach that he had never met an atheist (DNR 39–40). He certainly knew himself of men who styled themselves atheists. Cf. NHR 36n. On the sense of "atheism" in Hume's time, see David Berman, "David Hume and the Suppression of Atheism," *Journal of the History of Philosophy* 21 (1983): 375–87.

40. This is an argument that Hume places toward the end of both the *History* (Chapter 14) and the *Dialogues* (Part 12).

41. "There is no question of importance whose decision is not compriz'd in the science of man; and there is none, which can be decided with any certainty, before we become acquainted with that science"; Hume, *A Treatise of Human Nature*, ed. L. A. Selby-Bigge, 2nd ed., ed. P. H. Niddith (Oxford: Oxford University Press, 1981), xvi. See E. C. Mossner, "The Religion of David Hume," *Journal of the History of Ideas* 39 (1978): 653–63.

42. So, e.g., Hume argues that there is no natural obligation to obey promises, but that the utility of posing such an obligation has come to be seen; *Treatise of Human Nature*, 2.5 to end.

43. *Summa theologiae* 2.2.85.1.

44. Cf. Cicero's definition of *religio*, repeated by Aquinas in *Summa theologiae* 2.2.80.1.

45. Hume in fact has some perceptive things to say about the religious function of ceremonies; see DNR 13.

46. *Summa theologiae* 2.2.81.7.

47. See F. J. Crosson, "Structure and Meaning in St. Augustine's *Confessions*," *Proceedings of the American Catholic Philosophical Association*, vol. 63 (Washington, D.C.: American Catholic Philosophical Association, 1989): 84–97.

Chapter 9

This essay was read at the annual meeting of the Natural Law Institute, on April 14, 1988, at the University of Notre Dame Law School.

1. Lloyd L. Weinreb, *Natural Law and Justice* (Harvard, 1987), p. 99.

2. For an interesting presentation of this view, see Colin Turnbull, *The Mountain People* (New York: Simon & Schuster, 1972). I have discussed this view and Turnbull's argument in "Natural Rights and Anthropology," *CCICA Annual* (1984): pp. 19–33.

3. Helmut Koester, "Nomos Physeos: The Concept of Natural Law in Greek Thought," in *Religions in Antiquity* (The Hague: Nijhoff, 1977). For a later discussion, cf. R. A. Horsley, "The Law of Nature in Philo and Cicero," *Harvard Theological Review* 71 (1978): pp. 35–59.

4. It is, indeed, the conventional interpretation of Cicero that he is the "great popularizer of the natural law philosophy of the Greek Stoics": Michael Bertram Crowe, *The Changing Profile of the Natural Law* (The Hague: Nijhoff, 1977), p. 36. Crowe concedes that it "has been argued . . . that the Stoic natural law is a creation of Cicero's—at least in the sense that the older Stoics, according to our admittedly defective knowledge, were no more natural law theorists than, say, Plato or Aristotle": ibid., p. 37. My argument is that Cicero himself was not more a natural law theorist than Plato or Aristotle.

5. *Op. cit.*, 1.18 (Loeb translation): *lex est ratio summa insita in natura, quae iubet ea, quae facienda sunt, prohibetque contraria. eadem ratio cum est in hominis mente confirmata et confecta, lex est.* Compare the definition in *de Rep.* 3.22.33: "True law is right reason in agreement with nature." (*Est quidem vera lex recta*

ratio naturae congruens.) Subsequent references to Cicero's text are to the *de Legibus*, unless otherwise stated.

6. Even Leo Strauss, who constantly stressed the distinction between natural right and natural law, seemed to consider Cicero a teacher of natural law. Cf. *Natural Right and History* (Chicago, 1953), p. 154.

7. Philo of Alexandria, *de Opificio Mundi* (Loeb translation) 1.3, 55.143, 61.172.

8. H. Koester, *art. cit.*, p. 533.

9. Augustine, *On Free Will*, 1.5.13, 1.8.18; *Contra Faustum* 22.27.

10. ST 1.2.71.

11. ST 1.2.71.1.

12. *Metaphysics* XII.10, 1075a11–25.

13. ST 1.2.73.7.3.

14. *Summa Contra Gentiles* 3.122: *non enim Deus a nobis offenditur nisi ex eo, quod contra nostrum bonum agimus.*

15. ST 1.2.17.1.

16. For a powerful analysis of the consequence of the voluntarist view for the emerging natural science, see Hans Blumenberg, *The Legitimacy of the Modern Age* (MIT, 1985).

17. Gregory wrote, "If, *per impossibile*, the divine reason, or God himself did not exist, or that that reason were mistaken, still if one were to act against right reason, angelic, human or any other if such there be, he would sin." Quoted in M. B. Crowe, *op. cit.*, p. 208.

18. F. Suarez, *Selections from Three Works*, vol. 1 (Oxford: Clarendon Press, 1944), *op. cit.*, Bk. II, chap. 6: *An lex naturalis, sit vere lex divina praeceptiva?* For a discussion of this chapter and its influence on Grotius, cf. Charles S. Edwards, *Hugo Grotius* (Chicago: Nelson Hall, 1981), pp. 54–60.

19. *Op. cit.*, ch. 2, sec. 6.

20. Ibid., ch. 8, sec. 96. For Aristotle's argument, cf. *Politics* III.11.

21. *On Liberty* (Liberal Arts Press, 1956), p. 81. See, for a further discussion, my "Mill's Dilemmas," *Interpretation: A Journal of Political Philosophy* 16, no. 2 (Winter 1988–89): pp. 229–45.

Chapter 10

1. *Op. cit.*, ¶¶ 32, 34. Text quoted is from *The Church Speaks to the Modern World*, ed. E. Gilson (New York: Doubleday, 1954), pp. 222–24.

2. Ibid., ¶ 7. See the discussion of Locke's influence on some of the content of the encyclical in Richard Camp's interesting work *The Papal Ideology*

of Social Reform (Leiden: Brill, 1969), pp. 54–56, and more extensively in E. Fortin's article "'Sacred and Inviolable': *Rerum Novarum* and Natural Rights," *Theological Studies* 53 (1992): pp. 203–33, from which the above quote is adapted (p. 219). Mary Ann Glendon has argued (*Rights Talk: The Impoverishment of Political Discourse* [New York: Free Press, 1991]) that "rights" language is not well-fitted for the discourse of citizens in democratic civil societies.

3. From her commentary on *Populorum Progressio* in *Encyclical Letter of His Holiness Pope Paul VI on the Development of Peoples* (New York: Paulist Press, 1967), p. 21.

4. *Populorum Progressio* #59.

5. Cf. ibid. #78: "Who does not see the necessity of thus establishing progressively a world authority, capable of acting effectively in the juridical and political sectors?" John Paul II comments in *Centesimus Annus* that there ought to be "effective international agencies which will oversee and direct the economy to the common good." #58.

6. *Man and the State* (Chicago: University of Chicago Press, 1951), p. 202.

7. Ibid.

8. Ibid., p. 203.

9. Allen Bloom, who was not a religious person to say the least, once told me that he thought his students who came from homes that divorce had divided learned from that painful situation that "number one comes first." Bloom was concerned about this as a lesson for future citizens.

10. Ibid., p. 209. My emphasis.

11. Ibid., p. 208.

12. *Immortale Dei* (1885) #6 in Gilson, *op. cit.*, p. 164.

13. *Longingua Oceani*, reprinted in *The Great Encyclical Letters of Pope Leo XIII* (Rockford, Ill.: Tan Books, 1995), p. 323.

14. Ryan and Boland, *Catholic Principles of Politics* (New York: Macmillan, 1940), pp. 316–21.

15. Ibid., p. 321.

16. I shall be discussing this final position (if it can be described as "final"). For a very clear and responsible tracking of the development of Murray's thought, cf. Keith J. Pavlischek, *John Courtney Murray and the Dilemma of Religious Toleration* (Missouri: Thomas Jefferson University Press, 1994).

A recently discovered memorandum that Murray wrote for then-Cardinal Montini contains a very brief and lucid statement of his position in 1950. Cf. J. C. Murray, "The Crisis in Church-State Relationships in the U.S.A.," *Review of Politics* 61, no. 4 (Fall 1999): 687–704.

17. *The Problem of Religious Freedom* (Westminster, Md.: Newman Press, 1965), p. 65. (Henceforth referred to as PORF.) Similarly: "These Popes [Pius

and John XXIII] laid aside the more Aristotelian, ethical conception of the state that is to be found in Leo XIII." Cf. "On Religious Liberty," *America* 109 (Nov. 1963): 706, quoted in Pavlischek, p. 187.

18. PORF, p. 66. Note that this quote and the longer quotation that follows it in PORF are taken from wartime radio addresses.

19. Ibid. (My emphasis.) Murray calls this "a badly needed *aggiornamento* of the official political philosophy of the Church." Ibid., p. 67. Nonetheless, he also quotes later texts from Pius XII on religious freedom that he admits "are in continuity with Leo XIII." Ibid., pp. 13–14.

20. Ibid., p. 56.

21. Ibid., 42–43; cf. 29–30: "public morality, as determined by moral standards commonly accepted among the people." This measure of morality does not seem substantially different from that of an eminent proponent of the limited liberal state, John Stuart Mill, who also allows restrictions on freedom of action on the grounds of what is deemed to be indecent.

22. "The Issue of Church and State at Vatican II," *Theological Studies* 27 (Dec. 1966): 598. Emphasis mine. I have left out of consideration here the (ironic) fact that, coincident with Vatican II, the First Amendment protection of religious freedom was being interpreted by the Supreme Court to include the right not to be religious, and so not to have to be forced to be present at religious exercises. I refer to the school prayer cases, beginning with Abington School District vs. Schempp (1963).

23. Cf. his commentary on the Declaration in *Documents of Vatican II*, ed. W. Abbott and J. Gallagher (New York: Fordham, 1966), p. 682, quoted in Pavlischek, p. 181.

24. *Vatican II: An Interfaith Appraisal*, ed. John Miller (Notre Dame, Ind.: University of Notre Dame Press, 1966), p. 580 (cf. p. 572). Murray quoted his own translation: the Latin is *bonum commune*.

25. PORF, p. 31. At the Notre Dame conference, Murray's paper—written a month or so before the meeting—contained the assertion that "freedom is not only the primary method of politics; it is also the highest political goal." When I questioned him about whether that was consistent (as he had argued) with the Preamble to the Constitution, he replied that I might not have noticed that when he delivered the paper at the meeting, "I left out 'highest political goal' because I am not at all sure freedom is the highest political goal." *Op. cit.*, pp. 574, 580.

26. So theologians like Charles Curran have claimed. See the discussion in Pavlischek, p. 194.

27. "It is religion itself, not government, which has the function of making society religious." "The Issue of Church and State at Vatican II," *loc. cit.*

28. MacIntyre, *Whose Justice? Which Rationality?* (Notre Dame, Ind.: University of Notre Dame Press, 1988), p. 336. Emphasis mine. The whole of chapter 17 is relevant to the issues here discussed.

29. Ibid. Similarly in the liberal market economy, preferences are the form that reasons for action—production, marketing, etc.—take. If enough people prefer some direction for the market, i.e., if the price can be paid, then the voices are heard.

30. Ibid., p. 338.

31. Ibid., p. 342.

32. See MacIntyre's remarks in *After MacIntyre* (Notre Dame, Ind.: University of Notre Dame Press, 1995), pp. 302–3. I should add that his position is that the "culture of liberalism" is only the historical form that our nation-states have assumed, and that the very nature of the modern nation-state and its size and organization prevent any genuine political community from emerging within it. Cf. ibid. and "Poetry as Political Philosophy: Notes on Burke and Yeats," in *On Modern Poetry*, ed. V. Bell and L. Lerner (Nashville: Vanderbilt University Press, 1988), pp. 145–57.

33. *Op. cit.* #47. See also *Evangelium Vitae* #4: "Choices once unanimously considered criminal and rejected by the common moral sense are gradually becoming morally acceptable."

34. *Evangelium Vitae* #70.

35. *Centesimus Annus* #46.

36. *Acta synodalia Concilii Vaticani II Period II*, 2.530–32.

37. Richard Rorty has a wonderful Gordian knot solution to this dilemma: just define the truth as what comes out of free discussion.

38. For a discussion, cf. my "Mill's Dilemmas," *Interpretation: A Journal of Political Philosophy* 16, no. 2 (Winter 1988–89): pp. 229–45.

39. *The Lincoln-Douglas Debates*, ed. H. Holzer (New York: Harper-Collins, 1993), e.g., p. 258: "I believe that slavery is wrong, and [I believe] in a policy springing from that belief that looks to the prevention of the enlargement of that wrong, and that looks at some time to there being an end of that wrong." Compare the politician who says "Personally I'm opposed to (such and such) but I'm not going to impose my views on others."

40. E.g., *Sollicitudo Rei Socialis* #10 *et passim*.

PUBLICATIONS OF FREDERICK J. CROSSON

This list of publications is based on documents that were originally created by Frederick J. Crosson and then checked and revised by Michael J. Crowe.

EDITED BOOKS

Editor (with Kenneth M. Sayre). *The Modeling of Mind*. Notre Dame, Ind.: University of Notre Dame Press, 1963. Reprint, New York: Simon & Schuster, 1968.

Editor and contributor (with Kenneth M. Sayre). *Philosophy and Cybernetics*. Notre Dame, Ind.: University of Notre Dame Press, 1967. Reprint, New York: Simon & Schuster, 1968. Translated into Japanese, 1970. Translated into Spanish, 1971.

Editor. *Science and Contemporary Society*. Notre Dame, Ind.: University of Notre Dame Press, 1967. Translated into Portuguese, 1969. Translated into Spanish, 1970.

Editor and contributor. *Human and Artificial Intelligence*. New York: Appleton-Century-Crofts, 1970.

Editor. *The Autonomy of Religious Belief*. Notre Dame, Ind.: University of Notre Dame Press, 1981.

ARTICLES

"On the Ground for History in the Classical Philosophy of Human Nature." *Modern Schoolman* 39, no. 4 (May 1962): 359–71.

"Formal Logic and Formal Ontology in Husserl's Phenomenology." *Notre Dame Journal of Formal Logic* 3, no. 4 (Oct. 1962): 259–69.

"Plato's Statesman: Unity and Pluralism." *New Scholasticism* 37, no. 1 (Jan. 1963): 28–43.

"Phenomenology and Computer Simulation of Human Behavior." *Proceedings of the American Catholic Philosophical Association* 38 (1964): 128–36. Reprinted in *Catholic Psychological Record* 2, no. 2 (Fall 1964) and in *Philosophy and Science as Modes of Knowing: Selected Essays*, edited by Alden L. Fisher and George B. Murray, 160–69. New York: Appleton-Century-Crofts, 1969.

"Natural Law and Contraception." In *The Problem of Population*. Edited by Donald Barrett. Vol. 1, Moral and Theological Considerations, edited by Donald Barrett, 113–31. Notre Dame, Ind.: University of Notre Dame Press, 1964.

"Phenomenology and Realism." *International Philosophical Quarterly* 6, no. 3 (Sept. 1966): 455–64.

"The Concept of Mind and the Concept of Consciousness." *Journal of Existentialism* 6, no. 24 (Summer 1966): 449–58. Reprinted in *Phenomenology in America*. Chicago: Quadrangle Books, 1967.

"Personal Commitment as the Basis of Free Inquiry." In *Academic Freedom and the Catholic University*, edited by Edward Manier and John Houck, 87–102. Notre Dame, Ind.: Fides Press, 1967.

"Memory, Models, and Meaning." In *Philosophy and Cybernetics*, edited by Frederick J. Crosson and Kenneth M. Sayre, 183–202. Notre Dame, Ind.: University of Notre Dame Press, 1967.

"Information Theory and Phenomenology." In *Philosophy and Cybernetics*, edited by Frederick J. Crosson and Kenneth M. Sayre, 99–136. Notre Dame, Ind.: University of Notre Dame Press, 1967.

"Liberty and Authority in the Church." In *Law for Liberty: The Role of Law in the Church Today*, edited by James E. Biechler, 147–55. Baltimore: Helicon, 1967.

"Psyche and Persona: The Problem of Personal Immortality." *International Philosophical Quarterly* 8, no. 2 (1968): 161–79. Reprinted in *New Themes in Christian Philosophy*, edited by Ralph M. McInerny. Notre Dame, Ind.: University of Notre Dame Press, 1968.

"The Computer as Gadfly." *Boston Studies in the Philosophy of Science* 4 (1969): 226–40.

"How Is a College Catholic in Practice?" *Delta Epsilon Sigma Bulletin* 20, no. 2 (May 1975): 54–59.

"Philosophy, Religion, and Faith." *Proceedings of the American Catholic Philosophical Association* 52 (1978): 168–76.

"Religion and Faith in St. Augustine." In *Rationality and Religious Belief*, edited by Cornelius Delaney, 152–68. Notre Dame, Ind.: University of Notre Dame Press, 1979.

"Proof and Presence." In *Experience, Reason, and God*, edited by Eugene Thomas Long, 55–77. Studies in Philosophy and the History of Philosophy 8. Washington, D.C.: Catholic University of America Press, 1980.

"Geopolitics and Reichenbach Falls." *Baker Street Journal* 31, no. 1 (March 1981): 6–9.

"Maritain and Natural Rights." *Review of Metaphysics* 36, no. 4 (June 1983): 895–912.

"Father Brown, Sherlock Holmes, and the Mystery of Man." In *A Chesterton Celebration*, edited by Rufus William Rauch, 21–33. Notre Dame, Ind.: University of Notre Dame Press, 1983.

"Droit Naturel et Anthropologie." In *Droits des peuples, droits de l'homme*, edited by Roberto Papini, 77–87. Paris: Centurion, 1984. Reprinted in *CCICA Annual: Publication of the Catholic Commission on Intellectual and Cultural Affairs* (1984): 19–33.

"Psyche and the Computer." In *A Century of Psychology as Science*, edited by Sigmund Koch and David Leary, 437–51. New York: McGraw-Hill, 1985.

"*Fides and Credere*: W. C. Smith on Aquinas." *Journal of Religion* 65, no. 3 (July 1985): 399–412.

"Man and the Meaning of the Whole." In *Beyond Mechanism: The Universe in Recent Physics and Catholic Thought*, edited by David L. Schindler, 51–64. Lanham, Md.: University Press of America, 1986.

"Intentionality and Atheism: Sartre and Maritain." *Modern Schoolman* 64, no. 3 (March 1987): 229–45.

"The Philosophy of Accreditation." *North Central Association Quarterly* 62, no. 2 (1987): 386–97.

"The Role of the Faculty in Accreditation." *Academe: Bulletin of the American Association of University Professors* 74, no. 4 (July–Aug. 1988): 18–22.

"Religion and Natural Law." *American Journal of Jurisprudence* 33 (1988): 1–17.

"Mill's Dilemmas." *Interpretation: A Journal of Political Philosophy* 16, no. 2 (Winter 1988–89): 229–45.

"The Structure of the *De Magistro*." *Revue des Études Augustiniennes* 35, no. 1 (1989): 120–27.

"The Semantics of the Grammar." *Faith and Philosophy* 7, no. 2 (April 1990): 218–28.

"The Analogy of Religion." *American Catholic Philosophical Quarterly* 65 (1990): 1–15.

"Reconsidering Aquinas as Post-Liberal Theologian." *Thomist* 56, no. 3 (July 1992): 481–98.

"The Laws of Nature and of Nature's God." *Vera Lex* 11, no. 2 (1992): 10–11.

"Newman and Augustine: The Narrative of Conversion." In *Tradition and Renewal: Philosophical Essays Commemorating the Centennial of Louvain's In-*

stitute of Philosophy, edited by David A. Boileau and John A. Dick, 265–78. Leuven: Leuven University Press, 1992.

"Rejoinder to Bruce Marshal." *Thomist* 57, no. 2 (April 1993): 299–303.

"Show and Tell: The Concept of Teaching in St. Augustine's *De Magistro*." In *"De Magistro" di Agostino d'Ippona*, 13–65. Palermo, Italy: Edizioni Augustinus, 1993.

"The Thomistic Tradition and the Intellectual Worker." *CCICA Annual: Publication of the Catholic Commission on Intellectual and Cultural Affairs* 15 (1996): 39–48.

"Hume's Unnatural Religion (Some Humean Footnotes)." In *Modern Enlightenment and the Rule of Reason*, edited by John C. McCarthy, 168–86. Studies in Philosophy and the History of Philosophy 32. Washington, D.C.: Catholic University of America Press, 1998.

"Catholic Social Teaching and American Society." In *Principles of Catholic Social Teaching*, edited by David Boileau, 165–76. Milwaukee: Marquette University Press, 1998.

"Structure and Meaning in Augustine's Confessions." In *The Augustinian Tradition*, edited by Gareth Matthews, 27–38. Berkeley: University of California Press, 1999.

"American Reflections on a Century of Catholic Social Teaching." In *One Hundred Years of Philosophy*, edited by Brian J. Shanley, O.P., 95–110. Studies in Philosophy and the History of Philosophy 36. Washington, D.C.: Catholic University of America Press, 2001.

"Philosophy and Belief." In *Gladly to Learn and Gladly to Teach: Essays on Religion and Political Philosophy in Honor of Ernest L. Fortin, A.A.*, edited by Michael P. Foley and Douglas Kries, 17–28. Lanham, Md.: Lexington Books, 2002.

"Book Five: The Disclosure of Hidden Providence." in *A Reader's Companion to Augustine's "Confessions,"* edited by Kim Paffenroth and Robert P. Kennedy, 71–87 and 237–39. Louisville: Westminster John Knox Press, 2003.

"Fanaticism, Politics, and Religion." *Philosophy Today* 47, no. 4 (Winter 2003): 441–47.

"Esoteric versus Latent Teaching." *Review of Metaphysics* 59, no. 1 (2005): 73–93.

TRANSLATIONS AND OTHER WORKS

Lorenzen, Paul. *Formal Logic.* Translated from German by Frederick J. Crosson. Dordrecht: Reidel, 1965.

New Catholic Encyclopedia (New York: McGraw-Hill, 1967):
"Consciousness." Vol. 4, 208–9.
"Objectivity." Vol. 10, 608–9.
"Phenomenology." Vol. 11, 256–60.

Cambridge Dictionary of Philosophy, edited by Robert Audi (1995):
"John Henry Newman." 528–29.
"Noetic." 536.
"Pre-existence." 640.

Finally, as noted by Frederick J. Crosson at the end of his most recent bibliography, "literally hundreds of book reviews and speeches."

ACKNOWLEDGMENT OF SOURCES

Of the ten essays by Professor Crosson included in this volume, nine were previously published, the Cicero essay being the exception. The ten essays by Professor Crosson are:

1. "Esoteric versus Latent Teaching," *Review of Metaphysics* 59, no. 1 (2005): 73–93.
2. "Book Five: The Disclosure of Hidden Providence," in *A Reader's Companion to Augustine's "Confessions,"* ed. Kim Paffenroth and Robert P. Kennedy, 71–87 and 237–39 (Louisville: Westminster John Knox Press, 2003).
3. "Show and Tell: The Concept of Teaching in St. Augustine's *De Magistro*," in *"De Magistro" di Agostino d'Ippona*, 13–65 (Palermo, Italy: Edizioni Augustinus, 1993).
4. "Philosophy and Belief," in *Gladly to Learn and Gladly to Teach: Essays on Religion and Political Philosophy in Honor of Ernest L. Fortin, A.A.*, ed. Michael P. Foley and Douglas Kries, 17–28 (Lanham, Md.: Lexington Books, 2002).
5. "Cicero and the Philosophy of Religion." Unpublished manuscript.
6. "Newman and Augustine: The Narrative of Conversion," in *Tradition and Renewal: Philosophical Essays Commemorating the Centennial of Louvain's Institute of Philosophy*, ed. David A. Boileau and John A. Dick, 265–78 (Leuven: Leuven University Press, 1992).
7. "Proof and Presence," in *Experience, Reason, and God*, ed. Eugene Thomas Long, 55–77, Studies in Philosophy and the History of Philosophy 8 (Washington, D.C.: Catholic University of America Press, 1980).
8. "Hume's Unnatural Religion (Some Humean Footnotes)," in *Modern Enlightenment and the Rule of Reason*, ed. John C. McCarthy, 168–86, Studies in Philosophy and the History of Philosophy 32 (Washington, D.C.: Catholic University of America Press, 1998).

9.   "Religion and Natural Law," *American Journal of Jurisprudence* 33 (1988):
     1–17. Reprinted in *CCICA Annual: Publication of the Catholic Com-
     mission on Intellectual and Cultural Affairs* (1989): 75–95.

10. "American Reflections on a Century of Catholic Social Teaching," in *One
     Hundred Years of Philosophy*, ed. Brian J. Shanley, O.P., 95–110. Studies
     in Philosophy and the History of Philosophy 36 (Washington, D.C.:
     Catholic University of America Press, 2001).

     For permissions for the republication of these essays, we are indebted to
the original publishers (listed above).
     We are also deeply indebted to the University of Notre Dame's Institute
for Scholarship in the Liberal Arts for a subvention that assisted the publication
of this book.

Rev. Nicholas R. Ayo, C.S.C., is a priest in the Congregation of Holy Cross. He holds an STL degree in theology from the Gregorian University in Rome (1960) and a PhD in literature from Duke University (1966). After many years teaching literature at the University of Portland in Oregon, Father Ayo became the director of novices for the Congregation of Holy Cross in North America (1974–80). He then taught in the Great Books Program at the University of Notre Dame from 1981 to 2004, when he retired to professor emeritus status. Among eleven authored books are several published by the University of Notre Dame Press.

Michael J. Crowe did his undergraduate studies at Notre Dame, receiving degrees in both the Program of Liberal Studies (where Fred Crosson taught him) and the College of Science. He also earned a doctorate in history of science from the University of Wisconsin. In 1961, he joined the faculty of the Program of Liberal Studies and eventually became the Rev. John J. Cavanaugh, C.S.C., Professor of the Humanities. He also taught in Notre Dame's Graduate Program in History and Philosophy of Science, which he founded. He is author or editor of nine books, including *A History of Vector Analysis*, *The Extraterrestrial Life Debate, 1750–1900*, and *Calendar of the Correspondence of Sir John Herschel*. In 2010, the American Astronomical Society awarded him its LeRoy E. Doggett Prize for lifetime contributions to the history of astronomy.

Mark Moes did his undergraduate studies at Notre Dame from 1969 to 1973, receiving degrees in both the Department of Philosophy and in the (then-called) General Program of Liberal Studies. Abroad his sophomore year in Notre Dame's Innsbruck Program, he was never able to schedule a class with Fred Crosson, but he heard him speak many times and conversed a great deal with students who took Fred Crosson's classes. After ten years outside of academia, he returned to Notre Dame in the 1980s and was awarded a PhD in philosophy in 1991. He is currently associate professor of philosophy at Grand Valley State University in Grand Rapids, Michigan. He is the author of *Plato's Dialogue Form and the Care of the Soul* and various articles on Platonic dialogues. He teaches courses on the pre-Socratics, Plato, Aristotle, Plotinus, and Augustine. He also teaches a philosophy of religion course on Hume and his epigones and respondents.

Mary Katherine Tillman is professor emerita in Notre Dame's Program of Liberal Studies, in which she taught from 1973 to 2006. She served a term as assistant provost of the University and she is the 1985 recipient of the Charles E. Sheedy Award for Excellence in Teaching in the College of Arts and Letters. She has published and lectured in seven countries and fifteen states on the thought of Blessed John Henry Cardinal Newman, especially on his educational philosophy and his theory of knowledge. In addition to dozens of articles and two monographs on Newman, she has recorded two series of audiotapes on his thought. Her graduate degrees are in philosophy from St. Louis University (MA, 1966) and the New School for Social Research (PhD, 1974).

INDEX

Frederick J. Crosson (1926–2009) was the Rev. John J. Cavanaugh, C.S.C., Professor Emeritus of Humanities in the Program of Liberal Studies at the University of Notre Dame.